Shadows in the Field

Shadows in the Field

New Perspectives for Fieldwork in Ethnomusicology

Edited by
Gregory F. Barz
& Timothy J. Cooley

New York   Oxford
Oxford University Press
1997

Oxford University Press

Oxford   New York
Athens   Auckland   Bangkok   Bogota   Bombay
Buenos Aires   Calcutta   Cape Town   Dar es Salaam
Delhi   Florence   Hong Kong   Istanbul   Karachi
Kuala Lumpur   Madras   Madrid   Melbourne
Mexico City   Nairobi   Paris   Singapore
Taipei   Tokyo   Toronto

and associated companies in
Berlin   Ibadan

Copyright © 1997 by Oxford University Press, Inc.

Published by Oxford University Press, Inc.
198 Madison Avenue, New York, New York 10016

Oxford is a registered trademark of Oxford University Press

Library of Congress Cataloging-in-Publication Data
Shadows in the field : new perspectives for fieldwork in ethnomusicology /
    edited by Gregory F. Barz and Timothy J. Cooley.
        p.   cm.
    Essays ; most originally prepared for the year-long colloquium series
"Fieldwork in contemporary ethnomusicology" sponsored by the
Graduate Program in Ethnomusicology at Brown University.
    Includes bibliographical references and index.
    ISBN   0-19-510910-4;   ISBN   0-19-510911-2 (pbk.)
    1. Ethnomusicology—Fieldwork.   I. Barz, Gregory F., 1960-   .
II. Cooley, Timothy J., 1962-   .
ML3799.S5   1997
780'.89—dc20   96-12479

9 8 7 6 5 4 3 2 1

Printed in the United States of America
on acid-free paper

This book is dedicated to our teachers, friends, field contacts, colleagues, and students, from all "fields." All have challenged us to reconsider the fundamental nature of human relationships and understanding in research, fieldwork, scholarship, and life.

Acknowledgments

The majority of the chapters in this volume originated as papers given during a colloquium series titled "Fieldwork in Contemporary Ethnomusicology." During this colloquium series particular issues emerged concerning new perspectives for fieldwork in Ethnomusicology, and many of the contributors felt it essential to follow through with the development of these issues into full-length chapters. The year-long colloquium was conceived of by the two editors and sponsored by the Graduate Program in Ethnomusicology at Brown University in Providence, Rhode Island. The intention of the colloquium series was identical to the editors' desire for this volume: to initiate, encourage, and provoke dialogue between ethnomusicology, anthropology, and other fields that involve fieldwork by addressing issues such as ethics, politics, gender, and relations with the people studied in contemporary fieldwork environments. The series was funded by the Brown University Department of Music, Program in Ethnomusicology, and Graduate Student Council, and the editors are grateful for their commitment to the exploration of new directions in the field of ethnomusicology.

Contents

Contributors

CAROL M. BABIRACKI is assistant professor of musicology/ethnomusicology at Harvard University and formerly taught in the ethnomusicology program at Brown University. She received the Ph.D. in 1991 from the University of Illinois at Urbana-Champaign. A specialist in the music and dance of India, she has also published on topics concerning the music and dance of ethnic communities in North America and of the Middle East. She is particularly interested in issues of music and identity (politics, ethnicity, gender), field research and ethnographic methods, and public ethnomusicology.

GREGORY BARZ recently completed a Ph.D. dissertation at Brown University titled "Religious Syncretism and the Performance of Social Identity: An Ethnography of Post-Mission *Kwaya* Music in Tanzania." He conducted field research with Tanzanian Lutheran kwayas ("choirs") along the East African coast, where he sang, performed, and recorded as a member with the well-known kwaya *Kwaya ya Upendo* in Dar Es Salaam. His area of research is the coextensive moment in which music and religion interact with colonial and mission histories in contemporary East African church-based communities. He currently teaches ethnomusicology at the University of Alberta (Edmonton) and previously taught in the Department of Art, Music, and Theatre at the University of Dar Es Salaam.

NICOLE BEAUDRY teaches ethnomusicology at the Université du Québec à Montréal. She specializes in the musical traditions of North America's northern native cultures and is particularly interested in issues of performance and the relation among music, belief systems, and social behavior. She is currently working on the musical traditions of the Dene Indians in Canada's Northwest Territories.

PHILIP BOHLMAN teaches ethnomusicology at the University of Chicago, where he also serves on the faculty of the Committee on Jewish Studies. During 1995–1996 he was a guest professor at the University of Vienna and the University of Bologna. His most recent book is *Central European Folk Music: An Annotated Bibliography of Sources in German* (Garland 1996). He is Series Editor of Recent Researches in the Oral Traditions of Music (A-R Editions) and Co-General Editor of Chicago Studies in Ethnomusicology (University of Chicago Press).

TIMOTHY J. COOLEY studied at Brown University, Northwestern University, and Wheaton Conservatory and has done fieldwork in Eastern Europe, Papua New Guinea, and the United States. His primary interests include the use of music in the construction of individual and community identities, and the history of ethnomusicology as a field. He teaches in the music and anthropology departments of Rhode Island College.

MICHELLE KISLIUK is currently assistant professor in ethnomusicology at the University of Virginia, and received the doctorate in Performance Studies from New York University in 1991. Integrating theory and practice, she specializes in a performance approach to cultural studies, experiential field research, and ethnographic writing. Since 1986 she has researched the music, dance, daily life, and social politics among forest people (BaAka) from the Central African Republic and has also written about urban music/dance and modernity in Bangui (the capital city). In addition, her work extends to the socioaesthetics of jam sessions at bluegrass festivals in the United States. Her forthcoming book is titled *"Seize the Dance!" Performance and Modernity Among BaAka Pygmies.*

WILLIAM NOLL is a lecturer at the Kyïv Music Academy (formerly the Kyïv Tchaikovsky Music Conservatory) and is director of the Center for the Study of Oral History and Culture, a nonprofit research institute in Kyïv. He serves on the editorial board of Rodovid, a journal of cultural history, ethnography, and ethnomusicology published in Ukrainian, and was principle editor for two issues. He is co-editor of *Transformations in Peasant Expressive Culture and Civil Society: Repression of the Ukrainian Village During Collectivization* (Kyïv:1996) and is the general editor of a series of publications, Ukrainian Ethnography and Ethnomusicology, published in Ukrainian in Kyïv in 1996–1998.

TIMOTHY RICE, Professor in the Department of Ethnomusicology at the University of California at Los Angeles, recently published *May It Fill Your Soul: Experiencing Bulgarian Music* (University of Chicago Press, 1994). He served as editor of *Ethnomusicology,* the journal of the Society for Ethnomusicology from 1991 to 1984.

KAY KAUFMAN SHELEMAY is Professor of Music and Chair of the Music Department at Harvard University. Her publications concerning musical traditions of Ethiopia, the Middle East, and the urban United States have treated topics including music and ritual, historical and urban studies, and ethnographic method.

JEFF TODD TITON has served as Professor of Music and Director of the Ph.D. program in music at Brown University since 1986, where he teaches graduate seminars in fieldwork and in the history of ethnomusicological thought. His fieldwork with a group of mountain Baptists in Appalachia's northern Blue Ridge spanned many years and resulted in the publication of an ethnographic book, documentary film, and sound recording, each titled *Powerhouse for God.* In the 1990s, his fieldwork involves Old Regular Baptists in eastern Kentucky, as well as old-time fiddlers, while his writing has turned more to theoretical issues involving fieldwork, epistemology, phenomenology, and ethnomusicology's past and future. From 1990 through 1995 he was editor of *Ethnomusicology,* the journal of the Society for Ethnomusicology.

Shadows in the Field

Casting Shadows in the Field

An Introduction

A Crisis for Fieldwork

Music's ephemeral nature predisposes ethnomusicologists to embrace multiple realities. As Lévi-Strauss suggests, "music . . . bring[s] man face to face with potential objects of which only the shadows are actualized" (1969:17–18). Ethnomusicologists often feel as if they are chasing shadows in the field when striving to perceive and understand musical meaning. Musical meaning is often ambiguous or liminal, inviting ethnomusicologists into a dialogue of multiple realities—a dialogue now shared by social scientists endeavoring to understand other aspects of culture. With a spirit of unboundedness, this volume focuses on chasing shadows—on field-work—as a crucial link in ethnographic processes. The chapters presented engage issues in fieldwork from a stance of cultural relativism and ideological diversity while looking critically at new models for ethnography that populate this post-postmodern generation, including feminist theories, phenomenology, reflexive and dialogic ethnography, and others. Drawing from established disciplines, ethnomu-sicology enjoys the advantages of being a flexible academic field, seemingly in a perpetual state of experimentation, that gains strength from a diversity and plural-ity of approaches (A. Seeger 1987a:493–94; 1992:107). In this sense, ethnomusicolo-gists are in a unique position to question established methods and goals of the social sciences, and to explore new perspectives. These new perspectives are not just for ethnomusicologists, but also for all ethnographic disciplines.[1]

Why do we focus on fieldwork when the most lively debate among social sci-ences in recent years, especially in North America, has concerned the adequacy and legitimacy of our means for describing the cultural "Other" in writing? Though the literature that addresses this "crisis in representation" does give some attention to fieldwork, it also includes an implied or stated claim that the quality of fieldwork is less important than the scholar's ability to represent convincingly the Other (Mar-cus and Fischer 1986:8ff). In this first book-length response by ethnomusicologists to recent critiques of the ethnographic enterprise, we deliberately shift the focus of the resulting "crisis" from *representation* (text) toward *experience* (fieldwork broadly defined). Without denying the usefulness, and possibly the necessity, of the ethnographic monograph, we wish to reframe the critical debate within postmodern social science to consider more meaningfully the aspects of the ethnographic process that position scholars through their fieldwork as social actors within the cultures they study. By creating a reflexive image of ourselves as ethnographers and the nature of our "being-in-the-world," we believe we stand to achieve better intercultural understanding as we begin to recognize our own shadows among those we strive to understand. This interactively realized self-image will resonate more truly with those outside academia, including those individuals we study. If this proposed focus on the processes of doing fieldwork also results in better ethnographic monographs, all the better.

Because of the potential for truly participatory participant-observation (see Shelemay in this volume) through actively joining in a society's "music-culture" (sounds, concepts, social interactions, materials—a society's total involvement with music [Slobin and Titon 1992:1]), we believe ethnomusicologists are well positioned to offer unique perspectives on postmodern fieldwork processes for all ethnographic disciplines. By ethnography, we mean the observation and description (or representation) of culture; for ethnomusicologists the focus is on music-culture.[2] Fieldwork is the observational and experiential portion of the ethnographic process during which the ethnomusicologist engages living individuals in order to learn about music-culture. Participation for the musician, however, offers insight and introduces new problems, as we shall see. The researcher may also engage physical documents of a culture in an archive or on site in the spatial location of research interest, but this is generally a secondary technique. Bohlman and Noll provide different perspectives on the uses of historical documents in fieldwork. Though the authors focus on the observational aspects of ethnography, they do not artificially ignore the textual imperatives of our academic field. For some (Babiracki, Barz, Kisliuk, Rice, and Titon) fieldwork is a process in which observation is inseparable from representation and interpretation.

Fieldwork distinguishes ethnomusicology and ethnographically based disciplines from other social sciences, and ethnographers derive from fieldwork their most significant contributions to the humanities in general. However, the critiques of the ethnographic enterprise that engendered the earlier-mentioned "crisis in representation" link ethnographic fieldwork as well as representation to colonial, imperial, and other repressive power structures (Asad 1973; Manganaro 1990:27–28; and Willis 1972), and to related challenges to totalizing scientific paradigms (Rosaldo 1993[1989]). Since these critiques target the historical circumstances of fieldwork and the epistemological foundations of knowledge gained during fieldwork, can it be fieldwork that provides a path through these potentially damning criticisms? Or, should the ethnographic process with its reliance on fieldwork be abandoned? Although they recognize fieldwork as problematic and believe that fieldwork should be reconceptualized, even renamed (see Babiracki, Barz, and Kisliuk), the authors in this volume argue for fieldwork as an inherently valuable and extraordinarily human activity with the capacity of integrating scholar, scholarship, and life (see Shelemay). Additionally, several authors (Kisliuk, Rice, Shelemay, and Titon) suggest that the focus on performative aspects of culture, and our ability to engage music and individuals through substantive participation, increases both the value and necessity of ethnomusicological fieldwork for cultural understanding. Taking stock in criticisms of the ethnographic process, the authors in this volume forge new directions and provide new perspectives for fieldwork.

Why This Book Now? Five Centuries of Ethnomusicological Fieldwork

In the mid-twentieth century, fieldwork reemerged as a common practice among ethnomusicologists, and fieldwork methodologies have since multiplied to such an extent that a comprehensive history of ethnomusicological fieldwork in this century would alone fill a book. The late nineteenth century is often interpreted as the beginning of ethnomusicology, but that period was preceded by a long history of ethnographic inquiry into music—a history in which fieldwork was not unimportant.[3] This extended history contributes to our legacy as ethnomusicologists and as ethnographers in general. Few of us have the opportunity to undertake fieldwork in a region of this small world where this legacy does not precede us. Conscious attempts by some ethnomusicologists to distinguish themselves from present and past colonial administrators, missionaries, tourists, and other ethnographers recognize our connection, for better or worse, with this legacy. As Kisliuk writes in this volume, we may be required by the people we study to enter into a role cultivated in the colonial legacy even if we actively work to define for ourselves a different field stance. As individual fieldworkers, our shadows join with others, past and present, in a web of histories: personal histories, the histories of our academic field, and the histories of those we study. Interpreted within a broad framework of intellectual and political history, a brief (and by no means comprehensive) history of ethnomusicological fieldwork allows us to understand better the present condition of fieldwork and suggests why the issues addressed in this book are vital now.

A fieldwork model of collecting data for goals quite external to the field experience itself is strikingly common in the history of ethnographic inquiry. This model of fieldwork is consistent with the science paradigm of the modern era,[4] and this paradigm has persisted to the twentieth century. In this model, music was an objectively observable fact to be collected in the field and manipulated in the laboratory. However, a few very early examples of ethnomusicological literature stand outside this science paradigm, and I will begin this selected sampling of ethnomusicological literature with one such example.

In 1578 Jean de Léry published a description of the music of a non-European society based on firsthand observations—on fieldwork.[5] A Calvinist minister, de Léry traveled to an island in the Bay of Rio de Janeiro in 1557 to assist in the organization of a French settlement. After quarreling with the leader of the settlement, de Léry was in a real sense stranded on mainland Brazil for about ten months until he returned to France in 1558 (Harrison 1973:6). While in Brazil, de Léry took an interest in the indigenous people around him and sought opportunities to observe and document their culture, including rituals involving music. In his descriptions of what he heard and saw, it is clear that he was convinced that their music and ritual was linked with "pagan" religious beliefs, but he did not allow this to interfere with the fascination he felt toward what he observed:

> But those ceremonies having lasted thus almost two hours, these five or six hundred savage men not ceasing at any time to dance and sing, there was a tune of such a kind that, given that they do not know what the art of music is, those who have not heard them would never believe that they could sing so well together. And in fact, whereas at the beginning of this sabbath (being as I have said in the women's house) I had been in some fear, I had now as recompense such a joy that, not only hearing the consonant sounds so well rhythmicised by such a multitude, and above all in the cadence and refrain of the dance-song, at each verse everyone drawing out their voices, giving forth in this way, I was altogether captivated; but also every time that I remember it with beating heart, it seems to me that I still have them in my ears. (de Léry, quoted in Harrison 1973:22)

The clarity of de Léry's biases, his first-person prose, his stated fear followed by joy at the experience of unfamiliar music, and his expressed passion for the music he heard, resemble recent reflexive ethnography. These qualities also distinguish de Léry's writing from later ethnographies in the science paradigm, which, ostensibly in the service of scientific objectivity, do not admit passion. I believe de Léry's Calvinist beliefs allowed him to be skeptical of the emerging scientific paradigm. He sought religious truth, not scientific objectivity, and though in his mind the native Brazilians were mistaken, de Léry seemed sensitive to their efforts to express belief with ritual.

In contrast, European writers of de Léry's era, and for several centuries following, typically replaced enthusiasm for non-Western music with a pronounced bias for European music. For example, nearly two centuries later the French Jesuit missionary and pioneer ethnographer among Canadian Indians Joseph-François Lafitau expressed surprise at de Léry's passion for Native American music: "I have not felt at all such keen pleasure as Mr. de Léry did at our Indians' festivals. It is difficult for me to believe that everyone was as much impressed as he at those of the Brazilians. The music and dancing of the Americans have a very barbarous quality which is, at first, revolting and of which one can scarcely form an idea without witnessing them" (1974–1977:326 [1724:534]).[6]

A century after de Léry's Brazilian encounter, Athanasius Kircher published a theory of music including a systematic comparative study of musics from around the world. He gathered together available information about musics, Western and otherwise, including musics in the Americas, to ponder the cosmological origins of music structures in his 1650 *Musurgia universalis, sive ars magna consoni et dissoni* (Bohlman 1991:144–46). This treatise is an interesting early source of music scholarship that includes non-European musics, but is prone to errors and unsympathetic comments about musics outside Western traditions (see Shelemay and Jeffery [in press] for a critique of Kircher). Kircher maintained a conservative neo-Platonic theory of music as a numerical symbol of God's cosmic harmony, but he was forward-looking in his extension of the discussion to include music far removed from European practice (Buelow 1980:73–74). Yet Kircher did no fieldwork himself and based his comparative studies on the fieldwork of others—a model repeated by some comparative musicologists in the end of the nineteenth century.

Systematic early ethnomusicological praxis centered on the scholar's personal fieldwork is represented in several musical ethnographies from the eighteenth century, notably those of Jean Joseph Marie Amiot and Sir William Jones. A French Jesuit missionary, Amiot moved to Peking in 1751 and remained there until his death in 1793. His 1779 book *Mémoire sur la musique des chinois* is based on many years of firsthand observation of music practice and on older Chinese music treatises. Similarly, Jones's 1792 article "On the Musical Modes of the Hindus" draws from his experience in Calcutta where he was a colonial high court judge for many years. Like Amiot, Jones benefited from historic treatises, observation of current music practice, and consultations with Hindu music experts (see Jones 1792:62 for a fair statement of his fieldwork methodology). Amiot and Jones respected the music systems they described, and Amiot is exceptional for his efforts to convey Chinese music from a Chinese perspective (Lieberman 1980:326). The methodologies of Amiot and Jones are not unlike those of present-day ethnomusicologists who study music systems that have ancient, indigenous theoretical literatures—the "classical" traditions.

Like other colonialists who wrote about the music of colonized peoples, Amiot and Jones focused on description and explanation, not on understanding (see Rice and Titon in this volume). The asymmetrical relationships of fieldwork in colonial contexts make it unlikely that a fieldworker would understand or even be interested in, for example, the inner life of an Indian or Chinese musician. Asymmetrical relationships may have excluded the possibility of Amiot and Jones submitting themselves as apprentices to master musicians, a common learning technique today among ethnomusicologists studying classical traditions of Asia and the Far East. I do not question the quality and integrity of the pioneering work of these early scholars, but I wish to situate historically and socially their work and to suggest how their shadows impact present-day fieldwork. For example, several authors in this volume (Babiracki and Kisliuk) strive to define for themselves new roles as fieldworkers in the lingering shadows of colonialism.

Technological advances in the nineteenth century contributed to the institutionalization of cross-cultural music studies using a methodology mirroring science: fieldwork and laboratory work. The establishment of comparative musicology as an academic field in the 1880s was facilitated by the invention of the gramophone in 1877 and the creation of a pitch and interval measurement system by Alexander Ellis (Ellis 1885; see also Krader 1980:275–77). Mechanical audio recordings and measuring devices allowed for greatly improved objectivity in analyses of music objects and could separate the scholar from the inherent subjectivity of fieldwork, which involved unpredictable human encounters. Reflecting the emphasis on sound objects, early leaders in the field of comparative musicology concentrated their work in newly established archives of sound recordings—the laboratory—and often did little or no fieldwork themselves—so-called "armchair analysis" (Merriam 1964:38–39; and see Marcus and Fischer 1986:17–18, for a description of contemporary phenomena in other ethnographic fields). Carl Stumpf, with the assistance of his student Erich M. von Hornbostel and medical doctor Otto Abraham, founded the Berlin Phonogramm-Archiv around 1901 (Christensen 1991:204; see also Schneider 1976), the first large archive of non-Western music field recordings, but Stumpf himself did not travel outside Western Europe to make field recordings. Hornbostel, who was the director of the Phonogramm-Archiv from 1906 to 1933, did do limited fieldwork among the Pawnee Indians in North America and in prison camps during World War I. Yet, the conception of fieldwork as the collection of data to be analyzed in the laboratory and used in universal schemes—such as tracing the evolutionary origins of music or mapping global culture areas—is persistent throughout the work of comparative musicologists up to and including Alan Lomax's cantometrics project (1968; 1976). In the heyday of comparative musicology, the general attitude toward fieldwork was expressed by Jaap Kunst, who described fieldwork as a desirable and even exciting activity. However, true scientific work was still thought to occur in the laboratory (1959[1950]:19).

Fieldwork was better integrated into different early ethnomusicological models active in America and Europe at the same time that the Berlin school of comparative musicology emerged in the late 1800s. Motivated by a fear that Native cultures were vanishing, the Bureau of American Ethnology sponsored massive fieldwork projects around the turn of this century that included the collection of Native American music sound on wax cylinders and the documentation of musics in their cultural settings. J. Walter Fewkes, Frances Densmore, and German immigrant Franz Boas—scholars who worked for the Bureau of American Ethnology at some point in their careers—all recorded songs as well as other "cultural artifacts." The emphasis on fieldwork and data collecting contrasts their approach with the Berlin comparativists, but at least in the case of Boas, they were no less engaged theoretically. Boas was influenced by comparative linguistics and the Berlin comparativists, and by the evolutionary theories that underpinned much of their work, but he ultimately rejected evolutionary hierarchies as inherently racist. Through a rigorously empirical fieldwork-based methodology, he moved toward theories of cultural relativism (Stocking 1974:478–80; de Vale 1980: 823).

Musical folklore—an additional early ethnomusicological model practiced by Zoltán Kodály, Béla Bartók, and Constantin Brailoiu in Eastern Europe, and Maud Karpeles and Cecil Sharp in the British Isles—shares with comparative musicology a science paradigm that conceives of music as a collectable, comparable, and ultimately explainable object within an observable cosmos. Contrasting with comparative musicology, musical folklore focuses on the "folk" music of the scholars' native country rather than on universal comparative schemes. Musical folklorists, like folksong collectors before them such as Johann Gottfried Herder who coined the term *Volkslied* in eighteenth-century Germany (Suppan 1976) and Oskar Kolberg in nineteenth-century Poland (1961), were motivated by the concern that their national folk heritage was vanishing. Fieldwork was associated with romantic nationalism and a quest for the natural and the pure. Even musical folklorists, such as Bartók, who did significant fieldwork outside their native country tended to relate music from other countries (or other ethnic groups within their home country) to the folk music of their native country (e.g., Bartók 1976:146).

Nationalism motivated British and continental musical folklorists alike. Sharp endeavored to glean from folk music national (racial) traits of the English (Anglo) people (1932:xxiv–xxxvi; 1954:1). Bartók's analyses "scientifically demonstrate which [tunes] are pure Hungarian folk song types, and which are borrowed melodies or reflect foreign influence" (1976:157). The perception of "the common people" or "peasants" as cultural and national ancestors also linked the British and continental musical folklorists (Sharp 1954:xx, 16ff; Bartók 1976:71). Fieldwork within one's own country and among individuals who share the fieldworker's nationality might seem to exonerate the scholar from the critique of ethnography that seeks to describe the Other, but musical folklorists created an Other within their national boarders by creating cultural and evolutionary development boarders separating them from the individuals studied (for a musical folklorist's theory of evolution see Sharp 1954:16–31). Situated historically, it is evident that musical folklorists are implicated in the oppressive policies of colonialism and imperialism. The British colonial empire was at its peak when Sharp collected folk songs and used them to promote an Anglo racial identity. Perhaps he perceived a need to distinguish English colonialists from the subjects of the British empire. Similarly, before World War I, when Bartók was active searching for pure Hungarian folk music, Hungarians had authority over the Hungarian portions of the Austro-Hungarian empire and used this authority brutally to suppress all but ethnic Hungarians. The conceptual leap is small between "pure Hungarian" music and "pure Hungarian" authority.

In the first half of the twentieth century, events conspired to undermine the confidence in Western intellectual hegemony; relativity theory and quantum mechanics undid absolute confidence in science (Tarnas 1991:359), and the two world wars strengthened an ongoing challenge to the belief that rational thought would lead to a new and better world. The modern era was over, the science paradigm was challenged (though persistent), and in the mid-twentieth century the foundations for ethnomusicology began to shift, resulting in an experimental moment that this book seeks to expand on.

Two scholarly societies were founded shortly after World War II: the International Folk Music Council (IFMC) in 1947 (the International Council for Traditional Music after 1982) and the Society for Ethnomusicology (SEM) in 1955. The IFMC began as the organ of European musical folklorists dominated by the English, and has grown over the decades into a truly international society that encompasses diverse approaches to the study of music. In a sense, the founding of the SEM replaced (though not entirely), especially in North America, a fairly unified academic discipline—comparative musicology—with a diverse academic field— ethnomusicology—that borrowed from comparative musicology as well as from historical musicology, anthropology, and folklore.

Historians of the field have suggested that by the end of the 1950s in North America two camps within ethnomusicology emerged: the anthropological camp as represented by Alan Merriam, and the musicological camp as represented by Mantle Hood (Nettl 1964:21–25; Myers 1993:7). Regula Qureshi provides a different interpretation, describing ethnomusicology as a marginalized specialty bonded with musicology by a shared interest in music, but ideologically closer to anthropology (1995:332–33). In my experience, ethnomusicology moves between the disciplines of musicology and anthropology depending on the individual ethnomusicologist, but also draws from other disciplines and fields. For example, folklore studies were and continue to be a strong influence as can be seen in the writings of Charles Seeger in the 1950s (i.e., 1953 in 1977:330–34), and in the more recent work of Jeff Todd Titon (1988:xv), Philip V. Bohlman (1988b), and others. The study of performance practice as developed by folklorists is also a model used by some ethnomusicologists (see Abrahams 1970; Bauman 1975; Béhague 1984). Linguistics and semiotics provide additional approaches (see Chenoweth and Bee 1971; Nattiez 1990). Music departments and anthropology departments, however, presented the most viable academic homes in institutions for ethnomusicologists.

Both the anthropological and musicological camps are significant from the perspective of fieldwork—fieldwork was an essential methodology to both, but fieldwork of different sorts reflecting different goals. Merriam's desire to "understand music in the context of human behavior" (1964:42) or "music in culture" (1960:109) called for fieldwork that closely resembled anthropological methods including extensive fieldwork by ethnomusicologists themselves. He believed ethnomusicology must be defined, not by *what* music we study, but by *how* we study music. Like earlier science paradigm models, his methodological model still combined two separate components, field and laboratory work, but he envisioned a fusion of the two

(1964:37–38), and he objected to comparative musicology's fixation on the music object (taxonomies, scales, melodic and pitch phenomena, and rhythm). In contrast, Mantle Hood advocated a very different fieldwork method that reflected his training as a musician. Without denying the importance of studying music in its cultural context, he shifted the focus back on the music sound object with his call for "bi-musicality," a corollary to the anthropologist's bilingual challenge (1960; 1982[1971]:25–40). In the 1970s and 1980s the anthropological and musicological methodologies and theories were merged in the work of some ethnomusicologists (e.g., Berliner 1993[1978]; Feld 1990[1982]; A. Seeger 1987b), and continues to be fused today as evident in the chapters by Babiracki, Barz, Kisliuk, Rice, Shelemay, and Titon.

As we approach the twenty-first century, ethnomusicology is in a unique position to reflect on our rich heritage as a field and to draw from the diversity and plurality of approaches that characterize present-day ethnomusicological practice. The fieldwork methodology of collecting data to support goals external to the field experience is no longer considered adequate. This model has not been replaced by a single new model or single methodology, but we have entered an experimental moment when new perspectives are needed. If the claim of an objective stance from which to analyze and compare the musics of the world's peoples can no longer be made, what can be known by the practice of ethnomusicology? Is it possible to engage in fieldwork that is not tinged with exploitation? Do ethnomusicologists—and ethnographers generally—have anything to offer humanity? As fieldworkers *and* musicians, do ethnomusicologists have particular obligations and opportunities? These are the types of questions that populate the post-postmodern atmosphere and motivate this book.

New Perspectives for Fieldwork in Ethnomusicology

The authors in this volume engage the many challenges to present-day ethnomusicology by focusing on the personal interactive processes of fieldwork in different, complementary ways. The shift in ethnomusicological method from a modern-era science paradigm toward more experimental forms of fieldwork is in part a response to changing world orders that challenge the superiority of Western worldviews. Instead of treating non-Western societies as cultures from which data can be collected to support Western theories of cosmic order, fieldworkers recognize the different and equally valid worldviews held by different societies. The shift in emphasis from classification, description, and explanation of music structures toward attempts to understand music as culture necessitates new fieldwork theories, methodologies, and epistemologies (Titon in this volume). Fieldwork in ethnomusicology has kept up with these changes, but the ethnomusicological literature on fieldwork has not.

Books devoted to the subject of fieldwork tend to be prescriptive field manuals that concentrate on techniques and technologies. For example, musical folklorist

Maud Karpeles's short booklet *The Collection of Folk Music and Other Ethnomusico-logical Material: A Manual for Field Workers* (1958), emphasized the collection and preservation of "folk" music, despite the fact that Karpeles witnessed during her long career a shift from the search for pure forms—the focus of her work with Sharp—to the inclusion of anthropological concerns for cultural context. A recent booklet published by the Society for Ethnomusicology updates Karpeles's booklet and is intended to "facilitate the effective collection and preservation of all kinds of data" (Post, et al. 1994:6). A more thorough prescriptive guide for novice fieldwork-ers is Helen Myers's collection of essays, *Ethnomusicology: An Introduction*, espe-cially her first two chapters, "Fieldwork" and "Field Technology" (1992:21–87). The first and only English-language full-length book by ethnomusicologists on field-work is Marcia Herndon and Norma McLeod's *Field Manual for Ethnomusicology* (1983). A valuable document that is sensitive to variables of human interaction in fieldwork, *Field Manual* is first a how-to manual that emulates scientific methods of hypothesis formulation and testing. A German-language book of collected essays, *Musikologische Feldforschung—Aufgaben, Erfahrungen, Techniken* [Musico-logical Field Research: Conditions, Experiences, Techniques] (Deutsche Gesellschaft für Musik des Orients 1981), foreshadows some of the issues dealt with in this volume but focuses on techniques for ethnomusicological fieldwork. Other attempts to establish ethnomusicological fieldwork methodologies were written by Nettl (1964), and the already mentioned Hood (1982[1971]) and Merriam (1964).[7]

Ethnomusicological literature that addresses issues closest to those in this vol-ume is often found in the prefaces or introductions to book-length ethnographies of music-cultures, or in journal essays. Notable examples include the introduction to Paul Berliner's book *The Soul of Mbira* (1993[1978]:1–7). Here, Berliner explains how he came to learn about the "nature of knowledge as privileged information" through his relationship with a master mbira musician. The postscript to the second edition of Steven Feld's *Sound and Sentiment* contains an evaluation of Kaluli interpreta-tions of Feld's interpretations of Kaluli, or "dialogic editing" (1990[1982]:240–44).[8] Kay Kaufman Shelemay's book *A Song of Longing* is a deeply personal, reflexive nar-rative that exposes the author's experiences as a female scholar of a "particular time, people, and place" (1991:xxii). Titon reflects on his varying positions in communities in which he has done fieldwork in an article, "Stance, Role, and Identity in Field-work among Folk Baptists and Pentecostals" (1985), and in the introduction to *Pow-erhouse for God* (1988), he offers an unusually thorough description of his fieldwork relations with the congregation of a Baptist church in Virginia's Appalachians. Jane K. Cowan based her ethnography of dance in Northern Greece on her personal experience of social life as publicly enacted in dance events (1990). Timothy Rice's recent book, *May It Fill Your Soul: Experiencing Bulgarian Music*, responds to those who believe one's own experience is irrelevant to an understanding of another tradi-tion by arguing "that personal experience is neither free nor individual; it is con-strained by interaction with the tradition" (1994:308).

Folklore literature is used by many ethnomusicologists. This literature is often in the form of how-to manuals and most useful for working with communities in the fieldworker's native country. Kenneth Goldstein's *A Guide for Field Workers in Folklore* (1964) is a classic how-to manual written with the intention of establishing a fieldwork methodology in folklore. Edward Ives's *The Tape-Recorded Interview: A Manual for Field Workers in Folklore and Oral History* (1980) is a readable guide with useful, if dated, information for audio recording. Some of the methods are not appropriate for producing high quality recordings of music. For me, the most useful book is Bruce Jackson's 1987 *Fieldwork*. More than the other folklore manuals, *Fieldwork* addresses some of the interpersonal human aspects of the fieldwork process. Of particular interest for the ethnomusicologist is a substantial, detailed, yet readable section on audio recording and filming.

Anthropological literature on many aspects of fieldwork has blossomed since the 1960s, when the decolonization of the traditional world regions of ethnographic interest contributed to problematizing fieldwork (Stocking 1983:4, 8). Oral and published discourse about fieldwork increased dramatically with the publication of the field diary of Bronislaw Malinowski, the anthropologist often credited with establishing the present-day ethnographic fieldwork method (1989[1967]).[9] Though the initial reaction among anthropologists to the publication of Malinowski's diary was ostensibly concerned with its effect on the reputation of the author and his scholarship, its most pervasive effect was to shatter the heroic myth of the empathic and objective observer of the Other (Stocking 1983:8–9). As Raymond Firth suggested in his second introduction to *A Diary in the Strict Sense of the Term*, the most pressing issue was and is the position of ethnographers in the life of the societies they study and realization that a scholar "both affects that life and is affected by it" (Firth in Malinowski 1989[1967]:xxviii).

The political climate of decolonization and the publication of Malinowski's diary encouraged a flowering of anthropological literature about the "epistemological, methodological, psychological, ethical, and political implications of fieldwork" (Stocking 1983:9). A thorough review of this literature is beyond the scope of this introduction, but a few items that share issues raised in this volume bear mentioning. Critical of colonial fieldwork methodologies, Paul Rabinow's *Reflections of Fieldwork in Morocco* (1977) and Jean-Paul Dumont's *The Headman and I* (1978) stress interactive communication between a researcher and cultural Others (see also Marcus and Fischer 1986:34). Essays in *Fieldnotes*, edited by Roger Sanjek, attempt to unpack the act of inscription of notes in the field and its impact on and implications for the ethnographic process (1990; see also Barz in this volume). Several publications address issues of gender and its influence on the fieldwork process and the products of fieldwork (e.g., Bell et al. 1993; Warren 1988; Whitehead and Conaway 1986). John Wengle's *Ethnographers in the Field: The Psychology of Research* begins with the premise that psychological change affects fieldwork and that an important aspect of fieldwork in anthropology is "its self-psychological import for the individual" (1988:xx). *Observers Observed: Essays on Ethnographic Fieldwork*, edited by George Stocking (1983), contains essays on historical developments in fieldwork of American academic anthropology since 1880. Essays in *Fieldwork in Cultural Anthropology* (Zamora and Erring 1991) address, among other issues, intervention during fieldwork, a heightened ethical self-awareness in recent fieldwork, and issues related to studying one's own culture. The authors of *In the Field* (Smith and Kornblum 1989) raise complex issues concerning the ethnographers' personal relationships with the individuals they study, and the challenges these bring to standards of objectivity. In *Fieldwork Under Fire* (Nordstrom and Robben 1995) the authors seek insight from fieldwork conducted in the context of violent wars that pervade the recent and present-day world. The young and diverse field of performance studies is providing new perspectives toward performance-approach ethnographic methods (see, for example, Schechner and Appel 1990; Turner and Bruner 1986). Others have called for the inclusion of our entire sensory experience in ethnographic representation (Howes 1991). Still more anthropological and related ethnographic literature is cited by the authors in this volume.[10]

The value of anthropological and related literature on fieldwork for the ethnomusicologist is not disputed here, but it fails to address fieldwork problems that are specific to ethnomusicology. For example, issues of representation multiply for ethnomusicologists, who must devise ways to transcribe music sound accurately. Audio recording technologies facilitate this process, but methods of adequately representing music sound are still debated in the field (see, for example, Ellingson 1992a, b; England et al. 1964; List 1974; Herndon 1974; A. Seeger 1987b:102; Shelemay and Jeffery 1993:2–3). Related to experience and the representation of that experience is a gap between musical experience and language experience (C. Seeger 1977:16–30). The authors in this volume dwell on the experience of music-culture itself in the fieldwork situation. The problem they address concerns how to arrive at some level of understanding of music that is like a shadow, a presence that conveys immediately experienced meaning, but whose meaning resists description.

The chapters are grouped in three sections. In the first part, "Doing and Undoing Fieldwork," the authors evaluate their own fieldwork and challenge readers to reconsider what it is they do when they do fieldwork, or "field research," a phrase preferred by Babiracki, Barz, and Kisliuk. Based on field research among BaAka pigmies in the Central African Republic, Michelle Kisliuk calls for writing that fully evokes experience. She notes that research focusing on the ethnography of musical performance stands to bring scholars in other ethnographic disciplines closer to more effective ways of writing about and understanding research and cultural processes. Whereas Kisliuk is concerned about the representation of experience in writing, Gregory Barz considers the impact of writing on experience. He wrote his contribution to this volume while "in the field" in Tanzania, East Africa. By looking self-critically at his practice of taking field notes, he realized that the activity of writing about experience was actually affecting his experience. The field journal, therefore, not only stands between experience and interpretation, but is also inter-related with experience and interpretation. Nicole Beaudry believes fieldwork is first of all an extraordinarily human research methodology—after all, it is humans that fieldwork brings together. In a candid and personal essay based on her field-work among Inuit, Yupik, and Dene communities in Canada, Beaudry describes how the humanity of the fieldwork enterprise caused her to question classic field techniques (participation-observation, interviewing, and translation) and to develop her own nonmodel approach.

The second part, "Knowing and Being Known," highlights the diversity of roles, identities, and self-reflexive experiences in ethnomusicological fieldwork. Jeff Todd Titon proposes an epistemology for ethnomusicology in which fieldwork is defined as "knowing people making music," an experiential, dialogic, participatory way of knowing and "being-in-the-world." This musical way of "being-in-the-world" and knowing differs from models of ethnomusicology that emphasize the contemplation in the laboratory (library, sound archive, study) of a text collected in the field. Timothy Rice adapts the phenomenological hermeneutics of philoso-pher Paul Ricoeur to mediate between field experience and field method. In the process, Rice challenges categories of insider and outsider, emic and etic, and the metaphorical notion of the field. He bases his views on transformative moments in his experience of Bulgarian music-culture, and on his personal process becoming a *gaidar* (bagpipe player). Carol Babiracki critically considers reflexive theories and feminist theories of ethnography as she seeks to develop research methodologies and writing strategies that bridge the chasm between the field experience and writ-ing about the field experience. In her chapter she investigates the impact of her identities and gender roles on her own research in village India, beginning in 1981 and renewed in 1993. The influence of these different gender identities and roles is manifest both when doing fieldwork in India and when writing in an American academic setting.

The chapters in the third part, "The Ethnomusicological Past, Present, and Future," comprise quite different challenges to the notion of synchronic field-work—the ethnographic present. Philip Bohlman used fieldwork methodologies to reconstruct the musical landscape of Jewish musical life in the Austrian border province of Burgenland, where Jewish religious life flourished from the late seven-teenth century until 1939, when Jews were expelled or deported as a first stage in the Holocaust. Based on these experiences, Bohlman suggests that the past not only lends itself to the fieldwork process but that certain historical conditions require a fieldwork approach. Based on the memory of present-day residents of Burgenland and on the surviving physical spaces of past practices, he theorizes fluid boundaries between the ethnomusicological past and present. William Noll's fieldwork involves history in a very different way. Questioning the tendency of some ethnog-raphers to follow prevailing academic fashions and to discount the research of ear-lier generations, Noll explains how in Poland and Ukraine he engages in fieldwork among many interpretive voices—the voices from the long history of ethnographic research in these regions of Eastern Europe. This ample body of ethnographic literature and the extensive collections of sound recordings enable Noll to interpret his fieldwork in the ethnomusicological present within the context of the ethnomusicological past. Bohlman uses fieldwork to understand the ethnomusicological past, Noll dovetails the ethnomusicological past with the present, and Kay Kaufman Shelemay examines the role of ethnomusicologists in the transmission of the music they study to the ethnomusicological future. The ethnomusicologist, while seeking to document the transmission process of music-culture, becomes a part of that music-culture. An event during Shelemay's research with Jews of Syrian descent living in Brooklyn, New York, pushed her toward recognizing the ways in which ethnomusicologists are implicated in the process of transmission.

The arrangement of the chapters into these three groups suggests only one of many possible paths through this book. The chapters stand independent of each other, but are woven together with the threads of issues and concepts. For example, if the authors represented in this book believe fieldwork is an important and central feature of present-day ethnomusicology, they do not all concur about what constitutes fieldwork and "the field." When Carol Babiracki first traveled to India, she carried with her a common conception of fieldwork as "clearly bounded by time, space, 'culture,' and language."[11] Babiracki wonders if she can avoid the disjuncture between the field experience and the rest of life, including hours spent writing about experience. Titon raises a similar issue related to his domestic fieldwork and writing. He tries to achieve integration by circling hermeneutically back and forth between texts and experience, musical knowing and musical being. In a complementary process, Shelemay experiences an integration of life and scholarship through fieldwork. Rice challenges the boundary between the field and home, suggesting that the field is a metaphorical creation of the researcher. Kisliuk questions whether "fieldwork" is a construction to distance ourselves from "real life," creating an artificial boundary between here and there, home and field, us and them. She prefers the phrase "field research" and defines the "field" as a "broad conceptual zone united by a chain of inquiry." For Jeff Todd Titon, fieldwork need not involve travel to a distant place—"fieldwork" can be playing music with other individuals and the "field" that shared experience. Noll and Bohlman extend the temporal realm of fieldwork into areas of inquiry normally left to historians.

Reflexive ethnomusicology is another pervasive theme in this volume. No longer are ethnomusicologists content to record music in the field—to collect data for later analysis in the laboratory. The shift in interest away from music as an object toward music as culture has renewed emphasis on "reflexive, nonobjectivist scholarship" (Kisliuk, this volume). Reflexive ethnography responds to two related aspects of our ethnomusicological heritage. First, it works to redress colonial ethnography that positions the ethnographer outside the culture studied in an Archimedian vantage point from which he or she may view and represent the

Other, resulting in what Gourlay called "the missing ethnomusicologist" (1978:3). Second, reflexive ethnography rejects the science paradigm that conceives of human culture as objectively observable (see also Myerhoff and Ruby 1982:15; Clifford 1986b:22). Instead, ethnographers attempt reflexively to understand their positions in the cultures being studied and to represent these positions in ethnographies, including their epistemological stances, their relations to the cultures and individuals studied, and their relationships to their own cultures. Reflexive ethnography is keenly aware of experience and of the personal context of experience. Though one objective of ethnography is to understand others, reflexive fieldworkers realize that "we get to know other people by making *ourselves* known to *them*, and through them to know ourselves again, in a continuous cycle" as Kisliuk describes the process. Rice constructs an epistemology mediated with experience that positions all understanding within the realization of self-understanding. The challenge is to avoid self-indulgent and "confessional" ethnography, and to focus on the ethnographically relevant (for critiques of reflexive ethnography, see Babiracki, Barz, and Kisliuk in this volume). Locating the reflexive moment in shared music performance is one method pioneered by ethnomusicologists for achieving relevant understanding (see Rice and Titon in this volume).

As ethnomusicologists, the authors in this volume believe they have much to offer other ethnographic disciplines when it comes to the ethnography of experience. As Kisliuk writes in her chapter, "because of our participation in performance, ethnomusicologists are especially aware that there is much one can only know by doing." Shelemay describes ethnomusicologists' tendency to participate in music-culture as "truly participatory participant-observation." The methodological advantages of participating in the music practice one is studying were first advocated by Mantle Hood (1960), positioning ethnomusicologists as leaders in the ethnography of performance, or performance practice. However, sharing music with the people one is studying is a practice that preceded Hood. Indeed, de Léry sang for the native Brazilians in 1557, a reciprocal act that seems to have been greatly appreciated (Harrison 1973:6). More recently, David McAllester wrote eloquently about the advantages of sharing songs with the Navahos from whom he was learning songs (1973[1954]:84–85), and Paul Berliner found his skills at playing an African mbira gave him entrée to a music-culture of Zimbabwe (1993[1978]). Music participation is not simply a means for gaining access to cultural information. Anthony Seeger discovered that it was part of his duty to reciprocate with songs when working among the Amazonian Suyá—he was called on to share music from his own culture, not simply record and document Suyá music (1987b:19–23). Seeger, like de Léry, practiced participant-observation, not only by doing what the Other does, but also by opening a window for the Other on the musical world outside their own (see also Shelemay in this volume).[12] Apprenticing oneself to a master musician is an established ethnomusicological fieldwork technique, especially among scholars of Asian art musics. The experience of knowing people through "musical being" is central to Titon's epistemology of musical knowledge. Taking feminist epistemology as a working model, Titon grounds musical knowledge in "musical being," rather than in introspective self-reflection. However, performance participation is not a panacea: It does not produce perfect musical ethnographies. In her work in village India, Babiracki participated in music and dance, but believes her performance resulted in skewed interpretations of music-culture, and performance certainly affected her gender roles and identities. Using their own fieldwork experience for negative as well as positive examples, the authors of this volume demonstrate what ethnomusicologists in particular can contribute to a better understanding of fieldwork practices for ethnographic disciplines in general.

This volume is not a how-to manual for fieldworkers, but is motivated by issues in fieldwork that are essential for the continued contributions of ethnomusicology and related fields. Rather than an intermediary step toward an ethnographic monograph in which culture is represented, fieldwork is potentially an inherently valuable model for "being-in-the-world." Doing fieldwork, we weave ourselves (or are woven by others) into the communities we study, becoming cultural actors in the very dramas of society we endeavor to understand, and vice versa. At this "experimental moment" in the field of ethnomusicology, we have unique opportunities to reconsider the theories, methods, and epistemologies of fieldwork. Toward this end, the essays in this volume offer diverse approaches for chasing the shadows of music-cultures and of cultural understanding generally. We hope they will ignite in readers a passion for knowing and a desire for understanding that can be achieved only through the experience of human interaction.

Notes

1. I owe a debt of gratitude to the authors of this book, most of whom provided helpful comments on the introductory chapter. I am especially grateful to Carol M. Babiracki, Philip V. Bohlman, Kay Kaufman Shelemay, and Jeff Todd Titon, who were particularly selfless with their assistance. Finally, I acknowledge my friend and co-editor Gregory F. Barz, who is responsible for much that may be good and useful in this chapter, and innocent of that which falls short.

2. See for different but not incompatible definitions of ethnography Marcus and Fischer (1986:18) and Feld (1990[1982]:x).

3. The numerous histories of ethnomusicology generally interpret the 1880s and comparative musicology as the beginning of the field. For example, see Merriam 1960; 1964:3–16; 1977; Nettl 1964:12–24; 1986; Krader 1980; Myers 1993:3–15; and Shelemay in this volume. In this introduction, I join a more recent trend and suggest a longer history for ethnomusicology. See for example Bohlman 1988a, 1988b, 1988c, 1991; Harrison 1973; and Shiloah 1995:ix.

4. By the "modern era" I refer to the time initiated by the scientific revolution in the sixteenth century and extending to the disillusionment with the hegemony of Western scientific thought in the twentieth century. This use of the root "modern" differs from twentieth-century literary and aesthetic use of the words "modern*ism*." "Modern*ity*," and "modern*ist*,"

terms about which there is little agreement (Manganaro 1990:4–7). In other words, I distinguish between the "modern era" and "modernism" (unlike Miller 1994:60–64). However, a mundane interpretation of "postmodern" as that which reflects the changes in how experience is perceived (primarily by Westerners) after the modern era is not incompatible with other attempts to characterize "postmodernism."

5. In 1552, a few years prior to de Léry's departure for Brazil, Mariano Vittori published a theory of Ethiopian musical practice. However, unlike de Léry, Vittori probably did not do fieldwork (Shelemay and Jeffery 1996 [in press]). Jeff Todd Titon first brought to my attention the unusual qualities of de Léry's writing about the experience of music.

6. De Léry's writings were known to subsequent scholars of non-Western music and societies. In addition to Lafitau, Montaigne used de Léry in his 1580 essay "Des cannibales" (see 1952) and Jean Jacques Rousseau used three tunes transcribed by de Léry in his *Dictionnaire de musique* (1768), but Rousseau mistakenly credited Marin Mersenne.

7. Additional literature that considers fieldwork is briefly annotated in the "Fieldwork Method and Technique" chapter in Schuursma's *Ethnomusicology Research: A Select Annotated Bibliography* (1992).

8. See also Clifford (1988a:41–44) for a discussion of "dialogic" or "discursive" models for ethnography.

9. See the first chapter of Malinowski's *Argonauts of the Western Pacific* (1962[1922]) for a fair description of this fieldwork method.

10. See Gravel and Ridinger's *Anthropological Fieldwork: An Annotated Bibliography* (1988) for an introduction to additional relevant anthropological literature. For additional and briefly annotated examples of fieldwork literature in ethnomusicology, see the "Fieldwork Method and Technique" chapter of Schuursma's *Ethnomusicology Research: A Select Annotated Bibliography* (1992).

11. The dislocation or "culture shock" associated with entering that "bounded" realm called "the field" is the topic of several books and articles on anthropological fieldwork (e.g., Cesara 1982; Lawless 1983; Wengle 1988).

12. I thank Philip Bohlman for pointing out this aspect of Anthony Seeger's participation in participation-observation.

PART I

Doing and Undoing Fieldwork

(Un)Doing Fieldwork

Sharing Songs, Sharing Lives

In the ethnography of musical performance we are particularly challenged, as writers, to present or re-present the experiential since performance *is* experience. The project of aligning form and content—writing and experience—is one way in which a focus on field research is reshaping ethnography. One might argue that all ethnography be considered ethnography of performance, since culture itself is at some level inevitably enacted. But the relative specificity of music, while always embedded in and enabled by other performance modes, can provide a heightened example of performance processes. A focus on the ethnography of musical performance—overdue in the ethnographic arena—can suggest incisive ways of researching, writing about, and understanding cultural processes.[1]

The renewed emphasis on experience is part of a continuing seachange in the humanities that is moving us toward reflexive, nonobjectivist scholarship (and, not by coincidence, distancing us from historically colonialist approaches). During our most in-depth and intimate field experiences, ethnographers and the people among whom we learn come to share the same narratives (as Edward Bruner has noted, 1986:148; also Geertz 1988); the deeper our commitment in the field, the more our life stories intersect with our "subject's," until Self–Other boundaries are blurred. The "field" becomes a heightened microcosm of life. When we begin to participate in music and dance our very being merges with the "field" through our bodies and voices, and another Self-Other boundary is dissolved.

In this chapter I address three interrelated questions, drawing illustrations from my own experience with the singing, dancing, and everyday lives of BaAka pygmies in the Central African Republic:[2]

1. Is there a way to determine what is or qualifies as field research, or to distinguish between who is or is not a field researcher? Should there even be a distinction, and if so, why?

2. What new approaches to writing are suggested by the changing, developing relationship between field experience and the ethnography of performance, particularly musical performance?
3. Are there aspects of personal experience that might not be appropriate to an ethnography, and how do we determine when to include or describe such matters?

The first question can illuminate what field research is by discovering what it isn't. How might it differ from other kinds of research, or from tourism, missionization, or journalism?[3] What *is* "the field"—is it spatially or temporally defined, or defined by a state of mind or attitude, an openness and readiness to see, to experience, to interpret? Who does or does not do fieldwork, and why might we say so? Ethnographers use tactics different from those of travel writers, for example, to define who they are in the "field." They also create themselves as ethnographers within the narrative itself, and thereby define their experience as "fieldwork." But are we using the term "fieldwork" to bring us closer to—or to distance ourselves from—our "real life"? Fieldwork *is* often intensified life, but part of a life-flow all the same, and it is inseparable from who we are. We might, therefore, begin to look for a term other than "fieldwork" (field research, field experience?) that implies seriousness and rigor without a scientistic/objectivist or colonialist connotation—incorporating the simultaneous vulnerability and responsibility of fully human relationships.

The second question suggests that one of the goals (or results) of a renewed emphasis on field experience in ethnography is to erase the dichotomy between "experience" and "scholarship," between "fieldwork" and "writing." The question is: How does ethnographic writing, and field experience itself, need to change and develop in order to facilitate the kind of writing we need to evoke experience fully? How might we integrate ethnopoetics, ethnoesthetics, and reflexive, narrative ethnography, along with the latest forays into the ethnosensorium (Stoller 1989; M. Jackson 1989; Howes 1991), moving toward more effective strategies for describing performative interaction, feeling, sound, and movement?

With the third question I come to wonder what can or cannot, should or should not be included when translating from field experience into ethnography. Since performance-oriented scholars have acknowledged that experience is central to both research and writing, and have thereby dismantled the taboo against the "subjective," the floodgates of experience have opened. We need to stem the tide, to rethink and perhaps redraw the boundaries of the ethnographic. Where is the border between getting at *truth* and going into a realm of the personal that is unnecessary or inappropriate for ethnographic purposes? The politically or personally sensitive, intimate points, or serious and profound self-doubt that throws one's whole project into question, spiritual crises and transformations, ethical dilemmas—when and where must they be included to present a full, evocative ethnography and how do we determine? Ethnography, like any creative enterprise, is a re-presentation, a re-formation of experience, and we need to develop tools that help us sense when and what to include when re-presenting a part of life—of our lives.

The Elusive Field and Fieldworker

The construction of "the field," and ourselves as "fieldworkers," helps us to frame and delimit our inquiries and our identities. But the fiction of these constructs has become increasingly more apparent, to the point where the edges and borders crumble and we allow our identities and our inquiries to flow between the cracks. While in the field, we are constantly in the process of defining ourselves, of modifying and deepening our identities in relation to others. Life itself is, of course, such a process as well, but when we remove ourselves from a home environment, pay special attention to culture and identity in our research, and grow to become participants in cultural performances, the process of identity making surges to the forefront of awareness.

Following is an edited excerpt from the middle of my ethnography, at a critical moment when questions of identity, research method, relationships, and theory all peaked at once. I chose to focus on a BaAka women's music and dance form, called *Elamba*, and took a long journey to the Congo to meet the originator or "mother" of that dance. To best learn and participate, I had been initiated into *Elamba* (this entailed receiving special herbal mixtures rubbed into tiny cuts in the skin at strategic points on the body). On returning to the home region of my research, however, I had some trouble finding how to proceed with my chosen focus. This excerpt takes place at a dance event hosted in a camp several kilometers away from the camp where I was living with an extended BaAka family (Bagandou region, Central African Republic):[4]

> As the Mabo *dancing continued, Djolo and Sandimba arrived at the host camp. During a long break between rounds of dancing, the two of them appeared to be negotiating with the hosts about something. Soon I realized that they were trying to stir up enthusiasm for* Elamba. *This effort, I feared, was expressly for my sake. I suspected that they had interpreted my numerous questions about* Elamba, *coupled with my pilgrimage to Mopoutou [in the Congo], as a request to organize that dance especially for me. But now I just wanted to settle in slowly and get to know the people and the dances better. I found, however, that what I actually wanted was rarely of much consequence. In Mopoutou my wishes seemed relatively compatible with those of my potential teachers, but here in Bagandou signals ended up crossed more often than not, and events simply took their own course.*
>
> *After some resistance from the hosts, it looked as though Sandimba and Djolo—with the assistance of Elanga and Bondo—had succeeded in mustering some cooperation for* Elamba. *I wanted to let them know that I did not want them pushing* Elamba *for my sake, but I appreciated their intentions and was hesitant to discourage or confuse them. I decided to relax and see what would happen, so I moved to sit on*

The author in home camp near Bagandou in 1989. Her neighbor, Koma, sits at center with her twin babies. The other women and children are relatives visiting from a nearby camp. Photograph by Roy Kisliuk.

the ground with the women who had gathered to sing. Bondo sat at my side and asked whether I would dance. I said that I probably would not because I first wanted to watch a few more times. She seemed disappointed and I wondered if I had made the right choice. Maybe they had already promised the others that I would dance—since, after all, I had been to Mopoutou to be initiated—and my declining would make them look foolish. But I wanted to dance well on my first try because I believed that how well I danced would establish my reputation as a serious learner. I had not yet seen enough to dance well.

It took awhile for the singing and drumming to warm up. "Mama Angeli" was the opening song. I listened to the drum rhythms, trying to memorize the pattern, which I sometimes found elusive.[5] As I sat there singing along, a young woman who happened to be sitting beside me suddenly pointed to her leg and told me to tend to her infected cut. I was taken aback. I gave her an exasperated look and told her that we were in the middle of a dance and, besides, I was not a doctor (I did often spend hours, mornings, trying to meet the constant demand for first aid). She looked back at me defiantly and I kept singing. Sitting on my other side, Bondo had not noticed the interaction and smiled approvingly at the part I was singing.

My frustration and confusion as to how the BaAka viewed me and how I should view myself had peaked. In retrospect, the young woman with the cut may simply have approached me in the only way she knew how. But I was frustrated by being pulled into an encounter more consistent with the earliest stages of fieldwork, and especially during a rare Elamba dance, while I was trying to communicate with Sandimba and the others. I had a sudden sense of panic that interactions like these would repeatedly interrupt my access to performance as it unfolded. I felt squeezed within a paradox. My experience as a researcher of music and dance helped me feel close to BaAka as performers, while strangers like the woman beside me resisted my efforts to move beyond being stereotyped. She approached me as though I were a nurse-on-demand, undermining, I felt, my developing role as an apprentice by insisting instead that I conform to her image of white people with medicine. Even my friends from Ndanga, who had tried to understand what I wanted (that is, "to participate in Elamba"), and had attempted to arrange it for me, did not realize that I—unlike most other non-pygmies they knew—hoped to pursue my interest not by grabbing at it greedily, but through patient interaction with them. Though I had developed what felt like effective communication with people like Sandimba and Elanga, it was becoming clear to me that even they had yet to understand what I hoped to do as well as had Bongoï and Kuombo in Mopoutou, and perhaps they never would.

But what really baffled me was the challenge of merging two roles: the silent new apprentice and the interacting partner in a cross-cultural dialogue. To learn a new expressive form, I first had to watch and listen. I wanted to absorb the repertoire as a quiet apprentice, but at the same time I puzzled with how this stance could fit with the interactive model of ethnographic enquiry within which I had also framed my project. My aim as an apprentice was to experience BaAka performance culture without radically transforming "it." I did not want to block my own access to learning about music and dance because other people's preconceptions about me were making my presence disruptive. At the same time I knew that I needed to understand those disruptions as part of a palpable context I had helped to create, set within historical circumstances beyond my control.

What does it mean to define oneself as a field researcher, ethnographer, or apprentice? The dialectic of defining oneself or being defined by others is the cornerstone of social and cultural politics (see Williams, 1980). In any role or profession, in order to act upon the world we need to continually re-express our identities; we get to know other people by making *ourselves* known to *them*, and through them to know ourselves again, in a continuous cycle. In field research this task is broken down to its basics, and magnified, and the micro and macro politics of social life are revealed. When I first began interacting with BaAka, I named myself (rejecting the name "white person," which some assigned to me) and redefined myself, so as to try and break from the legacy left by other people with white skin (colonialists, missionaries, and anthropologists) and other visitors (villagers and people from the capital city). It was a long road getting to a place where I could define myself as an ethnographer and student of music and dance, let alone assert my particular personality. The basics of language acquisition and just the time it takes to get to know people made for long-term and formidable obstacles to identity building, and there were continual setbacks, such as those described earlier.

Having a close friend and research assistant to help me define myself was crucial. A man named Justin Mongosso, from the village of Bagandou, had worked with BaAka and researchers in the past and was particularly interested in my project. He taught me the BaAka language, guided me through the forest, and often mediated between me and people's assumptions about me. But this relationship also had to stand continual tests. Establishing the economic and ethical base of our partnership was the first, early challenge:

After the day's heat had dissipated, I took a walk down the road with Justin. We discussed how to arrange the logistics and finances of our working together. The forest loomed on each side of the mud-tracked road as we walked, and black-and-white toucans crossed above, cawing. . . . The way to oppose the lingering effects of the colonial past, it seemed to me, was to take hold of the historically defined relationships imposed upon myself, Justin, and the BaAka with whom we would work, and knowingly struggle against that history, reshaping our relationships to fit our respective values and actual situation. Justin and I decided that the money for my project would be available for our collective necessities instead of me paying him a "salary." For Justin, this arrangement had several advantages. It liberated him from a social obligation to give his money to undeserving but insistent relatives who would otherwise assume, because he was working with me, that he always had extra cash. This way we could instead apply the funds to our projects (my learning, his farming) as required, while keeping on hand emergency resources—first aid supplies and petty cash—for family, friends, and neighbors in need.

Through this arrangement I was spared the untenable role of being my host's employer and was better situated to construct my own identity and relationships free from the weightiest colonial baggage. It might have been simpler (and in fact cheaper) just to establish a fixed salary, the way other researchers and business people usually do. Our way, by contrast, would require a constant effort to renegotiate financial matters according to changing mutual obligations, fluctuating priorities, and emerging circumstances. But, I felt, such negotiation would arise in response to those very real circumstances, and would therefore suit our living relationship.

Only a few days after our talk along the road, however, a gap between theory and practice was already emerging. As I watched the last of my recently purchased wheat flour being baked into pan-bread for Justin's children, I was wondering why Justin and his family could not seem to keep provisions around for any length of time. Why did they need to use the flour I had bought all at once? I ended up sharing the flour and other provisions with everyone in Justin's family compound, not to mention visiting passersby. And I noticed them giving away my emptied "ziploc" baggies. I would have liked to reuse them. "I know sharing is the thing here," I wrote in my journal. After all, they were sharing most of what they had with me (and what I had with others). "But how can I keep my head above water this way?" I wondered. I could not spend all of my time and energy worrying about provisions. "And I hope the money will hold out," I wrote. But my concerns were as much about the social inter-pretation of property as they were about money—about culturally defined boundaries of private property and its connection with definitions of "Self" or community. How I would construct my "Self" here depended on being flexible and examining those boundaries, first with Justin and his family, and then with BaAka.

Gradually, over two years and more, shared experiences and defining moments helped me to situate myself. The actual writing of the ethnography was also a process of identity formation, one in which I could sift my experiences and frame them ethnographically. I returned to my research area after having written the ethnography, with a strong but ever-evolving sense of my place in that particular social landscape.

But in fact the borders of my research area—the field—were not fixed but mutable. During visits to the capital city, Bangui, for example, I learned about the relationship of villagers to pygmies in the national context of the Central African Republic while watching the children of Bagandou farmers—at high school in the city—produce amateur comedies about the pygmies back home. And when Justin visited the United States in 1993, I saw in his reactions yet another reflection on his home world and mine. So, although we may imagine a "center" to our research area, the field is a broad conceptual zone united by a chain of inquiry.

Time itself plays a role in shaping the field and the fieldworker. The relation-ship we have to past research experiences tends to change, and the changing (hope-fully maturing) theoretical and intellectual environment of the mind affects how we take in and interpret new field experiences. The following extended example illustrates this process: During my initial project—which consisted of two years of research between 1987 and 1989—I became familiar with and participated in the current repertoire of hunting dances and women's dances in the area where I lived—the Bagandou region of the southwestern Central African Republic (Kisliuk 1991). I spent most of my time with one particular extended family, but I also trav-eled to gain a sense for the flow and exchange of new dance forms and songs com-ing in and out of the area. In 1989, during the later part of those two years of research, I encountered the effects of recent missionizing efforts by evangelists from the Grace Brethren Church. An American woman, named Barbara but called Bala-bala by the BaAka, focused her "church-planting" work on a permanent BaAka settlement, called Dzanga, west of the area where I had spent most of my research time. I briefly visited Dzanga to get a sense for the choices BaAka in differ-ent areas were making in response to this new missionizing activity.

I tried to keep an open mind, but when I got to Dzanga I could not help but be shocked and saddened by what I saw. The BaAka there had completely stopped per-forming the current repertoire of music and dance forms—with which I had become

BaAka at Dzanga during a church service in 1989. The man at far right wears a Muslim gown and sunglasses. The man standing at center tries to accompany the singing with a homemade guitar. Photograph by Michelle Kisliuk.

very familiar over the two years. Whereas in neighboring areas BaAka were hotly debating the value of what the "Christians" were saying,[6] at Dzanga all of the BaAka had been convinced by Bala-bala and her Central African evangelists that their own music, dance, and traditional medicine were "satanic." BaAka at Dzanga told me proudly— assuming that I would approve since I am white like Bala-bala—that they now performed only one kind of *eboka* (the word meaning singing, dancing, and drumming— *beboka* plural). Now they would only sing hymns to the Christian god in "church." These hymns were not in their own language, Diaka, but in Sango, the national language and the language of missionaries, which many BaAka do not understand (especially the women). What I saw and heard then looked to me like a slavish imitation of the missionaries—like a kind of cultural genocide—even though I tried to focus on improvisational aspects such as one BaAka churchgoer wearing a Muslim bubu gown, another sporting huge sunglasses and holding his Bible upside down, and the "preacher," trained by Bala-bala, reading haltingly and uncomprehendingly in Sango.

When I next returned to Central Africa in 1992, I saw a somewhat different situation. Three years earlier, the BaAka from my home camp had been arguing the validity of the Christian material, whereas now the controversy had settled. My old friend Djolo explained that the "god dance" is just one among many *beboka*, that they could dance their own dances and still "pray to god." They had begun to place the "god dance" within a BaAka system of values.

At the permanent camp at Dzanga, although BaAka were still rejecting BaAka song and dance forms, they too had begun to recontextualize radically the Grace Brethren Church material. At a "god dance" one evening I saw the dancers, mostly children and teenagers, move in a circle, using steps and drum rhythms just like the recreational dances popular among non-pygmy teenagers in neighboring villages. Many adults stood by, some joining in the dancing, others watching enthusiastically and singing along. The Grace Brethren songs were preceded and followed by hymns from various Christian sects practiced by neighboring Bagandou farmers, including Baptist, Apostolic, and even Catholic hymns. They not only blended all that into the same dance, but also mixed in recreational song styles and rhythms from the neighboring Bolamba people, and even pop song snippets in Lingala (from radio tunes from Zaire and the Congo). They called the entire mixture the *nzapa* (or "god") dance (*nzapa* meaning the Christian god in Sango). Ironically, Barbara and the Grace Brethren do not allow dancing in their religious practice, but they do introduce hymns; and since BaAka do not draw a line between music and dance, in Bala-bala's absence the hymns provided the basis for a new dance form.[7]

As I listened to the performance at Dzanga, I saw this developing expressive form as a means of addressing *modernity*. In an effort to reinvent themselves as competent in a changing world, these BaAka were claiming any "Otherness" that surrounds them and usually excludes them, and mixing it into a form they could define and control. But nevertheless I remained concerned, since at Dzanga BaAka were still trading in distinctively BaAka expressive forms for an idea of the "modern."

While making my way deeper into the forest beyond Dzanga (along with my research partner and friend Justin from Bagandou village), I met BaAka who, never having seen Bala-bala but only having heard of her, assumed I was she and clapped their hands over their mouths in wonder as though encountering a living legend.[8] I told them I was not Bala-bala, whom I heard them refer to for the first time as a *ginda*, the BaAka term for master teacher of an esoteric dance form! These people didn't even know the real Bala-bala, and although the disturbing idea (to me) that BaAka things are satanic had made it as far as this forest hunting camp, something else seemed to be going on if enthusiasm for the "god dance" was catching on at this distance—budding into a BaAka fad. At present, the majority of BaAka I know are including the "god dance" within a wider, dynamic BaAka repertoire, where it is poised uneasily among several expressive forms vying to define an emergent identity.

Over time, the "field" itself—the ongoing cultural landscape—changed, as did my ideas about how missionary culture was affecting BaAka. Also significant and more difficult to realize, my effort to understand was inextricably linked with my struggle to distinguish my own identity from that of the missionary. As unsettling as it was, at first I could not articulate that distinction, even to myself. To local people I appeared similar to Bala-bala, even if at Dzanga they did observe that unlike the white evangelist, I helped cook my own meals, and unlike the missionaries, Justin and I thought to bring them emergency medicine. Of course, my involvement with BaAka *beboka* also distinguished me from Bala-bala, but sometimes only perceptive people or those who knew me well understood that difference. Over time, however, my experience broadened and deepened enough for me to establish my position, and by extension to better comprehend the developing ethnographic situation.

One obvious difference between ethnographers and missionaries is a difference in ideological and vocational ancestors, though one can argue similarities as well, especially in terms of the colonial history of Europe and Africa. As ethnomusicologists, our ancestors and our roles both diverge from and unite with those of anthropologists, missionaries, tourists, journalists, and artists, among others. But in each comparison there is a crucial difference, I've found, and that difference is rarely generalizable, but changes depending on particular circumstances and particular people. In one circumstance, excerpted earlier, I needed to show I was not a nurse, in others not a missionary, and in January 1992 I found that even a "performance artist" had a radically different agenda from my own. I was asked to help an African-American artist research a performance piece about "pygmies," and at first I thought we might share some interests: art, performance, cultural politics, and the richness of BaAka expressive culture. As it turned out, however, this person seemed not at all interested in BaAka themselves, but was interested in how they might serve her performance piece and her own romanticized version of what "pygmies" might symbolize. One anecdote sums it up: One day during her two-week stay in a BaAka settlement, the actress wandered off alone to find the "real pygmies," as she said. She returned a few hours later with a young BaAka man following her. She sensed that he had something very important and spiritually significant to tell her, but she could not understand him and needed help. When the young man spoke his mind, it turned out he just wanted her to give him a cigarette. Disappointed, she found him a cigarette and he left.[9] She spent the rest of her time snapping photos and trying to buy BaAka household objects, seeming more like a tourist than a researcher.

The location of the field, then, does not depend on geography, but on the self-constructed identity of the ethnographer in a given social landscape. Similarly, the emergent identity of a fieldworker depends not on a particular location or apparent resemblance to other investigators and interlopers, but on the quality and depth of research relationships and ultimately on the way we each intend to re-present our experiences.

Ethnographic Writing: Framing and Translating Performative Experience

The task of bringing experience to paper is in some ways like telling a story to friends, only more difficult—especially if one is attempting to interweave theoretical and aesthetic themes within an extensive, intricately crafted ethnography. The amount of space required to evoke experience exceeds that of other ethnographic modes such as the presentation of predigested theoretical observations or the "writing-up" of quantifiable "data." An ethnography of performance is in itself a meta-performance, requiring all the care, honesty, and detail that the subject matter—people and their expressive lives—demands. A focus on experience also helps to ensure that we as ethnographers explain both the entryways and the barriers to knowing. Being explicit about what one could not come to know, and why, can often be more useful than ostensibly unsullied cultural information.

Rather than seeing experience as two sided (either "my" story or "theirs"), it is more helpful to see the ethnography of experience as a conversation within which learning is located, both during research and while writing (where the metaphorical conversation is with the material and the reader—I take up this point again in the section following). The pretense of much anthropology—and some ethnomusicology in its footsteps—is that it claims to interpret reality *for* its "informants." Ethnomusicologists and other ethnographers have since learned to be suspicious of writing that adopts a self-appointed but unexamined ethnographic authority (Clifford 1988b). I can only presume to speak from my own experience, hoping that I have been a rigorous and sensitive enough researcher to have gained insight into a mutual dialogue. If I provide enough relevant information about my experience within the ethnography, the reader can decide whether to trust my insight and how best to use it.[10] Because of our participation in performance, ethnomusicologists are especially aware that there is much one can only know by doing. If, as noted at the beginning of the chapter, we have come to partially "share the same narratives"—and songs—with those whose expressive lives we hope to understand, then an account of our experience is indeed exactly where we should focus.[11]

Another argument in favor of experience brought to the forefront by the ethnography of performance is that research is to a great extent particularized by time, place, personality, and social circumstance. One of the most common errors in conventional ethnography is the tendency to generalize into theory based on experiences particular to a certain interpretive situation. The focus on experience helps us to situate readers within the fluctuations and particularities of performative circumstances. This leads us to the task of writing about performance in a way that evokes this immediacy and particularity; that means finding ways to capture what we've learned via our senses, our bodies. We must make our writing specific enough to convey in detail the social and technical aesthetics of a group or style, and perhaps most important, to evoke the meaning of a performed moment. The following edited excerpt from my ethnography is one attempt to convey performative experience ethnographically:

In Elanga's camp [my home camp], on January 5, 1989, I joined the dancing of Mabo for the first time. That evening I had finally decided I had been waiting in vain to be invited to join in the dancing. Elsewhere in Africa people had always called me in to dance, even when they knew I was not familiar with the steps. So I had been hesitant to impose myself on BaAka—who as yet had not asked me to join—without being reasonably sure that they really wanted me to dance with them. When I mentioned this problem to Justin's uncle, the Mayor of Bagandou, he laughed, saying that the BaAka would probably not ask me to dance with them.[12] They would assume that if I wanted to dance I would get up and join them. He added that he was sure they would be honored if I did. This shed a new light on things. But aside from this, I suspected that my campmates were hesitant for another reason. Justin once mentioned to me that some [non-pygmy] villagers think that a pygmy can place a curse on them by touching them imperceptibly if they join a BaAka dance. As with the Elamba and sorcery issue, the hesitation could have been that if they invited me to dance and then something were to happen to me afterward, they might be blamed. Whatever the case, I was restless and felt the time was long overdue for me to start dancing[. . .]

It was a cool night. As Mabo got started I stood near my tent watching, and considered whether to put on a single raffia skirt like some BaAka women wear while dancing Mabo [the special costume for Elamba, by contrast, requires at least three layers of skirts]. I had acquired some skirts in Mopoutou, where raffia is more plentiful, and now I pulled one out of my bag. The singing and dancing continued but I felt eyes on me, especially because I had, as requested, left a lamp sitting between my tent and the dancing circle. I tied the skirt over my jeans and moved a little self-consciously to join the dancing, stepping into the circle among Ndoko and Kwanga, women of about my age, who did not react visibly to my joining them. After the first short round three men, Djubale, Ndanga, and Duambongo, surrounded me, smiling broadly. They shook my hand vigorously and thanked me, "merci, merci . . . ." Then, to my bewilderment, Duambongo suggested that maybe I'd had enough. He might have been worried that something could happen to me for which they would be blamed. I did not think of this possibility at the time, and wondered instead whether despite his apparent enthusiasm, he just wanted me to stop.

But as the dancing started up again Ndoko immediately called me to join. She addressed me as "beka," a friendly term that BaAka reserve for each other.[13] Ndoko led me through some Mabo variations, along with pregnant Kwanga, and young Mbouya and Ndami in front of them. Mbouya introduced a variation, keeping up the heel-sole stepping to the dance beat emphasized by every third stroke of the drum. She crossed her wrists and swivelled them to the beat, crouching down progressively lower as she continued stepping, then gradually straightening upright again. Those of us behind her copied the movement in follow-the-leader-style, breaking into separate upright dancing when we tired of the variation.

Ndoko glanced at me, called my attention again by saying beka, and suggested that I move my neck more, loosen it up. She demonstrated, letting her own supple neck follow through as she stepped. This was the most specific dance instruction I ever got. After a while the distracting novelty of my dancing seemed to wear off. The focus shifted from me to the whole group, or maybe I just relaxed to the point where I could notice the whole group. Oka, oka! people called out, meaning "let's go!" [literally, "listen!"].

My senses tingled; I was finally inside the singing and dancing circle. The song was "Makala," and singing it came more easily to me while I danced. As I moved

*around the circle, the voices of different people stood out at moments, affecting my
own singing and my choices of variations. Ndami sang a yodeled elaboration I had
not heard before. I could feel fully the intermeshing of sound and motion, and move
with it as it transformed, folding in upon itself. This was different from listening or
singing on the sidelines because, while moving with the circle, I became an active part
of the aural kaleidoscope. I was part of the changing design inside the scope, instead of
looking at it and projecting in.*

*The physical task of executing the dance step melded with the looking, listening,
smiling, reacting, that kept us all dancing. Since our camp was built on a hill, it took
extra effort to dance the full-soled steps while going up or down hill. Running the bottom of my foot inchworm-like across the ground required the sturdy support of all the
muscles in my leg. All this while trying to stay loose enough to follow through with my
whole body—including my neck—and keep up with the beat. As I continued to
dance, trying to refine my step, I noticed more fully the inward and delicately
grounded concentration of the movements, like the mboloko [blue duiker] antelope.
Someone cried out,* sukele! *["sweet!" an interpretation of the French,* sucré].[14]

*Suddenly, a few people shouted rhythmic exclamations that suggested a shift to
the* esime *[the rhythmic section], and the singing stopped. Tina stepped into the center of the circle and walked in the opposite direction to the one in which we were
dancing. He shouted* Pipi! *[imitating a car-horn], and the group answered* Hoya! *[an
exclamation]. He continued, O* lembi ti? *["Are we tired?" in the Minjoukou lan-
guage], and we answered O* lembi (o)te! *["We aren't tired!"]. As the* esime *continued
people "got down" in their dancing, crying* heeya, heeya, *repeatedly on the dance
beat, and sometimes jumping forward with a scoot instead of stepping to the beat. At
one point the women grabbed the shoulders of those in front of them in line and
began chugging ahead on the beat. I joined in, finding it hard to jump up the hill
while trying to stay as close as possible to Ndoko, whose shoulders I held onto in front
of me. Someone was behind me, I don't recall who, but she had to grab my waist
because she could not reach my shoulders comfortably. It was unavoidably clear at
this moment that I was much bigger than everybody else [Ndoko, one of the taller
women, comes up to my chin], and I didn't exactly blend in.*

*I sat beside Kwanga and other women who were taking a break from dancing to
sing from the sidelines. I noticed that some singers repeated only one or two variations
of a melody during a given song, or dropped out for a while and then rejoined the
chorus later. Other singers skipped around between several elaborate variations and
then joined friends in emphasizing and repeating one particular melody fragment. As
a song continued, the entire group sometimes focused on only a few overlapping variations at a time, leaving out the initial melody entirely. This was sometimes confusing
to me because I could not always recognize the variations as having been inspired by
an underlying but now silent theme, and could no longer recognize the song.*

During this eboka *I realized that at least some individuals have signature song
and movement styles, phrases or tendencies in movement or melody that suit them,
and to which they return periodically. I first noticed this as I sat beside Kwanga while
both of us were taking this break from dancing. Though I had noticed her singing a
number of times before, this time I was fully conscious of her specially "bluesy" style.*

BaAka women dance Mabo *in 1988 in a camp near Bagandou, not far from the author's home camp. Festive* mandudu *leaves that bob while dancing are tucked into the woman's G-string. The men's part of the circle can be seen in the background. Photograph by Michelle Kisliuk.*

> *When the evening of dancing was breaking up, several friends crowded excitedly around me. Djubale told the women to show me all the* bisengo *[pleasures, i.e., of the dancing] because this is my* ecolie *[school, from French]. As I fell asleep I noted that it had been one year since that first dance at Ndanga when I had pictured what I might learn, and had determined to do so.*
>
> *The next morning people were very quiet. When I crawled out of my tent I felt eyes watching me from inside the huts. Duambongo came over and tentatively said* bala èe *["hi"]. When I responded in kind as usual, he reported aloud that I was* bodi bona *["still like that," still myself]. Sandimba also greeted me with a relieved smile. Considering all the rumors, they must have wondered about the effects of my dancing. They were clearly glad to see that I was safe and sound, and that no blame for any harm would fall on them.*

How should we proceed when we have experiences or flashes of insight that are essential to understanding, but which do not lend themselves to prose description? Occasionally metaphor can bridge the gap, for example at moments in Feld's ethnography, *Sound and Sentiment* (1990 [1982:216]). The use of metaphor raises the question of whether we can presume to translate experience from one domain into another, possibly foreign one. But ethnography itself is such a translation—we're already in that game in other words. By moving directly into the realm of metaphor we boost the risk of missing the mark ethnographically or obscuring rather than clarifying experience. But if we proceed with caution (and practice) we can use poetics—steeped in experience—to convey in writing what otherwise might never come across.

Certain junctures in our writing can call for full poems rather than brief metaphors. Anthropology has a relatively long, if marginalized, history of poetics (see, for example, Brady 1991), but such efforts are extremely rare in ethnomusicological writing. This seems ironic because one would think that music lends itself, even demands on occasion, poetic description (e.g., Cantwell 1984). The avoidance of poetry could have been part of the effort by ethnomusicologists to legitimize our young field in the eyes of those who tended to see music as frill rather than as core culture, and a reaction against unsubstantive but flowery music writers, travelers, or dilettantes. Now, however, especially since an academic green light of legitimacy has come with the acceptance of interpretive and literary anthropology (e.g., Geertz 1973a), we can begin to tackle the ineffable but crucial aspects of experience that can only be addressed poetically. Following is one attempt I made, early in my research time, to try to crystallize my field experience up to that point:

"To Ndanga and Back"

A stream to wash in.
On my way I displace three blue
Birds of paradise.
Through soapy hair
A monkey eyes me from above.

BaAka children run singing down the path
To the stream,
Leaving tiny raffia skirts
Perched on bushes.

At midnight I wake to a mother's
Heart crying mourning songs.
Later, sprawled on her daughter's grave:
"Ame na wa na mawa, mawa na mwana wa mou."
"I die of pitypain, pitypain for child mine."
Milk still drips.

The moon lights a dance for the baby's
Returning spirit.
Women move together,
Singing the collective mother's pain:

"Mawa na mwe,"
"*Pitypain mine.*"

On the return trail we eat
Antelope dinners,
Pass villager hunters who
Hold a baby chimp
Captive—
Pieces of its mother packed in a
Basket of smoked
Meat.

The last day of walking,
Too tired to reach the village,
We camp near a stream.
Dangerous spirits
Move by in the night.

By morning we remain, the
Big green of the forest
All around.

One challenge that often comes with the description of aesthetic phenomena is to walk the thin line between romanticization on the one hand and irony on the other. This issue is particularly present regarding descriptions of African pygmies, because writing in this area has been heavily romanticized. Following is an attempt I made to achieve a balance between romance and irony in an early description:

> *Periodically the forest path passed through BaAka camps and settlements. This being my first time in the deep forest, I was enchanted when I heard a falsetto BaAka melody,* diyenge, *ring out through the trees as we approached one camp. A few steps later I saw the man, singing from high in a tree where he was cutting palm nuts. This is it, I thought, this is that romantic "pygmy-singing-in-the-forest" image I had come to expect from reading Turnbull, Lomax, and Arom. The clearing was actually fairly barren and dusty, but the path led to a shady stream that ran through the center of the settlement. As we approached to cross the stream, a teenage girl who had not seen us coming was singing a brief, open-throated song that echoed on the water and into the trees.*

When writing about field experience we want to get as close to a truth as possible, but evocation means selecting among experiences and choosing among a variety of ways to convey them. When we move beyond an objectivistic style of writing, boundaries between fiction and nonfiction can become blurred. This blurring does not mean that we are now writing "fiction," it means that the *construct* of "nonfiction" has begun to crumble along with the objectivist model.[15] The more explicit we are in our efforts to evoke experience, the closer we can come to communicating that experience and what it might mean.

Ethnography: What's In and What's Out?

Critics of reflexive ethnography often point to the sin of self-indulgence as the fatal flaw of such efforts. These critiques have often been justified, since early attempts at reflexive writing often did not distinguish between a "confessional" mode and an experiential ethnographic mode.[16] The fear of self-indulgence and the label of unprofessionalism created an implicit taboo against writing that seemed too personal, but in the 1980s there was a turning point for some anthropologists. In his essay, "Grief and the Headhunter's Rage" (in 1993[1989]:1–21), Renato Rosaldo struggles with his realization that he only came to understand what Ilongot head-hunting meant in the Philippines when Michelle Rosaldo, his wife and research partner, tragically fell from a cliff to her death. At that moment he understood for the first time the grief and rage underlying the Ilongot practice. Even then, Rosaldo worried that he was being self-indulgent by invoking in his writing this realization and his personal loss. Most anthropologists and other ethnographers have not been trained to distinguish between self-indulgence and ethnographically relevant experience, and have thereby impaired themselves and their readers. The way to distinguish, I suggest, is to ask ourselves whether an experience changed us in a way that significantly affected how we viewed, reacted to, or interpreted the ethnographic material (and to write with those connections in mind). For example, my choice to include my grappling with the issue of the presence of missionaries among BaAka was linked to a sense that my own struggle paralleled how BaAka themselves were confronting the politics of expressive culture, power, and identity. My own confrontation with the situation significantly affected my interpretation and my choices while in the field.

Sometimes, however, we can sense that certain experiences are relevant to an ethnography, even though this relevance is not obvious at first. Field experiences can be like dreams or poems—overdetermined in pertinence to issues and ideas, but existing within a realm of intuition. In ethnomusicology we also may wonder whether our experience is pertinent to an understanding of "music." Musical expression is usually so interlinked with the very life that music and other expressive forms embody, that the intuition of the ethnographer who lived a particular field experience is sometimes the only determining factor. The following passage and poem provide an example of an experience that I felt was relevant to my ethnography but which took place in a physical realm unconnected to BaAka. I had been on a journey to a different region of the forest to meet BaAka who live near the Cameroon border, and was on my way back:

> *I returned toward Bagandou from the west, obliged by the limited road system to travel far out of my way to the north. Riding in the crowded vehicle through the barren north country, I began to miss the trees. I sat in the cab next to the Chadian driver, the singing of the BaAka still filling my mind. We had left the town of Carno early in the morning in a blinding rain storm, and now we were whizzing down the road. I*

was apprehensive because I had just heard about a head-on collision between two trafiques [passenger vehicles] in this area. There had been no medical aid available and many people had bled to death. I breathed a bit easier, therefore, when the driver slowed as we approached a small village lining the road. The village looked eerily empty. We slowed more when we came upon a huge truck stopped by the side of the road. From behind the truck sprang nine armed bandits—their faces disguised by charcoal—who halted us. They pulled the driver out of the cab and then began shooting at us. . . . When I returned to Bagandou I told some BaAka about this ordeal, and they covered their mouths in horror.

"Dream or Not"

A dream:

A smooth antelope, immobilized
Surrounded by hunters.
An antelope woman
Brown, gentle, strong,
Wearing fresh green leaves
Bent forward, hands behind her,
Moments pulsing into a final sinking capture.

Waking:

Cringing in a bus
Seized by thieves.
Motor running, knee on the gas.
Two sickening pops,
A quick breath,
Glass, blood, bullets
Aimed at someone
Black, gentle, strong,
Wearing leafy green fatigues,
Shot into
Unimagined death.

Me—but not the leafy ones—waking
briefly back to life.

Why include this in my ethnography? My experience on the bus influenced profoundly how I remember my research time, especially at that juncture. Moreover, the metaphor in the dream connected the bus ambush to my experience among BaAka and their cultural struggles, and on yet another level with the hunting that I witnessed (I had tried to suppress my reactions to the brutality of slaughter). All these factors together determined my decision to include that passage. We continually move back and forth from experience to a perspective on cultural processes, and back again, until the intellectual and experiential come together. Trusting our intuition to tell us when occasionally to describe experiences that are not obviously relevant can help us later when we discover why they were relevant indeed.

Conclusion

In summary, a focus on field experience is clearly essential to performance ethnography. The challenge to ethnomusicologists is to create ethnographies of musical performance that are fully experiential. To that end I have developed a checklist that can encourage interactive, performative writing: There are at least three levels of *conversation* (literal or metaphorical) in the ethnographic process, and they each need to be addressed. The first is an ongoing conversation between the field researcher and the people among whom she works.[17] The second is the researcher's "conversation" with the material of performance such as song, dance, storytelling, and ideas about politics, social life, and aesthetics. The third—the ethnography—is a re-presentation and evocation of the first two conversations, within an overall meta-conversation among the ethnographer, her readers, and the material and ideas she addresses. As noted earlier, there is no definable border between the field and the space of writing—we write when we are doing research, and we research while we write. An awareness, therefore, that field experience and ethnography are inseparable must infuse both.

A final excerpt from the end of my ethnography might synthesize the three interrelated issues addressed in this essay: the identity of a field researcher, ways of writing about field experience, and the problem of sifting and determining the relevance of those experiences:

> *I had thought, at first, that I could exist as a lone researcher/apprentice, outside the legacy of colonialists, missionaries, and anthropologists. But I found instead that I had constantly to confront my predecessors, even at the end of two years of research. I spent my final week, in June 1989, with the BaAka of Kenga—the first BaAka I had ever met. They were living in a hunting camp several hours into the forest from Kenga village. One afternoon the women in the small camp were sitting by a fire weaving baskets. Mumbling something among themselves, they turned toward me. Makanda asked me pointedly whether, where I come from, we have animals with bones, and, if so, whether we eat the animals and throw away the bones. Confused, I answered yes to both questions. They gasped in surprise. Soon I comprehended the reason for the question: An American archeologist had collected animal bones in their abandoned camps a few years earlier and had left them perplexed as to what she was doing and why—were bones worth something where she came from? This conversation led us to the question of where "white people" come from—they thought that we all live in Bangui. When I explained that the place I come from is so far away that even Mongosso [Justin] had not yet visited my home (they knew he sometimes traveled to the capital with me), they were flabbergasted. I said that I have to take two airplanes to get to where I live (they sometimes see planes flying above). I took out a pair of globe*

*Makanda, wearing globe
earrings, prepares palm-nut
oil in a forest camp near
Kenga in 1989. Baby Molube
steadies himself behind her.
Photograph by Michelle
Kisliuk.*

*earrings that I had brought as a gift, and I tried to use the little globes to illustrate this
new concept. Makanda donned the earrings.*

*That night, after we had all gone to sleep, a violent storm began to stir. I lay in
my tent listening to the wind roar in the canopy. Suddenly I heard Mabambo in the
next hut call out my BaAka name, Masoï, oupa, oupa! ("get out!"). Lungoo! ("violent winds that can fell trees"). I tied my sneakers and crawled quickly out of my tent.
Everyone was outside their huts, looking up. Lightening flashed intermittently, revealing the turbulently swaying trees. Handing me a stiff duiker skin to hold over my
head against rain and falling branches, Makanda lamented how frightful it was that
we should have such a storm while I was visiting. Her husband, Mabambo, stood
holding their little baby Molube. Clutching Molube affectionately, Mabambo looked
up at the swaying, roaring trees with a concerned, expert eye, occasionally telling me
to move in one direction or another. Although I was afraid, I felt I could trust
Mabambo to know what best to do. Gradually the winds subsided, the rain pelted
down heavily, and we all got back inside our shelters. Still shivering, I had gained a
visceral understanding of BaAka vulnerability and resilience. For me, Mabambo's
vigilance was a lesson and a metaphor: survival depends on knowing how, when, and
in which direction to dodge in the political and cultural "forest" that sustains us.*

By the time I finished writing the ethnography, I learned that my friend
Mabambo, young husband and father, had passed away from a sudden illness. The
fragility and ephemerality of his life and our own became even more evident. My
ethnography came to serve as memorial to those who had passed away since it was

written, and the quality of my effort to capture the life they expressed and shared with me was all the more important to me. Coming to "share the same narratives" also means that we have come to affect other people's lives, and that we ourselves have been fundamentally affected, often in ways we cannot control. Field experiences become worth writing about and reading as a result of full participation in the life of research. The challenge and opportunity of performance ethnography is to focus thoroughly on that aliveness.

Notes

1. Ethnographies such as those by Feld (1990 [1982]), Chernoff (1979), and A. Seeger (1987b) begin to fill the void.

2. The term "pygmy" should read here as "so-called pygmy." "Pygmy" is a problematic term often carrying a derogatory or belittling connotation until Colin Turnbull's loving celebration of the Mbuti pygmies of Zaire (1961). Nonetheless, it is the only term in English inclusive of the many socially, culturally, and historically similar peoples of the African equatorial rain forest, including the Efe, Mbuti, Twa, Baka, and BaAka, among others. These current or former seminomadic hunters and foragers name themselves in many different languages, but often use the general expression "forest people" (literally "offspring of the forest") to distinguish themselves from their village-dwelling neighbors. I use "forest people" and a variety of other terms here, but the term "pygmy" also becomes apt when invoking issues and attitudes that engage "pygmies" as a social and cultural category, defined both regionally and globally. "Pygmy" as a racial label is objectionable, however, and therefore I leave it lowercase.

3. Journalists often refer to being in the "field" as "on assignment," but do not use the term "fieldwork," which is associated more with the social sciences and some natural sciences (where the "field" is opposed to the "lab").

4. I have chosen the spelling BaAka instead of Aka—the root word used in much of the scientific literature to refer to these pygmies of the western Congo Basin (e.g., Bahuchet 1985; Hewlett 1991). BaAka themselves never say "Aka" but use a prefix, "Moaka" singular, "BaAka" plural, and I feel most comfortable using terms closest to theirs. BaAka have varying accents; some call themselves "Biaka" (a spelling I formerly used), others say "Bayaka." BaAka is a spelling that accommodates these accents while indicating the prefix/root structure of the term (the second A after the prefix is capitalized so that readers will rearticulate that A). The BaAka language, classified as a Bantu language, is called Diaka.

5. For transcriptions and analyses of the music I refer to in this chapter, please see my doctoral dissertation (1991) and book in preparation.

6. I had at first resisted showing BaAka in my home camp my bias against the missionaries, but I was eventually obliged to enter the debate myself (see Kisliuk 1991 and in preparation).

7. I was confused about this transition from hymns in "church" to dancing, and asked a BaAka man whether, as some claimed, Bala-bala had taught them this dance. He said, yes, and when I asked incredulously if she actually *dances* he answered in the affirmative, demonstrating by imitating her bouncing body movements as she played the guitar to accompany the hymns.

8. BaAka, like many other Africans, have associated dead ancestors—traditionally white—with people with white skin. Bala-bala's reputation and instruction, therefore, held a supernatural sway which, unknown to her, had nothing to do with the nature of her preaching.

9. The issue of distributing cigarettes to BaAka was already a burning one for me, since I had struggled at first to break with the longtime convention of trading cigarettes for hospitality, knowledge, or meat. I preferred to reciprocate with gifts such as spearheads, axeheads, salt, and first aid (see Kisliuk 1991 and in preparation), and had asked explicitly that this visitor comply with my program in exchange for my help.

10. I have also found that readers, especially student readers, are much more likely to care about the people and the expressive culture described if the process of learning is an explicit and constant part of the ethnography.

11. Interviews, preferably informal ones, and direct quotation have their place in our research and writing. But, particularly during the first few years of research with a new language, among new people, the focal point of an ethnography is still with the experience of the researcher.

12. Months and years later, when I became generally known as someone who joins BaAka dances, people did venture to suggest I dance.

13. To the west, in Bayanga, the term *beka* is used by villagers to refer to pygmies, but has a derogatory connotation. Not so in Bagandou.

14. A metaphor in wide use in Africa, the concept of "sweet" or sugary is applied to good music and dancing (see, for example, Stone, 1982). While BaAka often shout *sukele!* during Mabo, they do not use the Diaka word for sweet and/or spicy, *bolembelembe*.

15. Carlos Castaneda's early (fictional) work obliquely addressed this very question.

16. One of several notable exceptions is Colin Turnbull's classic book, *The Forest People* (1961), though the book is problematic for other reasons.

17. This does not imply, as some critics have contended, that power relations are somehow level in such conversations. To the contrary, power relations are continually shifting, multileveled, and resonant with history and circumstance. A focus on conversation (or dialogue)—during which power relations are in fact negotiated—obliges the researcher/writer to address and examine those relations. I discuss this paradigm in more detail elsewhere: see Kisliuk in preparation.

Confronting the Field(Note)
In and Out of the Field

Music, Voices, Texts, and Experiences
in Dialogue

Field research is performed. The performance of field research is one of the most meaningful processes engaged by ethnomusicologists to define themselves. And writing about field research—ethnography, field diaries, fieldnotes—is often part of the process of re-performing field research. In this period of post-postmodernism the social sciences can no longer claim that the fieldworker escapes significant participation in the total cultural performance of field research. Performance is, after all, according to Johannes Fabian, "not what *they* do and *we* observe; we are both engaged in it" (1990:xv, emphasis added). In recent literature on field research and representation, ethnographers assign greater importance to writing *in* the field; experiences are transformed into texts, and fieldworkers, informants, friends, and teachers emerge as actors in a social drama.[1]

Reflections on ethnographic writing often neglect texts produced while still in the field—fieldnotes. Fieldnotes are for many ethnomusicologists an essential aspect of knowing; they are not only critical in determining what we know, but also illustrative of the process of how we come to know what we know. In this chapter I suggest that fieldnotes are part of the process that informs both interpretation and representation, understanding and analysis of experience—*in* and *out* of the field. As John Van Maanen suggests, fieldnotes are "'of' the field, if not always written 'in' the field" (1988:95). Notes written in the field affect perception, memory, and interpretation and are a part of an individual's way of knowing (what do we know about musical performance?) and process (how do we know it?).

Throughout this chapter I draw on examples from my field research with East African *kwaya*s [Kiswahili for "choir"] to illustrate ways in which fieldnotes function as more than hastily scribbled lists, scraps of paper, sloppy or unedited observations, or the inscription of performance details.[2] Fieldnotes were an essential part of my emergent epistemology during my field research—fieldnotes inscribe action while simultaneously affecting and reflecting that action. It is a simple premise, one most ethnographers would not question or deny. Yet, fieldnotes seldom appear in our ethnographies; only rarely when we write about musical performance do we allow our readers to experience our individual processes of knowing, those paths we took to arrive at understanding, interpretation, or analysis. In this chapter I argue for the inclusion of fieldnotes in our ethnographies and suggest one possible way of introducing fieldnotes into the dialogue between experience and writing.

I present selected fieldnotes in tandem with other voices: First, my voice while still in the field; second, a voice of reflection after the note was written; and third, a voice more distanced from experience. I use an *italic typeface* to represent the initial fieldnote, the first voice (presented in the present tense). The second, reflective voice is often an inscribed form of what Simon Ottenberg refers to as a "headnote," a memory associated with a specific field experience (1990:144). This second voice is represented in capital and small capital letters (presented in the past tense). The third voice, more analytical and removed from the first two field voices, represented by a roman typeface, illustrates my interaction with my fieldnotes "out of the field."

As the following fieldnote illustrates, the process of writing notes in the field presents a significant opportunity to pivot between experience and understanding, explanation and knowing:

After returning from a kwaya *rehearsal, I sit at my small desk watching the pen in my hand, attempting to will it into motion. It is a warm morning—it has been warm for such a long time. The standing fan wheezes, moving the already thick air from one place to another. The smells of* ugali *and* mchicha *fill our small room quickly as Mona and Amani prepare our afternoon meal.* WHY DID I NEVER LEARN TO COOK UGALI AS MONA HAD? WHY DO WE "CONSTRUCT" OUR EXPERIENCES SO DIFFERENTLY?—WHY DOES SHE ENTER TANZANIAN "FEMALE" CULTURE IN SUCH A DIFFERENT WAY THAN I ENTER "MALE" CULTURE? I CONSTANTLY RETREAT INTO MYSELF, EXPECTING ANSWERS TO COME FROM WITHIN, FROM A CONNECTION BETWEEN MY HAND AND THE PEN. MONA RELIES ON "HEADNOTES" AND REVIEWS THEM LATER WITH ME. I CONTINUE TO KEEP FIELDNOTES AND DIARY ENTRIES—IS THIS THE BEST WAY OF "INTERPRETING" WHAT I EXPERIENCE? I read through my fieldnotes—stored in diaries and journals—and find myself frequently writing through my experiences, using writing as a way of triggering further thought and action as I reflect on notes taken "in the moment" and "out of the moment" [where do the borders begin and end?]. *I concentrate on two conflicting stories from the previous evening's rehearsal, but find it difficult to make sense of the issues, to resolve the disparity. The rain outside the screened windows distracts me for a while—constant and predictable for over a week now, cooling down the steamy afternoons.* I GLANCE DOWN AND MY PAGE IS NO LONGER EMPTY. MY HAND MOVES AS I CONNECT WITH MY EXPERIENCE, AND I FORMULATE A RESPONSE TO THE CONFLICT I ENCOUNTERED LAST NIGHT. I BEGIN TO INTERPRET WHAT MDEGELLA AND OBAMA WERE DEBATING, AND RELAX AS I REREAD MY FIELDNOTE AND UNDERSTAND MY EXPERIENCE.

This experimental form of re-presentation is just one of the many paths I could have chosen. I did not spend all my time writing in the field and do not mean to imply that I solved all the problems of my research agenda through writing. Nor do I suggest that writing notes in the field is the only such way of re-experiencing, processing, and representing experience. My observations of fieldnotes both in and out of the field create an ongoing dialogue for me that illustrates the process in which all three of these voices contributed to my understanding of and personal relationship with change and adaptation in Tanzanian kwayas.[3]

What Is a Fieldnote?

Before exploring the role fieldnotes play in the reflection on experience, I first pose a simple question—*what is a fieldnote?* Defining just what a fieldnote is and what it is not, however, is extremely complicated. According to Jean Jackson's survey of seventy social scientists, the concern of "what *is* a fieldnote" is widespread (1990). Jackson's informants generally agree that a fieldnote represents the mediation between experience and representation, but few agree on what form that note takes. For some, fieldnotes range from "'raw' data, ideas that are marinating, and fairly done-to-a-turn diagrams and genealogical charts to be used in appendixes to a thesis or book," whereas for others fieldnotes represent part of a larger process of interpretation, "a record of one's reactions, a cryptic list of items to concentrate on, a preliminary stab at analysis" (1990:6–7).

Fieldnotes—often personal and inconsequential, forgotten, and missing from archives and collections of field materials—seldom, if ever, assume an authority in ethnographic writing. Why then focus on something as mundane as fieldnotes— the scribbles in journals, copious lists of names and relationships on index cards, quickly written remarks in shorthand on scraps of paper, quick and dirty musical transcriptions and song texts, notations from pitch pipe readings? Why, indeed, if fieldnotes are so far removed from the experience of field research, the act of "retreating from data" as one of Jackson's informants suggests (1990:24)? Fieldnotes can be critical—whether implicit or explicit—in the ongoing analytical process of one's field research. Once the fieldnote is written (in whatever form), we enter a new process of interpretation. This process, an attempt to understand personal and social experience, is one that changes perspectives and relationships to experiences. Refocusing on the fieldnote in this way challenges how we represent interpretation, calling into question the very notion of "original" experience.

Field Research versus Fieldnote versus Ethnography

Margaret Drewal regards field research action as performance, "placing the emphasis on the participant side of the participant/observer paradigm" (1992:11). If ethnomusicologists act out their role as cultural participants, "performing" their participation, then fieldnotes—the products of observation and reflection, participation and interpretation, voices and sounds in the field—are also an integral aspect of social performance. Fieldnotes often act as ongoing and changeable scripts for the mediation between experience and interpretation/analyses, and in this way, field-notes join the process of performance as we continue to engage them in an ongoing process of interpretation. In the following fieldnote, my writing parallels the learning or "knowing" of a member of a *kwaya* I am working with:

> *After the session at Buguruni I go outside and chat with the* mwinjilisti *[evange-list]—very young with five children. Solomon sends someone off for a* pepsi baridi *[cold soda]. I drink half and hand the rest to Sampson who finishes the bottle. I go to find the rehearsal of the* kwaya ya vijana *[youth kwaya]. They work in one of the Sunday School classrooms behind the church. I walk in and sit on a bench in back. Mjema is teaching a new song, an interesting process to watch, although I feel Mjema begin to "perform" a bit when I enter the room. Someone (Mjema?) had written the text for the new song on the front blackboard, and everyone uses that as a guide. As is usual for a* mwalimu wa kwaya *[teacher of a kwaya], Mjema sings all the different voice parts in the appropriate register, cuing and making corrections, jumping from voice to voice part. At one point Mjema goes up to one of the younger* wanakwaya *[kwaya members] who is busily writing down the text, and snatches the pencil out of her hand, telling her that to learn the song she must listen with her ears, not with her pencil.* I REPLAYED MJEMA'S WORDS OVER AND OVER IN MY HEAD DURING THE LONG *DALA DALA* [BUS] RIDE HOME, AND BEGAN TO WONDER IF HE WAS ATTEMPTING TO COMMUNICATE THIS SAME SENTIMENT TO ME INDIRECTLY—I HAD ALSO BUSILY SCRIBBLED DOWN THE SONG TEXT AS I LISTENED TO THE REHEARSAL. *The pencil, the moving hand, the fieldnote in process—I was not the only one who used writing for remembering, as a trigger to later aid memory. Why can't I trust my ears, as Mjema suggested, to listen and to learn?*

As I reflected on this moment—during the process of writing the fieldnote—I began to challenge my peculiar, inscriptive way of knowing. Could I learn about musical culture just as efficiently with my ears as with my hands?

In the following passage from *African Rhythm and African Sensibility*, John Chernoff outlines his own view of the process of representation that occurs *between* experience and interpretation, *between* field research and ethnography. Chernoff experiences this process as a form of cultural translation:

> *The most important gap for the participant-observer, therefore, is not between what he sees and what is there, but between his experience and how he is going to communicate it. In attempting to do anthropological research, to translate the "structures" and "processes" which appear in another culture into the textual structures of his own, a social scientist must evaluate his own experience with flexibility. Finding the proper level of abstraction to portray with fidelity both the relativity of his own viewpoint and the reality of the world he has witnessed necessarily involves* an act of interpretation. (Chernoff 1979:11, emphasis added)

Although contemporary ethnomusicology no longer embraces the utopian desire to interpret *the* reality of the world, Chernoff nevertheless accurately defines the interpretative act as a process of abstraction. In this chapter I posit that fieldnotes serve as just such a critical "textual structure" in the initial stages of *epoché*, or an abstraction from and back to experience. Philosopher Don Ihde suggests that this process of *epoché* is a way of stepping back from "ordinary ways of looking, to set aside our usual assumptions regarding things," expanding our experiential horizons—much in the same way as writing notes in the field (1986:32). Experience in this sense includes much more than an "original" moment in time—it includes the moment of "texting" one's experience.

Writing Field Research / Writing Ethnography / Writing Experience / Writing Fieldnotes

Writing notes in the field is a highly interactive process of cultural translation, the engaging of a dialectic between the axiomatic and the observational. Yet, in this translation the paradox of the fieldnote first appears; to produce a fieldnote one must project forward in order to glance backward. A hermeneutic circle circumscribing interpretation occurs in the field; the fieldnote, a deliberate *epoché*, "changes" whatever experience it focuses on, whether through magnification, clarification, examination, or reduction. The fieldnote, the "heavy glop of material," as Van Maanen characterizes it, is an attempt at understanding, textualizing, and thus reinterpreting original experience.

The position and importance of fieldnotes are not often given enough air time in ethnomusicological ethnography; fieldnotes are most often represented within a linear model, seldom more than a stepping stone bridging the gap between field research and ethnography.[4] I posit that a more interactive model, one that locates fieldnotes in a position straddling the ranges of both field research action and ethnographic production, needs to emerge in writing on ethnographic field research theory and method.[5] In my own experience I have found that fieldnotes are integral to both the processes of field research and ethnography—they function as an intermediary point that links the processes of ethnography back to the processes of field research. With fieldnotes acting as such a fluid and malleable intermediary point, boundaries between experience and interpretation become less distinct, allowing ethnography to become more directly linked to experience, and field research to become an integral part of interpretation.

As a fieldworker, my ability to allow fieldnotes to function in these ways calls into question statements that attempt to isolate fieldnotes as "simply a form of writing" (Lederman 1990:73). Writing notes in the field is a much more interactive process, mediating between experience and interpretation (and between preconception and reflection). In the following dialogue with a fieldnote, I began to real-

ize that my usual process of writing notes in the field could take on greater significance when it was expected, anticipated, or even requested:

I LEFT FOR MSEWE LATE IN THE AFTERNOON TO INTERVIEW MACHANGE—THIS
TIME I WAS BY MYSELF. THE ROUTE WAS SIGNIFICANTLY DRYER, YET SEEMED TO
TAKE LONGER THAN BEFORE. TWO WEEKS WITHOUT RAIN MADE A CONSIDERABLE
DIFFERENCE—I COULD CROSS THE RIVER WITHOUT TAKING MY SHOES AND SOCKS
OFF. *I meet Machange outside the Holiday Bar, and we share a cold soda. After a
while Machange decides that it is too noisy to have a discussion there, so we leave the
village area and head down toward the Lutheran Church. We greet a group of elders
at the entrance to the church compound, and finally settle on a bench outside the
church since there is no electricity inside the building. I begin by asking him about the
uongozi ya kwaya [the leadership or organization of the kwaya], and he guides me
through the various offices of the kwaya's leadership and their responsibilities. At one
point Machange stops the conversation and asks that I make a note of all this information to insure that I understand correctly, despite the fact that I am listening,
responding, and recording the conversation.* EACH TIME MACHANGE FINISHED
DESCRIBING THE FUNCTIONS OF A PARTICULAR OFFICER HE WOULD THEN ASK IF I
HAD UNDERSTOOD HIM. EVEN THOUGH I REPEATEDLY RESPONDED AFFIRMATIVELY
HE WOULD TAKE MY HAND AND PLACE THE POINT OF MY PEN DIRECTLY ON THE
SPOT WHERE THAT OFFICER SHOULD BE PLACED IN THE ORGANIZATIONAL CHART I
WAS OUTLINING. *Only after I can map out the individual offices of the kwayas, and
repeat the entire structure to him in Kiswahili, is he satisfied that I understand.
Before I leave, he asks if I could come earlier the following week to see his cows, goats,
and chickens. I tell him that I would be honored to see his animals.* Why was it so
important for Machange to "see" me writing a note, a document of responsibilities
of the individual officers of the kwaya? It was as if only through creating a visual
record would Machange feel that I had come away from our conversation with a
true representation of his words.

It was clear in this situation that inscription was equated with understanding. On
reflection, I find it odd that my initial reaction to Machange's request to diagram
the officers of a kwaya was to become defensive—I could remember all that he said,
and I could transcribe and translate our interview from the audio recording I was
making. This defensive posture is equally odd given my admitted propensity for
linking "knowing" with "writing" in the field.

My ways of knowing in a field research situation are numerous, but they are
largely based on the approach of the participant-observation model. My interests
in the musical performance of individual and communal spirituality in Tanzanian
kwayas, for example, led my wife and I to become members of *Kwaya ya Upendo*
[The Love Choir], one of the kwayas supporting worship services at the Azania
Front Lutheran Cathedral, and one of most respected kwayas in Dar Es Salaam. A
relationship of interviewing and documenting, being interviewed and being documented was not sufficient for my primary field relationship—joining and singing

with the kwaya became the only mutually satisfying role I could assume with this community. The following fieldnote, in the form of a letter sent home, was written as I waited for an interview with the *mwalimu* of Kwaya ya Upendo, Gideon Mdegella. In the letter, and in a subsequent entry in my field diary, I began to understand a particular connection I was making with one aspect of my relationship with the men in my *kwaya:*

> As wanakwaya *["members of the* kwaya,*"] "insiders," we [Mona and myself] are fortunate to observe, experience, sing, pray, and participate in the everyday life of an East African* kwaya. *We are often invited to share meals in the homes of members of the* kwaya, *events that honor Mona and I and also our hosts, and give us the opportunity to get to know one another at a more intimate level.* Kwaya ya Upendo *experiences solemnity as well as exhilaration and laughter, and I take great joy at participating in the laughter and humor that is always present with the men in the* kwaya. It has taken a while for my Kiswahili to catch up to the communication and understanding of humor, but now when Mbala slaps my hand after I tell a joke I know that I've communicated something (whether it is what I intended to communicate or not). It has been difficult not having humor be a part of my everyday life. I never knew before how much I depended on it to communicate effectively.

Writing this letter triggered further understanding of my ability to participate in an important part of the everyday life of Kwaya ya Upendo, the constant joke telling of the male members.

In addition to preliminary expectations, such as that of humor, many of my initial, pre-field research hypotheses about musical performance in postmission kwaya communities were misdirected; I needed to redirect my field research project to consider the complexity of musical styles embraced by urban Tanzanian kwayas. Many of my early experiences of writing fieldnotes guided the future course of my research, serving quasi-therapeutic purposes, enabling questions to be asked and answered, problems solved. Eventually, my fieldnotes aided in the formulation of new ideas and responses. In my experience, the practice of writing daily—notes, diaries, journals—served a cathartic function, almost as an inner/outer dialogue with myself. The daily exercise of engaging in this dialogue allowed me to proceed, daily, through my field research experience. The primary role of fieldnotes in recording data (names, places, songs, etc.) perhaps becomes secondary at times when the fieldworker requires an outlet for introspection.

The following fieldnote excerpt not only documents a growing awareness of my increasing influence on Kwaya ya Upendo, but the process of writing also enabled me to formulate a question, and served as a reminder.

> The experience of *[Kwaya ya Upendo]* learning an African-American spiritual: *Mdegella asked me to select a piece, an American* wimbo *[song] that the* kwaya *could perform during the Easter season. I was, of course, reluctant at first to*

make such a suggestion, not wanting to "interfere" with the repertoire of the kwaya.
*Mdegella was serious—he has asked me on three separate occasions. I finally decided
that I couldn't refuse his request, and I suggested an African-American spiritual,
"Were You There When They Crucified My Lord?" Initially, Mdegella told me that he
would translate the spiritual's text into Kiswahili. However, when he began to teach
the piece several weeks later he informed the* kwaya *that we would sing it in English!
The* kwaya *received the news very quietly* [SILENCE IS UNUSUAL FOR THE KWAYA ANY
TIME DURING A REHEARSAL]*—and I could sense some resentment within the* kwaya.
Why would we sing a piece in English when few in the kwaya *speak or understand
English? Prestige? Elitism? Or, as I now suspect, could it be some token form of appre-
ciation of my presence in the* kwaya? *Simple solution—ask Mdegella!*

Through writing, a process of reassessing or stepping back from my initial
assumption of elitism, I began to see my experience from a different perspective. In
this case the fieldnote began by serving a purely descriptive function. The time
spent writing the note and reflecting on the experience, however, produced new
insight and led to further clarification. What I initially perceived as elitism was, as I
later confirmed by asking Mdegella, an attempt to include me—the English-speak-
ing ethnographer (and his spouse and field partner)—and my presumed musical
and cultural language in the repertoire of the kwaya. It was not the fieldnote, but a
combination of experience, time, reflection, writing, performing, and question asking that brought clarity to my initial experience of confusion.

The process of isolation inherent in writing fieldnotes—both physical and experiential—facilitates a change of focus. In a liminal state we become further separated
from the experience of field research—field research itself is a liminal act, a prescribed *rite de passage*.[6] Writing the fieldnote just cited helped me to recognize that I
could become (and ultimately act as) a responsible member of the very kwaya community from which I assumed I could maintain an objective distance. This excerpt
demonstrates the process I went through to realize that I could no longer deny the
power and authority my presence had to affect change in this kwaya community.

Fieldnotes stimulate reactions and remain an abstracted site for personal reflection and for the formation of original ideas, differing from other forms of reflection in
that notes involve the observer in a physical process of organizing thoughts, ideas, and
reactions to events in a uniquely visual way. In the following fieldnote written directly
following an interview, the way in which I created a visual, written image forced me to
see my questions from a different vantage point. I observe now, for example, that I
deliberately set certain words apart from the rest by placing them within quotation
marks. As my hand began to "see" my questions transform into words I began to question the consequences of a specific approach I had been adopting:

*I turned to Masanga, the mzee [elder] of the group and asked him, "can music cross
over to become 'muziki ya kienyeji' [indigenous music]? Can* kwaya *music ever
become 'muziki ya kienyeji'"? I was sure that he would respond negatively—but he
surprised me. He told me that the missionaries brought music from Europe a long*

time ago to his people, the Wanyamwezi of the Tabora region. The earliest mission efforts attempted to indigenize music, adapt it to Kinyamwezi expression. He went on to say that he thought kwaya *music of the Wanyamwezi should be considered* "muziki ya kienyeji." I INTRODUCED THE POLITICALLY CORRECT TERM, "MUZIKI YA KIENYEJI," AND MZEE MASANGA RESPONDED BY USING THE ENGLISH TERM, "TRIBAL MUSIC." YET IN MY NOTES I QUOTE HIM AS USING THE TERM, "MUZIKI YA KIENYEJI." WHY DO I PURPOSELY TRANSLATE HIS USAGE OF "TRIBE" BACK INTO "MUZIKI YA KIENYEJI"? WAS I TRYING TO PROTECT MASANGA BY SUPPRESSING HIS USAGE OF THE WORD, OR AM I MERELY AVOIDING THE ISSUE? *Now, was he saying this because he thought that was what I wanted him to say? Or, was his statement so emphatic because he suspected a hierarchy inherent in my question and deflected (it's not "one or the other, it's both")? I think the latter.* WHAT ARE THE CONSEQUENCES OF MY POSING THE QUESTIONS I ASK PEOPLE TO ADDRESS? AM I AFFECTING CHANGE THROUGH MY PRESENCE? BY ASKING PEOPLE TO ASSIGN LABELS TO THE MUSICAL EXPRESSION OF THEIR SPIRITUALITY AM I FORCING A JUDGEMENT AND EVALUATION? By using the term "African" earlier in our conversation did I communicate a hierarchy, attach a level of judgment to the concept? When they heard me say "African" or "European" did they hear me saying "good" and "bad"? By extension, do I mean "African—good" and "European—bad"? If so, I might have communicated that.

If such a thing as "original experience" exists, I thought mine in the scenario just outlined to be one of innocence; I was interested in identifying the symbiotic relationship of multiple cultural discourses, distinct musical styles existing side by side in many Tanzanian musical performance traditions. During the production of this particular fieldnote, however, I came to realize that what I communicated and what I felt could, in fact, be two distinct messages. My perspective on the original event—the conversation with Mzee Masanga—was redirected after engaging in the production of this fieldnote.

Fieldnotes are typically analyzed as data "accumulated, jealously preserved, duplicated, sent to an academic advisor, cross-referenced, selectively forgotten or manipulated later on" (Clifford 1990:63). In this way, fieldnotes are a step taken directly *after* a given experience and *before* representation in the form of ethnography. A simplified model for this generative, nonreflexive stance could be represented in the following diagram:

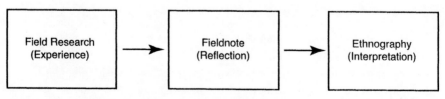

A simple model outlining a typical placement of fieldnotes in the ethnographic process of "doing" and "explaining" fieldwork.

This linear approach to the description process of what it is we do as fieldworkers denies a basic and continuing interaction between each of these three levels. At the same time, the model does not admit that changes in original perception may very well occur before the act of producing the fieldnote. Fieldnotes are locked into the original moment of writing in this model, not allowing for cross-influence(s). Where does "knowing" occur in this model? Although I acknowledge that the model as I have outlined it is an overly simplified reduction, it nevertheless, reflects common treatment of the abstraction of reflection about experience from that experience itself.

Perhaps a more productive way, a better model for viewing the relationships that exist among field research, fieldnotes, and ethnography—relationships that are experienced by most fieldworkers—would include a more fluid interaction between the three elements. One of the principal purposes of any fieldnote is to support the foundation of both initial experience(s) and ultimate interpretation(s), acting as an adjustable fulcrum of sorts. If we extend this fieldnote–as–fulcrum metaphor to account for the constant flux of musical performance, then, as the position of the fulcrum's pivot point—supporting field research and ethnography—changes, so do the perspectives of initial experience and later interpretation. With the addition of an adjustable fulcrum, our model of field research becomes more interactive, allowing time, reflection, and change to assume greater roles in the mediation of knowing. The three elements of the model offered here—Field Research, Fieldnote, Ethnography—are no longer static and locked into place:

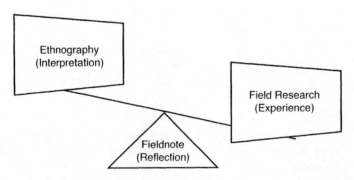

A model that introduces the fieldnote as a fulcrum, supporting both interpretation and experience.

Although this second model conceptualizes the fieldnote as a fulcrum supporting experience and interpretation, it also illustrates the ability of experience and interpretation to exist and interact without the aid of the fieldnote. This model also moves us beyond what James Clifford has suggested, that "turning to typewriter or notebook, one writes for occasions distant from the field, for oneself years later" (1990:64). Interpretation in this model is part of an ongoing process rather than a final product. There is, admittedly, something still missing from this model. It maintains individual experience in a position of alienation. This is rarely the case. Yet, the model does speak well to involving reflection in the overall process.

In the first, more linear model all arrows seem to point toward "Ethnography (Interpretation)" as the ultimate destination. Once reached, however, ethnography is seldom a comfortable resting place. One of the key reductionist points of the academic mission—to capture, categorize, structure, and discipline the practice of others into our own cultural system of the written ethnography—is downplayed in the second model. In this alternative model, the position of the fulcrum reflects the fieldworker's specific use of ethnography as an interaction with memory to understand how we can know what we know.

Talk of models, arrows, and fulcrums may obfuscate, however, what is understood by many to be a "natural process"—the fieldworker in the field doing field research. From my own experiences with musical performance, however, I am encouraged to explore an underlying concern with epistemology seldom approached by fieldworkers. The adeptness and artfulness behind the production of fieldnotes, specifically the inherently reflexive act of re-presentation, needs to be realigned with these epistemological concerns. What an individual fieldworker eventually selects to document is just as important as the methodology employed.

In *Powerhouse for God*, Jeff Todd Titon interacts with his fieldnotes in the process of writing ethnography. In the following excerpt, as Titon prepares his ethnography, his fieldnotes become increasingly interesting for what they do *not* contain:

> I failed to give enough thought to the likelihood that the members of the congregation would talk about us among themselves even after going along with our wishes. I look back over my field notebooks for signs of awareness and find almost nothing. An entry dated June 26 reads, "All extremely friendly." June 28, after attending a prayer meeting: "They were nervous about the recorder during the singing. As there were only 8 (& me) present I was conspicuous." They found out I played guitar and asked me to accompany their singing, but I refused, not wanting to intrude myself into what I was documenting (1988:18).

Titon's backward glances are a clear example of ethnography's interdependence with fieldnotes and memory, or "headnotes." Titon's fieldnotes function as more than "texts," more than words. In the example given here, his fieldnotes become a document of the absence of knowledge at a particular moment in the field. This example demands that we conceptualize fieldnotes in the second, more interactive model.

Other Voices, Other Texts

To support the alternate, more interactive model I now invoke the voices of others working within similar and different ethnographic models. The presence of the fieldnote can be felt in many of their ethnographic texts, and on closer examination we can determine the fluidity with which the fieldnote mediates between experience and interpretation. I begin with a brief didactic passage from a current popular introduction to the world's musics and peoples that outlines the uses of and need for fieldnotes in ethnomusicology:

> No matter how sophisticated your equipment is, you should carry a small pocket notebook. It will be useful for writing down names and addresses, directions, observations, and thoughts while in the field. . . . [N]otebooks are especially useful for preserving information learned in interviews . . . [Y]ou should make every effort to write down your detailed impressions of the overall field situation . . . your reactions and responses to the field experience as it takes place (Reck, Slobin, and Titon 1992:446).

Beyond the surface need for "preserving information," these authors suggest that fieldnotes—names, addresses, directions, and observations—support another, perhaps more significant process, the reflective process of responding to experience and interpreting experience through text. Although the process of writing notes in the field, specifically writing openly in front of colleagues, friends, and teachers, is not always considered the best method of documentation, the distance between jotting down information and taking the time to be reflexive is perhaps not all that great. It is also possible, however, to make the argument that writing fieldnotes while "in the field" can be a way of distancing oneself from experience rather than approaching it. As anthropologist Michael Jackson suggests, fieldnotes have their appropriate place, out of sight, or perhaps they should not be taken at all. Jackson suggests that only when we start to use our senses, "to listen, watch, smell, touch, dance, learn to cook, make mats, light a fire, farm," do we begin to make sense in our written notes (1989:9).

"Texting" one's experience is often a way of testing one's understanding of a situation. Anthropologist Edward Bruner suggests that an "ethnographic dialogue" develops when we enter into the practice of written interpretation (1986). The production of fieldnotes is a deliberate gesture, indicating a need for interaction, for "dialogue" with the various actors of social drama as well as with oneself. The "negotiation of the text," however, is just part of the reflexivity of fieldnotes, whatever form they take—whether entries in a field diary, scribbled notes on a scrap of paper, song texts, diagrams and outlines of performance spaces, or personal reflection (Bruner 1986:147–48). The process of producing a fieldnote is, of course, only one step in a complicated process of representation, and when combined with all the senses of experience a truly interactive ethnography emerges. The transformation of experience into discourse leads to dialogue between one's knowing and reflection on that knowing, and the transcription is not easy.

An act of interpretation that goes unseen and unpublished, fieldnotes are often of use only to the individual fieldworker. They are produced for a specific, personal reason, to function in a specific ongoing and reflexive ethnographic inner dialogue within the fieldworker. Fieldnotes are intended to be links between experience and the later "text" of ethnography, and are commentary on the secret and private lives of the observer and the observed, yet the fieldnote often must be combined with headnotes in order to make sense. Introducing headnotes, a form of unwritten fieldnotes, into the first, more linear Field Research–Fieldnote–Ethnography model could cause havoc with the directionality of the arrows. When in "constant dialogue" with headnotes, fieldnotes facilitate an interpretation that is never final, but always engaged in an ongoing process of re-evaluation.

Not everyone views fieldnotes and headnotes in tandem, however. In *Tales of the Field*, John Van Maanen maintains an objectification of fieldnotes, locking them into one specific moment of time in the field by claiming they are "only a tiny fraction of the fieldworker's own memory of the research period" (1988:117–18). This attitude continues to divorce the fieldnote from the process that produced it, reducing fieldnotes to ink on paper. Perhaps the most significant response to this would be to reflect on the changes in shelf life of my own fieldnotes. They seem to make increasingly less sense as time goes by, conveying less meaning now that I have been back from my field research for almost a year. Will they continue to degenerate in this way? Are all of my fieldnotes really as "incomplete and insufficient" as Van Maanen suggests (1988:117–18)? Probably so, but here again, I have fallen into the trap of treating fieldnotes as texts rather than part of my personal, ongoing process of interpretation and understanding.

Perhaps one of the principal reasons fieldnotes are so difficult to deal with in a post–field research situation is that they served their main purpose while still in the field, yet these "secret papers" live and breathe new life into many later studies based on "original" field research experiences. The fieldnotes one protects as carry-on luggage when leaving the field represent more than the negotiation between interpretation and experience; often, fieldnotes are a physical link, the trigger of memory, the sentimental reminder, or the source for new ideas and "translations." However, time seems to become the enemy of fieldnotes, creating an awkward distance between inscription and event. As Roger Sanjek has suggested, Malinowski was heavily dependent on his own fieldnotes while still in the field, using them as a form of analysis as well as for reflection and review, a way to spark new ways of interpreting experience, yet once out of the field they took on new meaning (1990:210). When I am in the field I ask many of the same questions that my historical colleagues asked. I believe that there are slight differences, however. Ethnomusicology now embraces so many wonderfully diverse ways of "being-in-the-world" musically, and I, as an ethnomusicologist, am comfortable exploring the periphery of shifting paradigms, so I am no longer concerned with defining what music is and what it is not.

Several not-too-distant disciplinary relatives in ethnomusicology entertained some of the same concerns with fieldnotes. In *The Ethnomusicologist*, for example, Mantle Hood includes several descriptions of the interaction between his headnotes

Male members of Kwaya ya Upendo *during a break from a recording session at the Tanzanian Film Company.* Front Row (seated): *Shadrock Kyambile, Goodvoice Materu, Jacobson Mmbaga, Gregory Barz, Charles Simpungwe.* Back Row (standing and kneeling): *Gideon Mdegella, Rishiael Tareto, Elioth Mujumba. Photograph by Mona Christenson Barz, also a member of* Kwaya ya Upendo.

and fieldnotes, outlining a fundamental interaction between experience and text. According to Hood, once ethnomusicologists involve themselves in the process of producing fieldnotes, they may "challenge" and further re-evaluate a particular experience (1982(1971):229). The arrows in Hood's field research model—the negotiation between experience, representation, and fieldnotes—point in many directions.

The Fieldnote as Object

I look at several recently developed photographs that document my final recording session with Kwaya ya Upendo. *I eagerly make my way through the stack several times. Each time I linger on one particular photograph—a group of eight male kwaya members of the* kwaya *(including myself) relaxing during a break in the session. We meet to discuss whether to include a* pambio *[call-and-response chorus] on the cassette. The composition of the photograph is curious—we look strange sitting on the ground with our feet in the water drainage ditch. The photograph is slightly underexposed, and not everyone appears to be aware of when the shutter was actually released. I remain focused on this photograph for quite some time.*

Just as I begin to move on through the stack I notice that I am holding a pen and

James Obama, the mwenyekiti *[chairperson] of* Kwaya ya Upendo, *and Gregory Barz. Photograph by Mona Christenson Barz.*

a small notebook in this photograph. The notebook, an inexpensive type, mass-produced for Tanzanian school children, is folded open. I often carried a small notebook while working with kwayas to scribble down quick notes—observations, names, ideas, and thoughts to expand on at a later time. *I look at this photograph now and see the actual process of producing fieldnotes taking form in front of me. I am clutching this notebook as if preparing to write something down as soon as the camera is put away. Or, have I already jotted down a quick thought or observation?* I HAD NOT BEEN AWARE DURING THE ACTUAL RECORDING SESSION OF THE NOTEBOOK APPEARING AS PROMINENT AS IT IS IN THIS PHOTOGRAPH. Maybe it wasn't. AND, I CANNOT RECALL IF I DISTANCED MYSELF AT ALL FROM OTHER MEMBERS OF THE *KWAYA* BY CARRYING THIS NOTEBOOK. How would I know? How would I ever know unless I ask? *I move on through the stack and come to a photograph of the kwaya's chairperson, James Obama, and myself sitting in the same drainage ditch later in the afternoon at the end of the long recording session—the notebook and pen are still firmly rooted in my hands.*

Curiosity led me to search through my various field research journals and notebooks to find the particular fieldnote that would have been written at the time of this photograph. Tucked behind a quick list of songs we were recording that day I found it. Even in its simplicity this note reveals an odd abstraction, an awareness achieved by pulling back.

How could I have ever seen myself as an intrusion? Kwaya ya Upendo doesn't need
me to document—they are perfectly capable of documenting themselves.

As if in answer to my earlier concerns as I worked my way through the stack of
photographs, I uncovered a transition I had originally worked through during the
recording session. I had addressed the very same issues at that moment as I do now
when I look at this photograph. Did I really think that I wasn't an intrusion—notebook or no notebook? Surely all fieldworkers are. The quick-and-dirty fieldnote
written hastily between takes at the recording studio suggests my realization that
my personal documentation, or stepping back from experience, was normative
within the kwaya; the kwaya was just as busy documenting itself—video and audio
recordings. In this case, taking notes during the kwaya's recording session was not a
way of stepping back from the kwaya, but a way of observing and reflecting in a
manner that was not outside the experience of the kwaya itself.

Fieldnotes: Beyond Text

"*Having* notes . . . is one thing . . . [b]ut *using* them is quite another" (Lederman
1990:90). Most ethnographers would agree with Lederman that the fieldnote is ultimately supposed to be of some use, that it must serve some purpose in the later
"writing up" stage, the construction of ethnography. A few authors have depended
heavily on fieldnotes as a principal source of documentation, often published with
little analysis, and there are also many who admit to not referring to fieldnotes at
all during their "writing-up" stage. Whether referred to or not, fieldnotes move
beyond text in their ability to communicate a sense of what was happening at a
particular moment "in the field." Beyond documentation, fieldnotes often communicate to an audience many of the frustrations, reactions, conflicts, and troubles
encountered in field research, communicating just how the fieldworker comes to
know what she/he knows.

Recently, while preparing an essay—written both in and out of the field—on
kwaya as popular music in Tanzania, I reviewed my fieldnotes looking for valida-
tion of what was to be the essay's main thesis: kwaya music is becoming a significant genre of contemporary Tanzania popular music. The strong feelings invoked
when I (re-)read the following note challenged me to represent the multiple worlds
in which kwaya music exists in Tanzania:

He is from Mbeya and didn't know anything about a Kwaya ya Maombolezo tradi-
tion there . . . When I asked him if his kwaya sang mapambio [improvised call-and-
response choruses] he said that usually only vijana [youths] and "born agains" sing
mapambio. *This seems like a generalization, but it is probably true. A little discour-*
aging was his read on the state of kwaya *music in Tanzania. When I asked him about*
music in his village in Mbeya he told me that the kwaya only sang traditional
Nyakyusa melodies with traditional harmonies, ngoma [drums], and other Tanzan-

ian instruments. I HAD TO FIGHT THE URGE TO TELL HIM HOW WONDERFUL THAT MUST BE! *He went on to say that his kwaya at home could not sing Bach and Handel the way his kwaya in Dar Es Salaam could.* AT SOME LEVEL THE RELATIVIST IN ME TOOK A BREAK AND ALLOWED ME TO FEEL A LOSS FOR HIS CULTURE. I ALSO FELT ANGER AT TRADITIONAL EXPRESSIVE CULTURE BEING RELEGATED TO A SECOND-CLASS STATUS, WHILE THE MUSIC OF THE WESTERN PENETRATION, COLONIZATION, AND CONVERSION PROCESSES RAISED TO NEAR WORSHIP STATUS.

Writing this fieldnote and rereading it now allows me to re-experience this moment, triggering many of the same conflicted emotions I felt when first talking with this young man: joy, anger, sadness, and frustration. This particular fieldnote served a therapeutic purpose at the time of writing, but now also reminds me of the need to embrace conflict in my interpretation of music in kwaya communities. The fieldnote in this case took me beyond the text, back to the field experience at the same time as it propelled me forward to interpretation.

Conclusion: Beyond "Keeping Good Field Notes"

No longer a marginal, or occulted, dimension, writing has emerged as central to what anthropologists do both *in the field* and thereafter. The fact that it has not until recently been portrayed or seriously discussed reflects the persistence of an ideology claiming transparency of representation and immediacy of experience. Writing reduced to method: *keeping good field notes*, making accurate maps, "writing up" results. (James Clifford 1986b:2, emphasis added)

The continuing presence of epistemological questions lurk close to the surface of my fieldnotes—"What do I know?" and "How can I know what I know?" As I continue to (re-)read the experiences entered as fieldnotes in my journals, notebooks, and diaries and listen to the many voices they contain, I am encouraged to renegotiate ideas, restructure hypotheses, question conclusions, and re-evaluate particular stances I have adopted. In this chapter I attempt to locate fieldnotes within an interactive system in which the production of fieldnotes continually affects and reaffects experience and interpretation, both in and out of the field. Fieldnotes play a major role in the overall performance of field research, and as such they are interdependent. The isolation of fieldnotes from the process that produces them denies change over time as well as the ability of experience to be continually re-evaluated. Writing in the field can move beyond what James Clifford suggests would be "keeping good field notes." Only when we release field notes from an objectification that reduces them to "heavy glop" and inexactness can we begin to include our reactions, responses, and ongoing interaction with notes in our interpretive processes.

In this chapter, I also challenged the construction of cultural translation while still "in the field" by sharing several experiences that led me in my own field research to reject a linear approach to ethnography—Field Research–Fieldnote–Ethnography.

Destabilization of this model allowed me to understand experience, understanding, and representation as interdependent. By focusing specifically on fieldnotes I actually focused on myself and on the epistemological processes of just how I came to know what I know. In a recent review essay of Roger Sanjek's *Fieldnotes*, anthropologist James Fernandez identifies the motivations of many fieldworkers searching for new field research/representation models to be a response to current "problems of reliability and credibility in ethnography" (1993:181). Although writing in the field may very well be just another way of "texting" one's experiences, it is, as I found out, a unique way to approach issues of reliability and readability.

Notes

1. Significant contributions to literature on relationships between ethnography and field research include: Clifford and Marcus 1986; Van Maanen 1988; Sanjek 1990; M. Jackson 1989; Atkinson 1990; and Emerson, Fretz, and Shaw 1995.

2. Earlier drafts of this chapter were read by Mona Christenson Barz, Timothy Cooley, Carolyn Schiller Johnson, Michelle Kisliuk, and Jeff Todd Titon. I am extremely grateful for their comments and suggestions.

3. I am indebted to Ellen Koskoff's presentation of ethnographic material of Lubavitcher women's song for the inspiration of presenting multiple styles/voices within an essay (1993).

4. See, for example, Bruno Nettl: "[T]here is no question that much of what I say is an interpretation of what they said, what I have read, and what I observed" (1989:x) and "In the most technical sense, ethnography describes culture synchronically" (1989:x, 8). Such a view creates a separation, divorcing experience from representation—in this case, the "ethnography" not the ethnographer does the description.

5. See, for example, A. Seeger 1987b for an example of the interactive field research-fieldnote-ethnography model. See also Feld 1990[1982].

6. I use liminality in this sense to refer to the separation of the field research from a "home" community while living in a "field" community. See Victor Turner for a discussion of liminality as the separation of individual from community (1989[1969]:102–8).

The Challenges of Human Relations in Ethnographic Enquiry

Examples from Arctic and Subarctic Fieldwork

> Once a journey is designed, equipped, and put in process, a new factor enters and
> takes over. A trip, a safari, an exploration, is an entity, different from all other jour-
> neys. It has personality, temperament, individuality, uniqueness. A journey is a per-
> son in itself; no two are alike. And all plans, safeguards, policing and coercion are
> fruitless. We find after years of struggle that we do not take a trip; a trip takes us.
>
> John Steinbeck, *Travels with Charley in Search of America*

John Steinbeck's wonderfully witty and judicious remark could easily apply to most
of my field experiences and probably to those of many other researchers. Although
it is seldom stated clearly in our writings, fieldworkers in any of the social sciences
frequently need to alter their research plans at the last minute. These changes are
felt to be beyond their command. Despite belief in the value of our scientific goals,
despite painstaking preparations and appropriate behavior, the fact that both
researcher and research objects are human beings cannot be dismissed. When
human beings of different cultural backgrounds are brought together, their interaction proves difficult to predict.

    This chapter explores some of the human dimensions involved in my own ethno-
musicological fieldwork in Arctic and sub-Arctic contexts, and their direct bearing on
my understanding of Inuit, Yupik, and Dene cultures. Within the field of ethnomusicology, this dimension of our work is infrequently discussed in detail, let alone analyzed. Perhaps this is so because it awakens raw emotions one hesitates to reveal publicly and perhaps it is also a consequence of our traditionally positivistic attitude toward
scientific objectivity that forbids the emotional realm to enter the rational realm.

    However, since Malinowski's time, when informants were referred to as the
natives or the savages (see, for instance, his *Diary in the Strict Sense of the Term*
1989[1967]), the trend has been reversed. Most anthropologists now openly recog-

nize and value the human reality and the vulnerability to emotions, enthusiasm, hang-ups, likes, and dislikes of their informants as well as their own, and their obvious impact in the field situation on interpersonal relationships. Most anthropologists also admit to the fact that entering a different cultural setting not only informs us about the "Other" but also in very significant ways enlightens us about ourselves. As Cesara states:

> [A]n anthropologist needs all aspects of his personality, not merely his drive to know; and he needs them under his command to produce good work. He is simultaneously an apprentice researcher and an apprentice human being until, that is, he has become a master of himself. (1982:100)

Although this is true of anyone, looking at oneself from outside one's habitual setting offers a privileged vantage point. In other words, the fieldwork experience and its introspective correlate accelerate personal growth. An anthropologist's work and writings should then reflect both his and his informant's humanity—an echo of anthropology's true mission as the study of humans.

Some anthropologists are particularly successful in this, and I am thinking here of Laura Bohannan [Eleonore Smith Bowen] (1964), Jean Briggs (1970), Manda Cesara (1982), Paul Rabinow (1983), Rosalie Wax (1971), and several others grouped under Peggy Golde's editorship (1986[1970]). Not only do these authors write about personal feelings and emotional responses, they are also able to weave their own and their hosts' personalities and expectations into their perception of the other culture. At the risk of presenting a candid portrait of myself, I firmly believe it is useful to investigate this further, and I shall try to describe and analyze some of my own explorations of other cultures. However, I wish to avoid what John Van Maanen's flippant irony designates as "confessional tales" because I do not wish to be drawn into a simple description of a "fieldwork odyssey" (1988:75). Furthermore, I have no doubt that this discussion is relevant because it helps demystify our sources of knowledge. This raises crucial epistemological questions about knowledge and knowledge acquisition through fieldwork—the same kinds we might ask of historical documents. The difference is that in the process of fieldwork we are face-to-face with the authors of our information.

Over the last twenty-odd years, since 1974, my experience as a field researcher in Inuit, Yupik, and Dene cultures parallels my growth as an ethnomusicologist and as a human being. My discussion here reflects the different stages I went through. For instance, moving from a research assistantship, to the writing of a doctoral dissertation, to autonomous research, represents academic growth. Over the same period, my resourcefulness as a fieldworker was tested by the immense cultural differences I found between each of the northern settings I had the opportunity to explore. In whichever northern context I worked, I perhaps grew accustomed to travel in small planes and by snowmobile, to eating unusual foods, or to sleeping in summer daylight and working in winter darkness. I have also learned, however, that the material aspects of cultures are less difficult to adapt to than different peoples' outlooks on life. The latter is what affected me most as a person. Thus, my growing experience was not merely a matter of developing adaptive mechanisms or of refining techniques for collecting knowledge—in or out of the field. More important, it meant a growing awareness of the variety and richness of human behaviors, including my own.

Prologue: A Bit of Human Geography

With a few small exceptions, my fieldwork experiences have all been northern, that is, in the northern part of the American continent, with the Inuit (in southern Baffin Land and northern Quebec), the Yupik (an Eskimoan group in southwest Alaska), and the Dene Indians (Canada's Northwest Territories). Some features typical of northern settings have had a direct impact on my stays and are therefore worthy of mention here.

First is the matter of isolation. My fieldwork is in small and distant communities, rarely connected by roads. Plane travel is available but rather expensive. If two communities are sufficiently close, that is, less than a hundred miles or so from each other, locals travel from one to the other by snowmobile in winter or by boat in summer. In some areas, winter roads on frozen rivers and frozen muskeg allow huge trucks to deliver construction materials and the store's dry goods for the year. During the three or four months that these roads are open there is a constant flow between communities and especially on weekends to and from communities where liquor is sold. In the dead of winter when roads (rivers and muskeg) are securely frozen, or during the short summer months when traveling by boat is easy, a community virtually empties on weekends, when people either go camping or visiting and drinking. Traveling is a vital component of northern peoples' traditional lifestyles and does not constitute a problem for them as it did for me in that setting.

As a fieldworker, weekends really mean very little to me—they might be used for work because days in the field are numbered. I am also accustomed to moving around at will. In the northern context, when no work can be accomplished and I am unable to travel, I feel like a prisoner. As a fieldworker, those weekends when the towns empty out are especially frustrating. Without my own truck, boat, or snowmobile it is difficult to go beyond the village limits. It is also difficult to catch a ride with another person because traveling conveyances quickly fill up with family and friends.

Besides, where would I go? Drinking trips frankly do not interest me, and the strangeness of the space makes it risky for me just to take a solitary walk. In some arctic communities I was warned about the presence in the area of polar bears, and people cautioned me against going out alone or without a gun. I mention this not to impress anyone with the exoticness of my experience. I simply want to emphasize the feeling of imprisonment and dependency throughout any such trip. Although there are some occasional snowmobile rides and picnics or outings with friends, weekends entail long hours of inactivity, hours spent fretting and wondering if something could be accomplished by being a little more imaginative.

Another interesting facet of the northern communities I visited is that, unlike most North American Native communities, these are not reservations. Despite the important social problems plaguing many of these small communities, people still proudly identify themselves as users and caretakers of their land. And beyond frequent expressions of resentment toward non-Native people, I never perceive that they—Inuit or Dene—feel dwarfed by a dominant culture. This means that in those areas, the non-Native is the outsider, a stranger in their land, on their home ground, trapped in a world where time and space take on unfamiliar meanings. A trapped stranger is what I become.

Another inescapable reality of any kind of northern project is the question of permits. One must request the Band Council's authorization to conduct research in a given community—in writing beforehand, and in person during a Council meeting as soon as one arrives. In some communities this is a mere formality; in others it requires veritable negotiations. These communities have been so often and so extensively "studied" by a variety of specialists that they are understandably fed up with the summer invasion of student-apprentice researchers, and wish to exercise some control over them. However, providing that a community is assured of reaping benefits from one's work, permission is usually granted, though this still does not guarantee people's participation. With each individual solicited another negotiation takes place, not only about the money offered for interviews but also about the ultimate goals of the work. We must constantly justify why we have come and explain our interest in these matters. This last concern will be discussed at length later.

The time of year is a also a factor to be considered. I personally prefer winter, partly to avoid the summer invasion of researchers, but especially to witness the predominant climatic reality of their lives. Summer trips, although physically easier, only yield an extremely reduced view of the northern life-style. Furthermore, the short summer inspires leisure—more than usual—sometimes making it a lot harder to get anyone to work for me on a regular basis. Just as it is in my milieu, gentler weather encourages family camping and picnicking and just taking it easy in general. On nice days, people just disappear. Although many drum dances and intercommunity festivals take place in summer, they last late into the sunlit nights with consequent disruptions of everyone's sleeping patterns, my own included. Thus, in northern regions I feel that the colder months teach me more about individual people's lives than the warm ones.

The Age of Innocence

When I look back on my first trip to the Arctic in 1974, I realize, somewhat uncomfortably, how little I knew about what I was getting into. At the time, I was a musicology student and working as a research assistant in a group intent on developing a rigorous analytical method that we hoped could be applied to any musical object, whatever the tradition or the source. To a degree this method would, from a "sound" point of view, neutralize any difference between, for instance, Debussy piano music and Inuit music. It was thus decided that three of the group's assistants would study Inuit throat singing, and a few months were spent discussing possible approaches to this material. However, we soon had to admit that our musicological training was of little use for a cross-cultural study. Consequently, we drastically changed our approach and enrolled in an Anthropology program specializing in Inuit culture and language. However, our first trip north took place before enrollment, armed with only a few days of special tutoring which consisted mainly in preparing an interview questionnaire and in learning how to handle tape recorders and microphones.

I believe it is useful to recall these details because they partly shaped the assumptions and expectations, both conscious and unconscious, we carried with us into the field. Looking back on and analyzing the roots of our development, even though in retrospect they appear naive and fragile, can be put to good use as long as the conclusions reached become a lesson learned.

We were literally sent on an errand. That is, each of us was sent to an Inuit community and expected to collect recordings of Inuit throat singing and some information about this unusual vocal form. One assumption was that this mission could be carried out as easily as a trip to the library with the additional merits of some physical discomforts. Consequently it was thought that a few weeks would yield enough information to allow the analytical process to begin. Another assumption was that we should focus mainly on what we were sent out to collect separately from anything else the culture had to offer. In other words, we thought we would deal with a well-defined object of study. Furthermore, we assumed that our object was Inuit "music," since the rare recorded samples of throat singing we could find were obviously "organized sound." We were still very much the products of musicological studies, and we had little awareness of the sociological implications of any expressive behavior such as singing and dancing. Neither did we have any idea what a psychological and intellectual impact these trips would have on our work and on ourselves.

Thus, each of us set off for a different community with a sense of responding to a challenge, both intellectual and physical—and, in my case, of responding to an attraction I had always felt for northern regions. But I remember our fears, not so much of the unknown but rather of falling short of expectations. We assumed that the difficulties encountered could result only from our own shortcomings because the informant was expected to be flawless. Within our assumptions the informant barely existed anyway—we were going to collect, and only incidentally to meet people.

I also carried other assumptions stemming from my own personality and from inexperience in a northern fieldwork context. For one, I believed it would be easy to convince people of the value of this project if I presented it with enough enthusiasm and adequate justification. Then, I assumed that I would be responsible for my work in the field and that six weeks would be plenty of time if all was well organized. I also took for granted that asking questions would generate responses. Finally, I had planned to address elders and other knowledgeable people, imagining that my interpreters would merely translate. Little did I know!

This first fieldwork experience taught me several lessons. Among other things, I came to understand that no expressive behavior exists in isolation from its cultural context and therefore that the shortest route toward real understanding is still the long way around—that I needed to see the forest as well as the trees. After a while, I also came to realize that my absorption with analytical concerns did not in the least interest the people I was visiting. More important, I awakened to the fact that "organized sound" did not automatically mean "music" and that the throat singing of the Inuit should rather be called "throat sound playing." Thus, it became irrelevant to examine these games in the light of Inuit singing traditions; rather, it was their playing traditions that shed light on many aspects of their performance.

I learned that I could not instruct people to work when and how I thought they should, even when I was paying them. In other words, even for money, my work was not a priority in their lives. On both my first and second trips to an Inuit community, I had to wait for two to three weeks before any concrete work could be accomplished. At the time, I was still unaware of the learning process that was taking place in spite of my apparent unemployment. I therefore had to adjust to other ways of gathering information and learning.

Finally, I began to understand that human relationships rather than methodology determined the quantity and quality of the information gathered. Social relationships within an Inuit community, which included me only during research periods, relationships between informants and interpreters, between myself, informants and interpreters, and between myself and the community at large—a below-the-surface human network of friendships, enmities, or rivalries over which I had little control—influenced my results in important ways. Subsequently, the human challenges this kind of research presented became one of the reasons why it has continued to attract me. I still prefer people to libraries!

The Nonmodel Approach

In subsequent years, the pattern of field trips was influenced by my first experiences. Familiarity with many ethnomusicological and anthropological paradigms concerning both methodology and ideology never erased, in my mind, the importance of human interactions and the development of relationships as the real sources of learning in the field. Thus, I very consciously resist the temptation of going into the field with a set theoretical model, although I never forget who I am and where I come from (both personally and academically), and the implicit analytic assumptions I necessarily uphold. Instead, having broadly outlined my interests, I feel that a more general preoccupation with ethnographic enquiry and an attitude of receptivity to whatever people want to teach me is more revealing than a very focused approach. This is not to be confused with lack of preparation. On the contrary, preliminary readings and reflections are essential, for although they frame my inevitable assumptions, they also pave the way toward the openness I wish to attain. Neither does my choice imply criticism of other fieldworkers' models. My point here and in the rest of this chapter is to demonstrate how major an influence human interactions are—interactions that can hardly fit into theoretical models. There are, of course, drawbacks as well as advantages to the nonmodel method—try, for instance, to write a grant application from a nonmodel approach, or to write up results without a theoretical framework to shape the writing!

By being as receptive as possible, I leave it to informants to choose the manner in which they wish to instruct me and to decide in which directions they will channel me. With some, this gets me nowhere at all, perhaps because it goes against the usual stereotype of sure-minded white people, but others acknowledge that I progressed since they last saw me and judge that I am ready to reach a little deeper into their culture.

I became especially aware of this while discussing with the director of the Dene Cultural Institute, a woman of considerable Western education, the types of narratives that were told to me on my first, second, and third visits to Denendeh. To her the progression was clear. Not only did the elders assess that my mind was ready for more information, but they also believed that I was handling the information respectfully—an attitude expected of all those learning, whatever their age. They were feeding my soul as well as my tape recorder.

Often, when hoping to record songs, I have been surprised (and, I confess, a little annoyed) at the number of stories the Dene always come back to. Had I been reluctant to listen to these, I would really have missed a lot. Not only would I have missed the narratives' content which is otherwise unobtainable, but I probably would have underestimated the importance of storytelling for the transmission of ethical values. Aside from teaching traditional tales, which recount mythological beliefs as well as historical events and heroes, these stories teach young Dene "to listen," an essential condition for the survival of body and soul. A youngster who does not "listen" does not learn survival skills, whether physical or social, and will probably "not live long"; therefore, elders might not even take the trouble to "talk" to this youngster. Hence, I was also being taught to *listen,* a quality I could never achieve by *asking* too many biased questions. Learning to listen is also learning to expect and to trust that truth, in due time, will reveal itself. Moreover, some Dene stories are of particular interest for ethnomusicologists because they teach about certain types of normally secret songs. In the context of stories, these songs find a secular outlet, which enables the listener to hear them and to absorb their textual and musical stylistic characteristics.

Another example drawn from my first visit to Denendeh illustrates how an "historical reconstruction" bias might have obscured the meaning of an important shift in the singing, drumming, and dancing tradition of the Dene. Right from the start, I was told repeatedly that "the drum started not long ago." I was puzzled, having assumed like many of us that the drum had been one of the most important and tenacious cultural items of America's First Nations over the centuries. On the other hand, a statement about their gambling game going back a "long, long time ago," a game in which drumming is essential, made the first statement appear like a contradiction. Only by listening to several apparently unrelated stories, by paying close attention to their wording, and by making observations in church, at drum dances, and in private homes, did I eventually understand that "not long ago" referred to the advent of Dene prophets. This occurred toward the end of the nineteenth century, simultaneously with the resolution of some intertribal conflicts. Thus, it was the drum's present usage and its relationships with a new spiritual mode that "started not long ago" (see Beaudry 1992). To have drawn attention to this historical contradiction or "error" by rushing into a series of questions with a need to "order" chronological events might have signaled that I doubted the storytellers or that I was still incapable of relating what they were telling me to real life.

Perhaps this nonmodel approach that I came to believe in is influenced to a great extent by the particular cultures I encountered. In other regions or in other cultures I may not have so strongly felt the thrust of their teachings. However, this approach, at first instinctive, not even well articulated, and reflecting my personal aversion to excessive planning, has proved valuable after all in northern settings. Many unexpected matters would have remained hidden had I not allowed this nonmodel approach to emerge. For instance, only time spent living with an Inuit family—when I became the butt of much teasing and laughter—gradually revealed (to me) the multifaceted importance of laughing and teasing in this culture and consequently helped me understand this most important dimension of the throat games (see Beaudry 1988). I really doubt this could have been uncovered by asking people why they laughed all the time or, worse still, by limiting my understanding to the "sound-producing" qualities of the individuals involved in the game.

Time Frame

Field trips were squeezed between academic terms and within the financial means at my disposal; thus, the length of the different trips ranged from six weeks to four months, with an average of two months per trip. This is different from the long-term, total immersion approach required for most degrees in anthropology or ethnomusicology; unfortunately, it could not be organized any other way. Nevertheless, some advantages derive from my fieldwork time frame.

One advantage is that I get relief from a situation with strong emotional overtones—a break that allows me to revert to my normal self while considering the field period with some perspective. I was then able to weave both in-situation and out-of-situation perspectives into a more objective whole that I transformed quite rapidly into a learning experience. Going away after collecting a certain quantity of information facilitates ordering that information, making it presentable and work-able, and seeing its strengths and weaknesses. It is a time for redefining issues. A subsequent field trip is then necessarily nourished both from the previous one and from the period of absorption following it.

As to the rough material collected—recordings of interviews and songs—I have always found it extremely difficult to synthesize and interpret what I was learning while I was in the field situation. I spent some apparently empty days rest-lessly fretting over wasted time because my days in the community were limited, rather than in intense intellectual reflection. Away from the field, on the other hand, there is time for making sense of an extremely varied collection of material. Directions appear that seem to have some emic significance, logical threads are revealed, connections are made possible between observations which at first seemed totally disconnected. It is a time for close examination of the informants' very words in search of clues to the meanings of things.

Practical and Methodological Issues

Working Through Interpreters

One of the drawbacks of the back-and-forth method of field travel is the increased difficulty of learning the language properly. In all three settings I developed some language skills but not enough proficiency to handle in-depth conversations and interviews. Therefore, I necessarily worked with interpreters. Some people I inter-viewed could talk to me in English; nevertheless, they felt more at ease in their own language because in this manner they felt they were addressing the people of their community rather than me.

Over the years I worked with a great many interpreters, and it is difficult to summarize this particular working condition simply. On the whole, it is my rela-tionship with them that caused me the strongest conflicting emotions—frustra-tion, anguish, and discomfort as well as joy, warmth, and thankfulness—in good part because these were the people that I spent the most time with. As I said earlier, I first assumed that interpreters would simply translate for me and that I would remain in control of my mission. However, in all three cultures explored, several things became apparent right from the start.

First, I now understand how in northern communities I come to depend on interpreters, not only for translation, but also for introductions to the right people and for advice about matters of etiquette, language, events, interesting subjects, plane schedules, and prices. The list is endless when it comes to things that have to be learned quickly. Moreover, interpreters are in touch with daily events and with the undercurrents of social life in the community. They know about the problems, the illnesses, the moods of the people I want to see. They are also in touch with the gossip and the rumors, some of which are directed at me. The success of my field trips is in their hands. Interpreters are even more than assistants; they assume the role of elder sibling as they help me to socialize and enculturate properly, although this happens within the relatively short span of each trip.

Second, the many hours I spend with interpreter-assistants leads to the development of varying degrees of friendship. Friendship ensures pleasurable work periods, but it necessarily entails reciprocal responsibilities. For example, being the one-from-the-south who comes to find something that the one-from-the-north can provide, I am expected to simply explain what I want and he or she sets out to get it for me. Conversely, I must be understanding, that is, not critical, when he or she gets up late, when a child is sick, when a sister needs help, or when he or she really doesn't feel like working. As a result, most times, the assistants' schedules define the work schedule. Furthermore, implicit equality among friends allows the assistants to feel free to substitute themselves for me. For instance, when we go on visiting rounds inviting people for interviews and singing sessions, sometimes little, if any, of the transaction between interpreter and informant is translated to me, and informants address their questions to the interpreter rather than to me. My role is often reduced to standing there, smiling, trusting that all is well, and thanking people without really knowing what is going on. When I insist on being included in conversations, some assistants make real efforts for a few hours but soon revert to their more natural manner.

Third, I developed a preference for working with middle-aged people. Younger people might speak English more proficiently, but many were educated away from their families and communities, and are thus somewhat estranged from their traditional culture. The English language skills of the middle-aged group might be weaker, but these people have a much better sense of their own language and culture, and of the older people's idiom, having been raised mainly "on the land" or "in the bush." However, the middle-aged people often have many children and responsibilities, and are involved in many adult activities. They have obligations and pressures of their own, and many of them refuse to work for me full time. Ideally, I must make arrangements with several people in order to fill my workdays. Matching their schedules with those of the informants sometimes constitutes quite a juggling act because they change all the time.

Fourth, as I said earlier, it is mainly on the assistants' terms that work gets accomplished, and this leads to many frustrating situations. Usually, the first week goes relatively well. We adjust schedules, spend time discussing the implications of the project, visit people who seem the most relevant and the most amenable to interviews, and generally learn to work with each other. Then the novelty wears off, daily life reclaims them, and my work and money take second rank. Children become a priority; visits to the health clinic become a priority; sleeping off all night card games becomes a priority; cutting wood becomes a priority; doing laundry before the water truck comes becomes a priority—all activities which for some reason can never be planned beforehand.

I often do not understand why an assistant does not show up for work, and I am always tempted to go look for him or her. I came to understand that insistence on my part is not appropriate. Instead, understanding their priorities demonstrates my respect for them. Secretly, though, I cannot help feeling that my own priorities are often not respected—a cause for private anger. To make this sound a little less paranoid, I must explain that northern Native cultures value autonomy and independence. When an assistant or an informant changes his or her mind about working with me, most of them assume that this is not a problem and that I will find something else to do. Assistants show their respect by recognizing (or assuming) my ability to function alone as well as with them.

When I realize that I have been "stood up," I then have the problem of finding something else to do. Just walking around, trying to stumble onto something interesting is a limited method when it is forty degrees below zero (−40° F) outside and windy! Ironically enough, they know about white people's need of structured time, and often, if I happen to be a bit late they do not allow for that. They might just take off, telling me later that I wasn't there! They aren't offended. They just go and do something else. This is all extremely frustrating for me because many hours are wasted just waiting for the person I am dependent on. It is all the more frustrating because being an adult I don't envision myself as dependent. It is also frustrating because my own culture values time "used" versus time "wasted," and frustrating in the particular context of short trips because in the researcher's world, funding agencies need tangible proof of our efforts—that is, recordings, photographs, and so on.

Still, visiting and recording are, in my experience, what the assistants like best. Other tasks such as retranslating a recent interview are often felt to be somewhat boring, and the success of these tasks depends completely on the relationship that develops between us, and between us and the informants.

Participant Observation

At this point, a brief discussion of some methods of information acquisition is in order because this is closely linked with the development of my relationships with the people in the community and with assistants in particular.

Early on, I was fascinated by the participant-observation approach. Nevertheless, once in the field situation I could not easily distinguish between participation and observation. Living in a community requires a twenty-four-hour-a-day involvement, which constitutes, in my opinion, a constant observation method. On the other hand, I attend many events that most of the community's non-Native people never bother to attend. Does that qualify as participation? It seems that the expression is at best superfluous. Perhaps it is more interesting to try to understand how people assess my presence and my activities in a community.

When I attend religious services (masses, funerals, weddings), feasts, or sports games, I might think I am "just watching," but the northern cultures I have worked in value someone's presence as much for pleasure as for the social gesture it implies. The Inuit especially assess an individual's mental health and well-being by the amount of interaction he or she engages in. Loners are suspect because they implicitly refuse interaction. However, watching a game does not mean one has to play. Individuals do as they please. Just being there is a demonstration of willingness to engage in social interaction that comprises both those doing and those watching. Just "watching" or "observing" in an anthropological sense is meaningless because in itself it is asocial and therefore threatening.

In Denendeh, when I attend Catholic masses people believe I do so out of conviction, although my purpose, which I can never really share with anyone lest they feel watched, is only that of observing. When attending feasts, I listen to speeches (which I don't understand) with all the others, wait with the others the prescribed amount of time, and then eat just as hungrily as the others. People don't talk to me very much, but I am there, my presence acknowledged by much hand shaking. In their terms, I am participating.

On some occasions such as group dances ("Eskimo dances," fiddle dances, or drum dances), again my status is mixed. My fancy recording equipment is more noticeable than all the other cassette recorders around, and this somewhat isolates me from the others. Even when I sometimes get up and dance with the others, a form of participation expected of me, the recording equipment makes people feel and sometimes resent that I am observing.

Recently, I started taking notes at drum dances mainly for the purpose of complementing my recordings. Every time I do so, it elicits strong reactions and causes malaise around me—"What's that?" "What's that for?" "Can I see what you're writing?" These questions come at me from children, adults, elders—from everybody. Everyone remains polite except for drunks, who, less inhibited, often get really angry at me. On one occasion, my note taking was even mentioned at a Band Council meeting. Although many understand that non-Native people's proverbial lack of memory forces us to write things down, this makes some feel more of an object than does recording or photographing. This is a touchy issue: by "just recording," I behave as a proper human being, a friendly and pleasant one at that, whereas with a notepad I become an observation tool, and in their assessment, not friendly and not pleasant.

Interviewing

Interaction with individuals constitutes my principal method of acquiring information. I spend a lot of time and money interviewing a lot of people, but it's well worth it. It is my shortcut into the transmission network. I put myself in a position where I am told things because I do not spend enough time in the community to learn it all by observation alone. Interviews usually take place in the presence of an interpreter-assistant and are conducted with one person at a time. Everything is recorded. Most of the interviewing is done inside people's homes where they seem to be more comfortable, even with all the disruptions this entails. Some recording sessions attract other members of the household and occasional visitors. On other occasions people take us to a quieter room. Nevertheless, because isolation is abnormal, children and other family members do not hesitate to come in with requests or simply to listen.

The format of the recorded interviews has changed over the years, ranging from my first year's prepared-questionnaire approach (which I quickly rejected), to loosely prepared questions, to semistructured conversations with attempts to initiate singing, to life-story telling, and to storytelling in general. As time goes by, my own development as a fieldworker allows me to relax when something is discussed that seems a bit remote from my interest in songs and musical event descriptions. But I must confess that deciding on the thrust of the conversation is often taken out of my hands. A discussion between my assistant and the person being recorded usually takes place at the beginning of an encounter. Often, little of this is translated to me, and I have learned over the years that I have to stand ready for anything. Sometimes, I am told to ask questions if I want, but often the answers are not translated, or are translated incompletely. At other times I can easily spend an hour recording someone uninterrupted by translation, trusting that all will be translated at a later time.

Asking Questions

Asking questions is problematic in northern cultures. First of all, if the assistants are considered young it is contrary to northern Native etiquette for them to ask questions. A young person should wait until he or she is told something, as it is up to the elders to decide when a young person is ready to hear things. However, when the assistant is old enough to discuss certain matters with elders, personal rivalries or gender differences prevent him or her from answering the assistant. With one male assistant an elderly woman protested that certain matters were too intimate to talk about and just giggled when I was with him . This same woman responded differently when I was helped by a woman. Most of the time it is difficult to analyze an elder's avoidance of one of my queries and to decide whether reluctance is caused by my outsider status or by the presence of the assistant.

Second, for the Inuit especially, asking questions is a mark of mental incapacity. In a culture that values learning by observation and imitation, only the village idiot goes around asking questions. As an outsider I am forgiven for asking questions, but the assistant remains reluctant to proceed like this, so ingrained is the habit of waiting for information to reveal itself.

Third, when the assistant does ask questions, another cultural injunction must be broken for my sake. Informants' answers tend to be lengthy, and in order to translate properly the assistant would have to interrupt the conversation—an impertinent behavior by any northern standard. Assistants are thus caught between their desire to show respect and my need to know what is going on. One assistant, even after weeks of working together, had never really come to terms with this problem. Time and again he entered into an untranslated conversation with an informant, then turned to me saying, "Do you want to ask another question?"

On my first trips, it was hard for me to let go of the question-and-answer format. Euro-Americans value the act of asking questions as a mark of intelligence and healthy inquisitiveness, and I feel the obligation of participating actively in the learning process. Besides, if I do not get an immediate translation I start to feel lost and not in control of the situation, fearing that informants might go off on tangents of their own. I trust certain people, but with others I find it difficult to hide my dissatisfaction, and in this way I make everybody uncomfortable. Though interference on my part often helps to straighten matters out, it sometimes destroys people's concentration.

It is significant that both assistants and informants dislike the question-and-answer format I occasionally adopt. There are several reasons for this. Many find this procedure so boring that they lose interest in the subject and provide only short, uninteresting answers. In keeping in close touch (through translation) with what is said, I lose out on the quality of the content. Furthermore, these are people that see each other nearly every day. Suddenly, through working with me, they are prevented from addressing each other naturally in an attempt to respect the rhythm of my conversation. Finally, middle-aged assistants are justified in feeling that they could give the answers themselves or that they could think of better ways of getting the information. Depending on their personalities and on the relationship that has developed between us, they may or may not take the initiative to ask questions on their own. When they do, the interview often switches to a conversation between assistant and informant.

Retranslating

Ideally, all my interviews must be retranslated. Even when things are translated during the recording, a lot is still missing. Assistants themselves say so when we leave someone's house. The near impossibility of interrupting an elder before reaching the end of a thought makes it very difficult for a translator to remember all the details of the longer stories. As was discussed earlier, the short question-and-answer format is severely limited in usefulness, and most of my recordings consist of fairly long statements that need to be retranslated after the interview.

When retranslating, the assistants often supplement the informant's answers with their own understanding and explanations. Retranslation sessions, as time- and money-consuming as they might be, represent the most precious moments of all my field experiences—times when I have learned the most. In addition, unless there are personality clashes, it is on these occasions that intimacy develops between an assistant and myself. We work hard—the assistant translating while I write down everything—but we also yawn, complain about boring bits, or laugh at humorous stories. Woven through hard work, stories about my assistants' lives and about mine are exchanged. After a while I even get the latest gossip. On a recent trip, my assistant, a woman of my age, started crying while listening to a song on the tape she was translating. Her grandmother had been singing this song at the time of her father's recent death, precisely at the moment he passed away. It is not the song itself that evoked such emotion but the occasion it recalled. For both of us there was room for emotion while working together.

During these sessions I relax. I am myself in a one-on-one relationship with someone with whom I can laugh, talk, and work. Beyond the pleasantness, I learn about what makes people laugh, complain, and cry. I learn through gossipy conversation who is friends with whom, who is lazy, who has been drinking, who is stingy (and therefore what stingy means), and who is generous (and therefore what generosity means). This is the next best thing to spending a lot of time in a community.

Ethical Issues

"What Do You Want?"

In the fieldwork setting professional motivations are often confused with personal ones. Over and over, acquaintances, friends, informants, interpreters, and assistants want to know why I do all this. As one Dene said to a white friend of mine during a late drum dance, "She looks so tired. Why doesn't she just go home?" In some cases, as when I lived with an Inuit family, the people can see that I am submitting myself to somewhat uncomfortable living conditions. Then, though I express wanting to know about the culture, I soon demonstrate that I am more interested in certain things. This is hardly congruent with their idea of learning the culture. What could I really want?

Northern people are now acquainted with masses of university students who come in search of dissertation material, and they wonder why they are targeted. For many elderly people and for most of the middle-aged generation, obtaining a university degree still represents something of a mystery. It means education, a lot of education, but beyond that the notion is hazy and seen only from the perspective of eventually getting a job. Knowledge for the sake of knowledge, and not for the sake of ensuring livelihood, is not a well-understood motivation. Within this perspective they feel as if they are being used like objects—observed, analyzed, written about, and left.

Working toward a degree nevertheless remains a fairly concrete motivation. It then appears even more surprising that when this degree business is over we start other similar projects, this time with no obvious reason. As researchers we are something of a puzzle, obtaining and spending a lot of grant money to accomplish something totally unrelated to our own community and lives. Thus, a suspicion arises that we must be doing it for money or for personal advancement. For a long while, we do not escape identification with some of the non-Native people who come to the North precisely for the purpose of making money. Will we be different? Will we interview them, pay them modest fees claiming that we have a small grant, and then return south where we will reap all kinds of benefits from their generosity?

This is certainly the sorest point in my relationships with the northern communities. It crops up regularly in all my trips and generates the most resentment and hostile remarks toward my work. It seems that I will never find the right way to explain the difference between exploration and exploitation. It is also embarrassing to tell them that however important and beautiful their traditions are to them, "down south" only a limited public will be really interested enough to buy the book I say I will write. If nobody is interested, then why am I doing it?

When they wonder about the possible benefits to the community—or to them as individuals—of this work they are even more surprised and suspicious when I invoke the argument of preservation. They may agree and feel that this is truly useful for their cultural survival, but what then does the researcher get out of it? Is it possible that, like missionaries, we do this strictly for altruistic reasons? Not likely!

Obviously, the problem is one of classification. Where do we fit? How do we tie into their lives? Neither nurse, nor teacher, nor Sister, nor social worker, nor government representative—what are we doing there? In one small Inuit community I stayed with a family into which I was adopted. However comforting it is to think that I was adopted because I was nice, in retrospect, I humbly understand that it was easier for that family to create a slot for me within its immediate social network if I was assigned a status as a member of the family. However, this status did not define me outside my adoptive family because I didn't stay long enough for that to happen. For the rest of the village I retained my outsider status—an outsider whose motivations were far from clear (as I will demonstrate).

The relationships we develop in the field are conditioned by the status we are finally given: the single woman visitor or student who must be helped; the researcher (whatever that means) with money enough for such an expensive trip, but not quite enough to achieve the prestige of a rich person; the priest's and Sister's friend; the recording person who does not represent any radio or television network; the "asker-of-questions" (a nickname the Inuit gave me); or the nice person. Strangely enough, I never achieved the status of employer, although I handled a lot of money and paid everyone that worked for me. Was it because I am a woman or because I remained such a dependent employer (as I explained earlier), or is my failure to be regarded as an employer a compliment? After all, in a colonial context an employer is rarely the best of friends. Maybe, then, they understand that, like them, I am first and foremost a human being.

From a human point of view, the transient nature of my involvement with northern communities stands in the way of the development of deeper friendships. Whether I remain in a community for six weeks or six months, everyone is conscious of the fact that one day I will leave. This aspect of faraway fieldwork has also affected me, and I, too, sometimes hold back, protecting myself as they might from the discomfort of separation. On the other hand, to some people outsiders such as fieldworkers represent a breath of fresh air, new ideas and new persons to whom secrets can be told without fear that they will eventually be known by all. It is precisely because we go away that we hardly represent a menace to privacy.

Although the professional benefits I will reap from these trips are apparent (to me), the communities' own interests are not so obvious. For one, there is a profound and unfortunately legitimate fear that once again, the researcher will take all this "cultural" material home, leaving them nothing, a fear that their trust, interest, and attention has been wasted, and a fear that they have been double-crossed. This has happened so often in the past that it is a wonder that they trust researchers at all, a witness to their enduring faith in human trustworthiness.

Who Do You Think You Are?

In spite of overall friendly relations, the suspicions and fears my hard-to-explain presence evokes lie close to the surface. In nearly every village I have visited I was taken for a spy of one form or another. There was one occasion when this accusation had particularly harmful consequences on my work. It happened in 1980 at Easter time in a very small community of Arctic Quebec. One afternoon, the community hall opened in preparation for festivities—games and dances—of the week-long Easter festival. For once I had the unusual and unexpected opportunity to prepare my own recording equipment in advance. This hall also housed the local radio station, and I socialized for a moment with the people there.

When I left the hall, a friend of mine, rather drunk and funny, followed me out. In his drunken state, he made lewd remarks and offers that I just walked away from without paying much attention. A few hours later, as people started gathering in the hall and I showed up with my recording paraphernalia, the Band Council leader came to me, unsmiling, and said, "No recording tonight!" I asked why with a smile but still got the same stony-faced reply, "No recording tonight!" From that moment I started noticing that nobody was talking to me, or even looking at me. This was very unusual because Inuit people are always outwardly friendly and smiling.

I put the recording equipment away but spent the entire evening there, determined not to look upset or guilty about anything. Inside I was bewildered and feeling sorry for myself, wondering what had gone wrong. My assistant came into the hall later in the evening, and she spoke to me naturally enough, but it was obvious that she was also very disturbed about something. She never said a word, did not play games, and never danced, although she stayed close to me all evening. I didn't have a clue what was wrong with her.

After twenty-four hours of this I discovered through the nurse's boyfriend that my drunken friend had announced on the radio that I had come to study their community and culture so that the government would learn how to trick them better. I was astounded at their reasoning because on that trip I had mostly been researching traditional games, in my view hardly a politically threatening subject. This occurred during the James Bay Agreement negotiation. This was one of the three Inuit villages against signing, and understandably they felt extremely vulnerable and small.

As for my assistant, I later learned that my drunken buddy had gone home after his announcement and beaten his wife—my assistant's sister—severely. My assistant had witnessed it all, incapable of doing anything. It is no wonder that she was too upset to help me, even though she knew what had been said on the radio was false. At least I had a firm friendship with her and I could express my fear of alienating my adopted family. I needed her urgently because talking myself out of this was beyond my Inuttitut skills. When she explained to them what happened they just laughed and said they never worried about the words of a drunkard. Although my family still trusted me, the rest of the community was another matter. We tried to resume work after the Easter festivities were over, but to no avail. People avoided me. One man even left his house in a hurry when I entered—a very meaningful avoidance tactic for an Inuit. Working with people had come to a standstill.

It took a few days for my friend to come out of his drunken state, remembering nothing. I described to him what he had done and what happened as a result, not asking him to do anything. That very same day, he went back to the radio station of his own free will and made a public apology, saying that when he was drunk he did not know what he was saying. He urged people to welcome me again into their homes. I was truly grateful for his gesture, but the harm could not be undone. My remaining fieldwork time was short. About half of the people became friendly again, and had I stayed long enough, things would probably have straightened out, but the work pattern was broken.

Beyond the distress such events caused me, there are things to be learned from the experience. For one, suspicions and fears about my motivations obviously lie close to the surface, ready to erupt instantly—and the community stands ready with self-protective measures. Also close to the surface were my own feelings of dismay and fear because I did not know what was going on, sadness at suddenly losing my friends, and anger, which I could not vent openly. There was not much I could do. I was getting a good taste of the Inuit's most powerful sanction: the deprivation of social interaction, which strips one of any social status whatsoever. Although frustrating professionally, the situation was even more upsetting personally. Although it was my work that had become suspect, it was my integrity that was being punished.

The fact that this happened was also a signal that I was perhaps getting too close, that I might be threatening to the Inuit in some ill-defined way. As one evolves from friendly guest to someone-who-knows-things, one's identity must be readjusted accordingly. This story was proof that I was seen differently than I had been before (this was my second trip there). Throughout that final period, I found it amazing that some people still believed in me. It was their own decision to believe the rumors or not. There was plenty of room for individual choice and action in this allegedly homogenous society.

On Whose Authority?

In none of the communities I visited was my "authority" taken for granted. On the contrary, this authority was constantly challenged, forcing me to question the frames I used for understanding. This is happening everywhere in the North. Julie Cruikshank, who has spent many years in the Yukon, speaks of a "recent explosion of critical local interest in ethnographic research in the North" (1988:27), which demonstrates that not only is one's approach to research scrutinized but that one's publications are also read by members of local communities. We have become accountable to our hosts.

In my experience, contestation took several forms, ranging from subtly voiced doubts about my capacity for ever understanding their culture, to resistance to the decisions regarding the content of interviews, and even to attempts at influencing my choices of kinds of material to look for and people to work with.

An example of this last kind of pressure happened during my first trip to Denendeh in 1987. For the first couple of weeks, meeting people and interviewing went fine. My assistant, a man a bit younger than myself and with whom I became quite friendly, was also the son and brother of two of my informants. After a while though, things came to a standstill, and a whole week went by without anything happening. My assistant had been on a drinking binge, and I had not yet found somebody else to work with. One day, still slightly drunk, he phoned me and told me that the men would not talk to me anymore because I paid the women as much as I paid them. They thought I should pay women less money than the men (!) because what the men were talking to me about was more important. I could hardly believe what I was hearing, and I became so angry that I could not continue the conversation. Fortunately, I was alone in my house at the time and I didn't have to keep my face from showing anger. I felt trapped ethically. I have always tried to be respectful of the beliefs and practices of the people I am working with, but this was going too far because it meant moving beyond my own principles.

I decided to downplay this incident and just ignore it. After all, my assistant had been drunk when he said this, and I took the chance that he would not remember what he told me. Luckily, the incident did not go any further, and I never had to take a stand one way or another. I certainly did not change my wage practice! However, once my anger had abated I was left with several questions and one partial answer. How, for instance, did my gender affect my relationships? Did the men's exclusivity in handling the drum and the drum songs prevent a woman from asking about them? What does one do when one is profoundly provoked, especially when working in cultures that value emotional restraint? How does one deal with requests that demand a transformation of one's own ethical values? How much of oneself must one hide in order to reach one's objectives?

If throughout this chapter I have neutralized my feminine identity somewhat, this was only meant to focus better on my human identity as opposed to my professional one, but is gender a matter that can ever be left aside? Was it only a matter of gender that was at stake in the scenario I outlined earlier? Were these men trying to tell me something about the importance of the drumming and prophet song tradition? It seems, as I understood much later, that they were pointing at a hierarchy in song and story statuses, something they felt I needed to pay more attention to. My attention to women's songs and stories made them wonder if I could understand anything at all and if I was worth "talking" to. Fortunately, my work was eventually resumed with other assistants and informants, and with those who originally contested me. It was brought home to me rather forcefully, though, that they wanted to assume control over what I was to learn and when. It was their decision that I should not leave their community with a distorted (in their view) picture of their traditions. I had no control over this whatsoever and never really understood what had gone on until several trips later. For a long time I was blinded by gender anger.

"Who Do You Think We Are?"

The development and fostering of human relationships, however close or "objective," raise another dilemma for fieldworkers: what is the status (for us) of those we relate to? It is easy enough to make a case for our own ambiguous status in the field, but only recently have anthropologists begun to question the dangers of mixing business with pleasure. I have no solution to offer, only the expression of my own disquiet. Indeed, it would be professionally simpler to retain a rather neutral attitude toward the people I work with, but because of my interest in them as human beings I am constantly shifting between recognizing them as either friends or informants and between my own roles as friend and observer. R. Laing identifies a distinction between "friends" and "organisms," that is, between people we see either as interacting with us or people as part of an organic process or system (quoted in Jay 1974[1969]:368). We need the friendships—they ensure the depth and truth of our understanding, but we also need to be able to detach ourselves from these same friends for the sake of observation.

This is particularly difficult when assistants become my friends. As explained earlier, they are the ones with whom I become the most intimate. But, what of the knowledge I gain from their intimate lives, their past and present sufferings, their opinions about other people in the community, and their emotional states? Such is the ransom for enjoying other people as human beings, as friends: discretion, respect for personal lives, and restraint in the information chosen for publication.

Furthermore, assistants often consider themselves to be the true specialists of their culture and sometimes question my decisions or my choice of directions. More and more they resent the fact that publications have not, in the anthropological tradition of the past, adequately represented the collaborative input of all participants. This represents (to them) a breach of professional etiquette and a breach of friendship. It is no wonder northern communities are ambivalent about our presence as researchers.

Again I turn to Julie Cruikshank's analysis of the evolution of anthropological research in the North:

> Increasingly, aboriginal people have their own ideas about the kind of relationship they want to establish with an anthropologist. Their expectations include considerably more sustained participation from the ethnographer than was the norm in the past. While this is certainly a contentious issue, it has to be addressed by every ethnographer working in the North.
>
> The model being negotiated in some northern communities is one based on collaboration between participants rather than research "by" the anthropologist "on" the community (1988:30).

Because of our university-oriented goals and the grant policies we work under, collaboration in the true sense of the word is sometimes difficult to set in motion. Although we take for granted that we are "in control" of our research goals, the physical and cultural distance we feel after leaving a community makes it difficult to implement fully collaborative measures. I hesitate to comment further on this aspect of my research because I have not yet resolved my dilemma, but I have been taught to recognize and value the intelligence and freshness of approach of the many highly dynamic individuals I have worked with.

This is an issue more directly concerned with the representation of a tradition and with the potential uses of analytical results, and perhaps this discussion belongs elsewhere. Let us not forget, however, that this has been fermenting for a long time in northern Native communities, and that it has underscored all my relationships in the field, whether or not it was consciously felt by me or by the host communities.

Conclusion

In spite of all the unanswered questions, I can only reiterate what I have already stated: Human relationships not only influence the quality of my work but are what makes fieldwork a meaningful experience. Allowing friendships to develop or simply enjoying people as they are is not as simple as it sounds: Friendship and camaraderie are tainted with the pragmatic uses that could be made of them. This is a moral issue, one that can only be answered by individual experience. Because we must remain in control of our feelings and emotions at all times in the name of our research objectives, we might feel that we are prevented from fully being who we are. Beyond the frustration of keeping oneself in check, fieldwork remains a challenging experience because it teaches us that there are many different ways for human beings to be themselves.

PART II

Knowing and Being Known

Knowing Fieldwork

Epistemology is that field of inquiry whose subject is the origins, nature, and limits of human knowing (see Rorty 1979:140). An epistemology for ethnomusicology is therefore concerned with the origins, nature, and limits of human knowledge concerning music in human life. An epistemology for ethnomusicology attempts to answer two basic questions: What can we know about music, and how can we know it?[1]

Not long ago, musical transcription was the distinguishing mark of our discipline, not only as a passage rite (Hood 1982[1971]; McAllester 1989) but as a generative practice. Transcription told us what we could know about music and how we could know it. Music was objectified, collected, and recorded in order to be transcribed; and transcription enabled analysis and comparison. Transcription—that is, listening to a piece of music and writing it down in Western notation—not only became a guild skill but also "wrote across" lived experience, eliminated the life-world, and transformed what was left (sound) into a representation that could be analyzed systematically and then compared with other transcriptions so as to generate and test hypotheses concerning music's origin and evolution. Today it is not transcription but fieldwork that constitutes ethnomusicology. Fieldwork is no longer viewed principally as observing and collecting (although it surely involves that) but as experiencing and understanding music (see Titon 1992[1984]:xvi). The new fieldwork leads us to ask what it is like for a person (ourselves included) to make and to know music as lived experience.

As it did most, if not all, ethnomusicologists, music caught hold of me before ethnomusicology did. In the late 1960s when I began formal study of ethnomusicology, at the University of Minnesota, I was already part of a blues musical community centered on Lazy Bill Lucas, an African American who was born in Arkansas and had a career as a blues singer in St. Louis and Chicago before moving to the Twin Cities in the early 1960s. Harmonica player Mojo Buford, who had been with Muddy Waters's band, bass player JoJo Williams, guitarist Sonny Boy Rogers, and pianist and singer Leonard "Baby Doo" Caston also visited Bill's apartment, the hub of this community; and we played music together, ate Bill's fried chicken dinners (he was a superb cook), drank Fox Deluxe beer, and became friends. I got to know them, their wives, and their girlfriends, and we passed time together. Later, in Alan Kagan's seminar in ethnomusicology, I learned about fieldwork. Then, fieldwork relied on in-person observation and on data gathering through structured interviews, a method derived from the Trobriand Island practice of anthropologist Bronislaw Malinowski during World War I.

Thinking about my blues musician friends, I wondered whether to do fieldwork with them. Why not? I thought, and I proceeded to interview Bill for a class project. Of course, I had already "observed" him for a long time (and vice versa). I had no difficulty speaking with them about their lives and careers, particularly because they felt that it might result in useful publicity—and it did. The publication of Bill's interview, for example, led a French blues enthusiast to produce two LP recordings of Bill's music (Titon 1969; Lucas 1971, 1972). In those interviews I asked questions such as when and where they were born, what kind of work their families did, when they first learned music, how their musical careers progressed, and so forth; and they answered them. I was doing oral history and was interested in obtaining facts of their lives. In a word, I was data gathering. As a result, my relationship with them added a dimension: I became someone who might be able to promote them, to help them in their careers, instead of just a young man hanging around older ones and trying to learn music from them. Besides friendship I now had a tacit contract with them.

I had discovered that my fieldwork thrust me into thinking about relationships; it wasn't just about surveying and collecting. Later, I also realized that structured interviews did not always result in my best understanding. Blues singer-guitarist Son House had come to the Twin Cities to do a concert, and I was able to get an hour alone with him and a tape recorder. I had my oral history questions ready, but I had decided to begin by playing him a tape of a blues recording from the 1920s by his friend Charley Patton, hoping to enlist his help in deciphering Patton's lyrics. (House later told me that you could sit at Patton's feet and not understand a word he was singing.) House listened to the tape, and I was ready to start asking questions, but before I could do so, he began to speak and reminisce about "Papa Charley" and those days. I forgot about my questions and listened to what he wanted to say. He told me a long and detailed story about how he "got religion" when he lived in the Mississippi Delta. He also spoke about the old times, and the bad whiskey they made and drank, and he acted out a story about how he got put in jail one night because he was so drunk he wouldn't let a Greyhound bus pass him while he was driving home. He told me how his white landlord had interceded with the sheriff and the judge to free him, but added a fine of indebtedness to his sharecropping arrangement. In telling the story he played the parts of the boss and sheriff. Boss (House whispers): "You got to let him out of there; he's so good with the tractor. I need him Monday morning." Judge (House whispers): "Well, all right, we'll tell him he had to pay such and such a fine." House (normal voice): "See, that's how they stepped in with each other" (Titon 1976).

I sat there raptly listening, wanting more. When House stopped telling stories from his life, I steered him through a series of oral history questions, hoping to get more stories; but now I was directing it by the questions I asked, and House no longer felt free to move in his own direction. And so began a long process in which I pondered the different kinds of knowing that arose from the structured interviews that were a part of the old fieldwork, versus those life stories told to sympathetic listeners or friends in a "real life" situation that could not, then, be described as fieldwork, but whose resultant texts I maintained ought to be valued, not as a form of data gathering, but as a means toward understanding (Titon 1980).

Continental European philosophy since the nineteenth century regularly distinguishes between two kinds of knowledge: explanation and understanding (Dallmayr and McCarthy 1977). Explanation is typical in the sciences, and understanding typifies knowledge in the humanities. We are all familiar with the scientific method of inference, hypothesis, and experiment; scientific explanations in their strongest form are expressed as universal laws of nature, such as the law of gravitation. Explanation gives us the kind of knowledge that enables prediction and control (Carnap 1966). Understanding, on the other hand, represents a different kind of knowledge. If explanation is directed toward objects, understanding is directed toward people. If explanation drives toward law, understanding drives toward agreement, sometimes, though not always, through lived experience (Gadamer 1992(1975); Schutz 1962). Explanation proceeds through analysis, understanding through interpretation. Explanation is a type of "knowledge-that," whereas understanding is a type of "knowledge-of." "Knowledge-that" is a typical concern of British and American positivist philosophers in this century, because in their view all meaningful knowledge-propositions can be expressed in propositional form as "I know that . . . ." (Of course, not all "knowledge-that" propositions are meaningful in a positivist sense.) Understanding's "knowledge-of," on the other hand, is more characteristic of an earlier view: knowledge of subjects, expressed in statements like "I know my friend William" or "He knows plumbing" or "You know ethnomusicology" (Rorty 1979:141).

Most writings about ethnomusicology as an academic discipline favor explanation theories of knowledge in which music is considered a type of language (see, e.g., Nettl 1964; Hood 1982[1971]; Kunst 1959; Meyers 1992). Ethnomusicology is said to have begun in the 1880s when it became a scientific project. At the time it was not called ethnomusicology but comparative musicology, reflecting its close kinship with similar disciplines such as philology (comparative linguistics). The person generally regarded as its founder, Alexander Ellis, set out to measure the musical intervals in selected non-Western musics. Most Europeans thought that these musics were more or less "out of tune." Ellis, representing the best tradition of ethnomusicological relativism, had another hypothesis: that the modes and scales of other nations had their own patterns, different from those of Western Europe, but coherent in their own terms. Measuring the intervals confirmed his hypothesis. Significantly, Ellis was tone-deaf and employed an assistant to make the measurements. That is, Ellis could not experience the musical intervals and had to rely on an external instrument to do so.

The most obvious application of explanation theories of knowledge to ethnomusicology came via linguistically based theories of music. Comparative musicology and musical folklore both rely on philology (comparative linguistics) for their methods. In this century linguistics has changed, but whether in the systematic musicology of Charles Seeger, the transformational ethnomusicology of John Blacking, the cognitive ethnomusicology of many of our European colleagues, or the semiotic ethnomusicology of Jean-Jacques Nattiez, the notion that music behaves and ought to be studied as a system like language continues to have a profound and shaping influence on our discipline, one that has affected my work as well as others'. Ethnomusicology, as a paradigm, owes a great deal to anthropology—after all, the Society for Ethnomusicology was originally planned at meetings of the American Anthropological Association—and anthropological linguistics is one of the four fields of traditional American anthropology. (Archaeology, physical anthropology, and cultural anthropology are the other three.)

Theories of knowledge based on understanding rather than explanation, on the other hand, find their philosophical defenders in a continental philosophical tradition that begins with Dilthey and includes Husserl, Sartre, Heidegger, Schutz, Merleau-Ponty, Gadamer, and Ricoeur. This tradition, an alternative both to Anglo-American positivism and to European structuralism, involves mainly two kinds of activities: phenomenology and hermeneutics. Phenomenology emphasizes the immediate, concrete, sensory lifeworld, and it attempts to ground knowledge in the world of lived experience (see Ihde 1986[1977]). Hermeneutics originated as a way of interpreting the Bible but has come to be a method for interpreting texts in general. In recent years, Paul Ricoeur has attempted to integrate the two into what he calls hermeneutic phenomenology. For Ricoeur, any meaningful action can be considered, or read, as a text; thus, a musical performance, for example, can be understood as the equivalent of a text (1981b). Clifford Geertz took up this formulation, likening cultures to "an assemblage of texts," and his work has enormously influential on American ethnomusicology in the past fifteen years or so. Although much of my work from the 1980s is based in hermeneutic phenomenology, I have more recently become critical of the poststructuralist tendency to textualize everything, musical experience included; and I have proposed that we stand Ricoeur on his head, that meaningful actions be experienced as music, not read as text (Titon 1995). In other words, I suggest that we change the metaphor we use for our interpretive acts. The world is not like a text to be read but like a musical performance to be experienced. But I must leave that for a future essay.

Ethnomusicology, in my view, has made use of four paradigms, or bedrock sets of assumptions, during the current century, of which comparative musicology was the first. The English translation of the second is musical folklore. It is typical in Eastern Europe, and was until recently in Britain. Although musical folklore involves collecting, transcribing, analyzing, and comparing, it adds four other features: an ideology of nationalism, an ethnographic emphasis on surveying social context, an ethical dimension that involves the preservation of music thought to be traditional and endangered throughout the world, and an educational aspect in which the music becomes part of the public school curriculum and is offered to adults as well. The collecting, classifying, and analytical works of Béla Bartók and of Constantin Brailloiu are representative of musical folklore.

The third paradigm is ethnomusicology itself, associated with the birth of the Society for Ethnomusicology in the 1950s, which grafted in American anthropology, with its emphasis on fieldwork and cultural immersion, rather than survey work; in addition, ethnomusicologists tend to distrust broad comparative generalizations and produce, instead, monographs based on detailed studies of particular music-cultures. Ethnomusicologists also distrust nationalism, rejecting it as ethnocentric, and they do not, by and large, emphasize preservation; rather, their focus is on acculturation and change. Nor do ethnomusicologists find much enthusiasm for public school music education; they think of themselves as scholars. (The late Alan Merriam used to dismiss the efforts of his world music colleagues in music education as "sandbox ethnomusicology.") The "native point of view" is important to ethnomusicologists, many of whom adopt in one form or another Merriam's three-part feedback model of music in culture: ideas, behavior, and sound (1964). For Merriam, and most of the ethnomusicologists of his generation, ethnomusicology nevertheless was about data, while the personal experiences of the ethnomusicologist, including all the relations with others in the field that not merely affected but constituted the meaningfulness of the data, were absent; ethnomusicology was to be, in his memorable phrase, "sciencing about music" (Merriam 1964:25).

The seeds of the fourth phase, for which we do not yet have a single name, were sown by those ethnomusicologists who brought master artists to American universities, where they led non-Western ensembles in which some graduate students found their most profound musical experiences. I have called this new paradigm the study of people making music[2] (Titon 1989, 1992[1984]), but it might also be called the study of people experiencing music. In retrospect it is apparent, also, that this fourth paradigm came from a generation transformed by the politics of the 1960s: the women's movement, the peace movement, and the Civil Rights movement. Because it is still emergent, this fourth phase is difficult to describe systematically, but some of its consequences are evident. An emphasis on understanding (rather than explaining) the lived experience of people making music (ourselves included) is paramount. Other emphases involve reflexivity and an increase in narrative representation that is descriptive, interpretive, and evocative (see, e.g., Kisliuk 1991); sharing authority and authorship with "informants" (who are now considered teachers, consultants, friends, or all three) (see von Rosen 1992; Guilbault 1993); a concern for history and with issues of power relationships, ethics, identity, and belief; a deconstructing approach to boundary concepts such as race and ethnicity; close attention to how class and gender operate within music-cultures;[3] skepticism toward the culture of science and engagement with feminist and third world perspectives; a willingness to explore various media, such as museum exhibits, festivals, film, video, and hypertext, to represent people making music; and an active involvement as musical and cultural advocates trying to help people in the music-cultures with whom we work have better lives in which their music can flourish (Sheehy 1992). All of these emphases are implicated in "the new fieldwork" and many are generated by its emphasis on human relationships rather than on collecting information. The new fieldwork does not abandon musical sounds and structures, it just repositions them as "texts" (subjects of interpretation) in a hermeneutic circle (Ricoeur 1981a). Musical sound is still documented, and if musical structure is an important aspect of the musical experience, as it so often is, then it is analyzed and interpreted as part of the matrix of meaning. Nor does the new fieldworker abandon documentation; if anything, documentation increases. But documentation, too, is repositioned, and is now considered reflexively, as an intersubjective product, rather than as the report and analysis of a witness.

If we enlarge the history of our discipline to include understanding-type theories, then we will be sure to attend to some of the writings of the early world travelers and missionaries whose understanding of native music took the form of an encounter with it. Jean de Léry, for example, a sixteenth-century missionary, narrated an account in which he told how he was "captivated" by native American music, and in doing so he weighted his narrative toward experience (Harrison 1973). In the revised histories we will emphasize "bimusicality" (Hood 1963, 1982[1971]), and ponder the nature of knowledge that comes through the human relationships developed through fieldwork. David McAllester's early work with the Navajo and cultural values will take on profound importance (1973[1955]; see also Mitchell 1978), and Kenneth Gourlay's articles on the ethnomusicological researcher become key early theoretical statements (1978; 1982).

Our approach, whether we favor explanation or understanding, will obviously depend on what we think music is. In my view, music is a socially constructed, cultural phenomenon. The various cultural constructions enable people to experience it as patterned sounds, aesthetic objects, ritual substance, even as a thing-in-itself. But to say that music is a culturally constructed phenomenon does not mean that it has no existence in the world, for like everyone I know, I experience my world through my consciousness, and I experience music as a part of my lifeworld.

In the rest of this chapter I offer phenomenological and reflexive answers to questions concerning what we can know about music, and how we can know it. I begin by examining experiences of music as they are presented to my consciousness. I proceed by examining experiences of fieldwork. Finally, I discuss some interactive strategies for representing these experiences so as to enlarge our understanding of music. Of course, there is no single phenomenology. Husserl's transcendental phenomenology is significantly different from Heidegger's existential phenomenology, which is different from Ricoeur's hermeneutic phenomenology. Nevertheless, they constitute a tradition and have certain common assumptions and emphases. In what follows, I will draw from this tradition without attempting to represent any single version of phenomenology. Indeed, I do not find any single version of it wholly satisfactory.

"Phenomenology insists that phenomena be investigated as they present themselves to consciousness" (Stewart and Mickunas 1990:91). Consciousness is always consciousness of something: in this case, music. How am I conscious of music? How am I "in the world" when my consciousness is consciousness of music? First, of course, my consciousness of music constitutes an experience of music, and this is culturally mediated; obviously, my experience of music is bound to be different from someone else's in another culture, not to mention others in my own. And I experience various musics differently over the course of my life. But for the moment, let me attend to my ordinary and current consciousness of music, both generally and in one particular case.

I take people making music as my paradigm case of musical "being-in-the-world." For me, making music is incomplete when I do it by myself; it is completed in a social group when I make music with others. You may or may not feel the same way, but I want to take making music with others for my paradigm case. I could have chosen making music in a string quartet, a gamelan, a blues band, an Old Regular Baptist church, or a Ghanaian drum ensemble, but for this exercise I choose making music in an old-time string band, with fiddle, banjo, and guitar—a peak experience which I consciously seek and find.

Here is how I would describe this experience phenomenologically. Desire compels me to make music. I feel this desire as an affective presence, a residue of pleasure built up from my previous experiences with music and dance that makes me seek it out in order to know it better. It is a curiosity of all my bodily senses and I feel it embodied in them: an embodied curiosity. Knowing people making music begins with my experience of music. Playing the fiddle, banjo, or guitar with others, I hear music; I feel its presence; I am moved, internally; I move, externally. Music overcomes me with longing. I feel its affective power within me. Now I have moved from what phenomenologists call the "natural attitude," the normal everyday way of being in the world, not to an analytical way but to a self-aware way. I feel the music enter me and move me. And now the music grows louder, larger until everything else is impossible, shut out. My self disappears. No analysis; no longer any self-awareness. The shutting out is a phenomenological reduction, what Husserl called *epoché*. It is a radical form of suspension. I no longer feel myself as a separate self; rather, I feel myself to be "music-in-the-world." Eventually music returns me through desiring to myself. That is, the be-ing of desiring brings me to myself, re-presents myself to consciousness. The "I" returns; I am self-aware, I see that I and others are making the music that I hear.

When I see that I and others are making the music that I hear, I want to know these others. For us to understand one another we must know one another. How may we know one another? Who are you? If you were an object I might come to know you as I know other objects. But you are a person making music and I come to know you as a person (see Code 1991:37). We seek to know one another through lived experience. Through common, intersubjective experience we enter the world of interpretation. Interpretation turns sound into music, be-ing into meaning.

When my consciousness is filled with music I am in the world musically. My experiencing mind tells me that I have a musical way of "being-in-the-world" when I make music and when I listen and move to music so that it fills my body. I call this musical being, and it is a mode of being that presents itself as different from my normal, everyday modes of experiencing, from my self-conscious modes of experiencing, and from my objectivizing modes of experiencing.

I would like to ground musical *knowing*—that is, knowledge of or about music—in musical *being*. I look, in other words, for an epistemology of music that is grounded not in a detached or objectivizing way of "being-in-the-world," nor in a reflexive, self-conscious way of being in the world, nor either in what phenomenologists call the "natural attitude" or everyday way of being-in-the-world. Rather, I think that musical being is a special ontology and that knowing music requires that we start from musical being.

Another way of saying this is that I ground musical knowledge in the practice of music, not in the practice of science, or linguistics, or introspective analysis. In my paradigm case of musical being-in-the-world I am bound up socially with others making music and when that music is presented fully to my consciousness it is the music of the whole group, not simply "my" music, although at peak moments I feel as if it is all coming through me.

This brings me to my experience of doing fieldwork, for it, too, is an experience of myself in relation to other people. For many ethnomusicologists, fieldwork is intersubjective and personally transformative. Like many of my colleagues, I experience fieldwork not primarily as a means to transcription, analysis, interpretation, and representation, although it surely is that, but as a reflexive opportunity and an ongoing dialogue with my friends which, among other things, continually reworks my "work" as "our" work (see also von Rosen 1993; Hutchinson 1993). Risking immodesty, I offer a recent example: a letter from one of my Old Regular Baptist friends in which he said, "Thank you for the way you have helped us look at ourselves" (Elwood Cornett, letter to Jeff Todd Titon, August 18, 1993). And I thank them reciprocally. My experiences of fieldwork have usually been intensely lived; in them I have become acutely conscious of my roles, stances, and identities; I have felt love, camaraderie, and anxiety. Most representations of ethnomusicological knowledge, of course, exclude expression of the experience of fieldwork, but a phenomenological approach to these representations requires its inclusion and the inquiry into values that it generates.

A reflexive look at the types of relationships fieldwork engenders reveals that fieldworkers, and those who are the subjects of fieldwork, bring identities to the encounter and are cast in a variety of roles (Titon 1985). By role playing I do not mean to imply inauthenticity, but rather to use the concept as the sociologist Erving Goffman developed it, to show how people behave socially in daily life. In the postcolonial world, when mere collecting is considered exploitive, and when some peoples simply will not cooperate with visiting ethnomusicologists, it is naive to think that the ideal field relationship will always result in friendship. Sometimes a kind of contractual relationship, implicit or explicit, in which each party helps the other, is more effective. Sometimes a combination of friendship and tacit contract is most effective. In another frequent role in the new fieldwork, the ethnomusicologist becomes student and the "informant" becomes teacher or wise elder. Infrequent and atypical roles include opposition, deception, lying, and spying—unethical under most circumstances, but rationalized on the grounds that the music-culture being understood and then exposed is illegitimate and corrupting (see Pillay 1994; Kingsbury 1988).

A phenomenological epistemology for ethnomusicology arises from our experiences of music and fieldwork, from knowing people making music. If we believe that knowledge is experiential and the intersubjective product of our social interactions, then what we can know arises out of our relations with others, both in the field and among our colleagues where we live and work, and these relations have an ineluctably personal aspect to them. The documents (texts) that we and our friends generate in the field have a certain immediacy to them—field notes, photographs, recordings—that remind us, when we are no longer in the field, of those relationships.

While we are with our friends, these documents appear—at best, and when they do not get in the way—not so much as objectifications but as extensions of our relationships. But when we are back from the field, in the university, in the library, or study, alone, particularly if our friends are far away, these field artifacts take on a very different cast. They substitute for experience by evoking our memories of it. Like a photograph taken or a brochure brought back from a holiday abroad, they are documentary and evocative at the same time. They traffic in nostalgia. In their presence, and the absence of the people I knew, I experience loneliness and longing. My task now is to represent the music-culture where I have worked, not only to students and colleagues, but also to the people in that music-culture. I search for forms of representing that will keep my experiences before me, in memory, and evoke the people making music whom I have known. Thus, I represent them to myself as well. The conventional representation that presents itself to me is narrative musical ethnography; two other forms that I will discuss are ethnographic film and hypertext/multimedia.

Narrative, of course, is the way we habitually tell ourselves and others about our experiences, and so it emerges as a conventional form in phenomenologically weighted representations of people making music. At its best, a narrative weighting in the descriptive ethnography of a music-culture invites the reader to share, imaginatively, in the experiences that are represented. Anthony Seeger's *Why Suyá Sing* derives much of its interpretive power and authority from narrative (1987b). Not that the book is entirely narrative, of course. For Seeger and others writing narrative ethnomusicology, ethnography becomes an experience-weighted genre in which narrative includes background information, interpretation and analysis, and above all one in which insights emerge from experience: one shows how one comes to understand (see also Feld 1990; Rice 1994). Narrative is not new to ethnomusicology. Mantle Hood's narrative passages in *The Ethnomusicologist* (1982[1971]) and Bruno Nettl's stories in *The Study of Ethnomusicology* (1983) are among their most telling. And experience-based narrative interpretation is increasing in cultural anthropology as well. Instances abound. Renato Rosaldo's *Culture and Truth*, for example, begins with his celebrated article "Grief and a Headhunter's Rage" (1989:1–21). Rosaldo could not understand how grief and rage "go together in a self-evident manner" for the Ilongot of the Philippines until his wife died as "she was walking along a trail with two Ifugao companions when she lost her footing and fell to her death some 65 feet down a sheer precipice into a swollen river below. Immediately on finding her body I became enraged. How could she abandon me? How could she have been so stupid as to fall? I tried to cry. I sobbed, but rage blocked the tears" (1989:9). Rosaldo had to experience a combination of grief and rage himself before he felt he could fully understand this aspect of Ilongot culture.

As Clifford Geertz has pointed out, writing good ethnography takes a great deal of rhetorical skill, and it forces us to face the fact that we are primarily authors, not reporters (1988). But if we are authors, we risk displacing the reader's interest from the people making music whom we are writing about, to ourselves. Autobiographical narrative ethnography has generated opposition from those who find it self-indulgent and unprofessional; indeed, the popular term for it, "confessional," indicates the problem of displacement. Yet narrative ethnography need not displace the attention from people making music to authors' consciousness. Instead, an author may skillfully work up a scene and cast herself or himself in the role of a bit player, someone whose participation isn't very important during the event, but whose reflections on it afterwards serve as a kind of interpretation. This, after all, is what Geertz does in his celebrated essay about a Balinese cockfight, although one may pause at Geertz's literary method of divining meaning and wish that it were more congruent with the Balinese people's own views. The prologue and first chapter of *Powerhouse for God* are also written as narrative ethnography, carefully utilizing tape recordings, photographs, fieldnotes, and recollections of my experience to recreate and evoke the scenes of a luncheon conversation and a homecoming worship service (Titon 1988). Finally, narrative ethnography is well suited to showing an ethnomusicologist in dialogue with people making music.

Film's (and video's) images and synchronized sound are conventionally understood to portray people making music and to place the viewer in the position of observer. Film's evocative power is extraordinary: we feel as if we are watching something real. Of course, it is possible to defeat the experiential aspects of film by making films that imitate books or by making films that represent scientific experiments, as much ethnomusicological filmmaking attempts to do. But a phenomenological approach to filmmaking attempts to involve the viewer by evoking and reflecting on the experiences and relationships that obtain in a musical community. This relationship between the filmmaker and viewer can take one of three forms: the filmmaker can place himself or herself in a fully authoritative position, usually through an omniscient narrator; the filmmaker can depart, ghostlike, from the film, making it appear that the viewer is merely looking at the action and eavesdropping; or the filmmaker can in the film itself interact with the subjects and the viewer, and both can reflect on the meaning of the film. It should be plain that interactivity and reflexivity is best suited to the kind of experiential understanding that arises from fieldwork and music making (von Rosen and Francis 1992; von Rosen 1993).

Hypertext and multimedia are a third means of representation that seem to me to do justice to an experiential bias toward people making music. Whereas a narrative text is a linear read, hypertext can be a weblike structure that allows readers to choose their own paths through the assembled information (Landow 1992). A computer is not required for hypertext, but a computer enables hypertext very efficiently. Interactive hypertext empowers readers ("authors-who-are-to-be," in hypertext fiction writer Michael Joyce's words) to comment on the information and thereby alter it for the next reader. Multimedia is often allied with hypertext to represent sound recordings, images, and movies. A carefully assembled hypertext is capable of representing the insights as well as the ambiguities of the experience of acquiring knowledge through fieldwork. For example, in the Davenport Hyper-Card Stack, a reader hears fiddle tunes and is told that they seem similar (Titon 1991). One path leads to musical analysis, and transcriptions demonstrate the tunes' similarity, but another path leads toward the fiddler himself and his demonstration that the tunes are different. The representation leaves it to the reader to resolve the paradox. Or not resolve it. A further development is hypertext fiction (see Coover 1993).

Not all hypermedia projects allow meaningful interactivity. Many "educational" hypertexts are nothing more than huge text-and-context assemblages with very efficient links, organized hierarchically rather than in a weblike fashion. The experience of such hypermedia "learning" environments is not much different from the experience of being in a library, where one seeks explanations. But the experience of a weblike hypertext is more like the initial stage of playing a game: one seeks to understand it.

In this chapter I have maintained that we have usually sought to explain musical sounds, concepts, and behavior rather than to understand musical experience. And yet our own most satisfying knowledge is often acquired through the experience of music making and the relationships that arise during fieldwork. It seems to me that in our ways of being musical, and in our ways of doing fieldwork, we, like the subjects (people) of our study, are open to transformations through experience. Furthermore, when we ask our musical friends for their "native" points of view or overhear what they say, they most often speak in terms of personal experience and understanding rather than offer systematic explanation.

If all of that is so, then an epistemology erected upon the ethnomusicological practices of music making and fieldwork as the paradigm case of our being-in-the-world, rather than upon collecting, transcription, and analysis as that paradigm case, will privilege knowledge arising through experience, ours and others'. And in our external representations of that knowledge, we seek those forms that best produce understanding. If we must rule out such unconventional representations as fiction or musical performances, because these are not available to scholars, at least not now, then narrative but not necessarily self-centered nonfiction writing, interactive and reflexive rather than authoritative or merely observational film, and weblike, interactive hypermedia are promising forms of representation that will convey understanding both in us, in the process of their formation, and in those with whom we seek to communicate. Yet I do not wish to dispense altogether with explanations as a form of knowledge, only to privilege understanding. I cheerfully admit that I continue to practice transcription and analysis, and to be curious about issues involving musical structures, history, and geography. An epistemology of musical knowing that follows from our musical being-in-the-world privileges experience and understanding, but it cannot possibly do without explanations because, after all, we also experience knowing by means of explanations, and we put those to work in daily life.

What of the future of fieldwork? If, as I have claimed, contemporary ethnomusicology rests epistemologically on fieldwork, then the poststructuralist challenge to fieldwork must be answered if the discipline is to continue. Indeed, some have called for the abolition of ethnomusicology. This critique is mounted on several grounds, three of which are central. The first is the charge, familiar since the late 1960s, that fieldwork-based enterprises rest on asymmetries of power and therefore involve the illegitimate use of the fieldworker's authority. In other words, fieldworkers have no legitimate right to represent their informants, for their purposes are not neutral—after all, ethnomusicologists' careers ride on these representations. The informants are the ones with the proper claim to authority, and they should be the ones to write—or not write—the ethnomusicological texts. A second charge is that fieldworkers enact a version of the heroic quest, although they do not realize this. The consequence is that musical ethnographies fall into a single pattern—the quest narrative, implicit or explicit. The problem is that the quest pattern, rather than the musical life of the culture under study, governs the representation and interpretation of the data. Thus, for example, music-cultures are viewed as utopian or dystopian, and ethnomusicologists become heroes, flawed heroes, or antiheroes (see e.g., Hood 1982[1971], where he writes of the importance of the ethnomusicologist's role in helping to build a large gong). Moreover, as a questing hero the ethnographer can scarcely claim authority to represent another music-culture: the hero has a different agenda. A third charge is leveled on epistemological grounds. Poststructuralist thought denies the existence of autonomous selves. The notion of fieldwork as an encounter between self and other is thought to be a delusion, just as the notion of the autonomous self is a delusion, whereas the notion of the other is a fictionalized objectification.

Neither the poststructuralist challenge nor a variety of answers can be considered here in the detail they deserve. But the beginnings of an epistemological answer may be found in the preceding phenomenological account of music making. Making music, I experience the disappearance of my separate self; I feel as if music fills me and I have become music in the world. But I also experience the return of the knowing self. The experience of music making is, in some circumstances in various cultures throughout the world, an experience of becoming a knowing self in the presence of other becoming, knowing selves. This is a profoundly communal experience, and I am willing to trust it. A representation grounded in this kind of experience would, I believe, begin to answer the poststructuralist challenge by reconfiguring the ethnomusicologist's idea of his or her own self, now emergent rather than autonomous. Autonomous selves enact heroic myths. Emergent selves on the other hand are connected selves, enmeshed in reciprocity. Connectedness is a value that challenges the postmodern critique of contemporary society. I am willing to assert this ecological value and its intimate relation with music-making and fieldwork on the grounds that the survival of far more than ethnomusicology depends on it.

Notes

1. This chapter is a revision of a paper presented at the annual conference of the Society for Ethnomusicology, Oxford, MS, October 25–29, 1993. Earlier versions were read in hypertext form to the Ethnomusicology Graduate Students' Colloquium in Fieldwork, Brown University, March 4, 1993, and to the Annual Conference of Finland's Society for Ethnomusicology, at the Sibelius Academy, Helsinki, April 1, 1993. The latter was published as Titon 1994. For an exchange of ideas I am grateful to Gregory Barz, Alan Bern, Timothy Cooley, Stephen Green, Katherine Hagedorn, Susan Hurley-Glowa, Patrick Hutchinson, Kathy McKinley, Jill Linzee, Nancy Newman, and Franziska von Rosen, students in the graduate seminars in fieldwork and in the history of ethnomusicology that I have taught at

Brown University since 1986, in which we have discussed paradigms, phenomenology, inter-pretation, and a more humanistic ethnomusicology.

2. "Making" in two senses: (1) producing the sounds that we call music, and (2) con-structing the cultural domain that we demarcate as music.

3. These boundary concepts continue to be discussed in an electronic conference on multiculturalism, primarily among ethnomusicologists, hosted since 1992 by Marc Perlman at Wesleyan University. The internet address is MC-Ethno@Eagle.Wesleyan.edu.

Toward a Mediation of Field Methods and Field Experience in Ethnomusicology

Fieldwork is so central to contemporary ethnomusicology that I would suppose nearly every graduate program devoted to training ethnomusicologists has a course on it, probably with a title containing the phrase "fieldwork methods." The three nouns in these courses' titles (method, field, and work) speak volumes about our collective understanding of theory and method in ethnomusicology, and thus provide the place where I would like to begin this reflection on fieldwork. I hope to show the limits of the usefulness of this phrase and the possibilities for an alternative view of where the field is and what happens in the field, a view that balances method and working with experience and playing. To do so, I move narratively between theoretical or philosophical reflection and some of my own fieldwork experiences, just as I do in practice.

Fieldwork Methods: Epistemological Solutions to an Ontological Problem?

Method

The word "method" implies both a pre-existing theory and a concern with the epistemological problem of finding, verifying, and knowing the truth within the frames of reference defined by theory. A course with the title "fieldwork methods" implies that ethnomusicology has a theory or theories for which fieldwork methods have been developed to test, and the existence of such courses implies that these methods can be taught. But does ethnomusicology have such theories, and, if so, what are they, and what are their associated methods?

One view of ethnomusicology is that it has been rather untheoretical in its orientation, especially since the mid-1950s when, in the United States, it broke away from comparative musicology and its theories of evolution and diffusion. This view is expressed by those who question whether ethnomusicology is a discipline (presumably disciplines have theories) and who, on the contrary, assert that it represents merely a domain of interest shared by a community of scholars. Those who support this theoryless view of ethnomusicology need only cite the myriad idiographic studies of individual musical cultures that dot the ethnomusicological landscape and the relative paucity of recent attempts to posit and test explicit theories. From this perspective, what passes for theorizing in ethnomusicology amounts for the most part to retrospective catalogues of what has been done and prescriptions for what might be done rather than statements of relationships to be explored in the field. This sort of theoryless ethnomusicology would have no use for methods; indeed, methods, whether applied in the field or in the laboratory, are impossible to define in the absence of theory. Perhaps professors with such views don't offer courses called fieldwork methods; rather, a title such as "things to do in the field" would suffice.

A second view of ethnomusicology acknowledges that, although no single theory predominates, ethnomusicologists currently work with many theories, and have woven a "polyphonic" theoretical fabric. If a discipline requires a single, unifying paradigm (Kuhn 1962), then ethnomusicology still might not qualify, but at least each of its contrapuntal theoretical lines would require a disciplined method. A multiplicity of theory would account for the plural form of the course title, "fieldwork methods." The polytheory view is advanced by those who claim that no descriptive work of the sort that minimally constitutes ethnomusicological writing can take place in the absence of some sort of theory. Alan Merriam made this point repeatedly in the definitional debates of the 1950s and 1960s. Bruno Nettl's *The Study of Ethnomusicology: Twenty-Nine Issues and Processes* (1983) provides a "book of lists" of ethnomusicological theories, although some of them predate the 1960s, when the idiographic, intensive studies based on extended fieldwork in one place, called for by Mantle Hood and others, became the norm.

To illustrate the point that multiple theories exist along with the correlative methods they require, I give three examples. One informal theory, for example, maintains that musical practices disappear, which leads to methods aimed at their accurate preservation as sound, film, or video recordings. A corollary of this theory-and-method combination is that a practice has been preserved when converted into a recording, that is, into a fixed text or monument—perhaps analogous to the way jam preserves fresh fruit. A second theory that undergirds some of our activity would state, if made explicit, that music exists as a "sound fact" to be interpreted and compared, at least by ethnomusicologists, using ordinary language description and Western musical notation. The main methodological questions raised by this theory concern accuracy (are the rhythmic durations and intervallic pitch relations correct?), systematicity (are the descriptive tools logically consistent and unambiguously understood?), and replicability (would others using the same tools produce comparable results?). A third theory states that music is a form of human behavior created within a coherent cultural system, and therefore possesses structures analogous or homologous to other culturally constructed forms encoded as art, architecture, everyday speech, ideas about natural sounds, and cosmological or religious beliefs about the nature of the world. The methods characteristic of this theory involve describing and then finding ways to compare radically different formal structures and behaviors, typically through a reduction of those differences to a common structural model borrowed from linguistics and semiotics or through the elicitation of native metaphors and key symbols that link two or more cultural domains into a coherent ethnoaesthetic (Ortner 1973). This theory minimally requires fieldwork methods that go beyond the accurate preservation and description of music as an isolated cultural domain to the observation, recording, and analysis of other cultural domains as well.

The third view of the field holds that a large number (but certainly not all) of its practitioners share a core set of theories or beliefs that constitute the field as a discipline. Even Bruno Nettl, whose list of twenty-nine issues fits his view that ethnomusicology may be less a unified discipline than a field of interest, boldly asserted ethnomusicology's "central question" (1983:234) and offered a four-part ethnomusicologist's credo (1983:9), both of which, although he probably didn't intend them as such, could provide a place from which to search for our discipline. The credo seems particularly suggestive as a source for theories and methods that unify the discipline. In analyzing it, I will not question whether these beliefs are in fact widely shared, but rather show what they reveal about the link between theory and method in ethnomusicology.

According to the first part of Nettl's credo, we believe that music systems can be compared, so we need methods to determine "what is typical of a culture" and distinguish those items from "the personal, the idiosyncratic, the exceptional." Whether the methods would be applied as analytic tools in the lab or as social measures in the field he doesn't say. Second, "we believe that music must be understood as a part of culture," but he provides no shared belief about the methods that would elucidate this theory, aware as he is of the methodological counterpoint on this problem. Furthermore, he acknowledges that "many pieces of research do not directly address this problem," which amounts to the troubling admission that, in ethnomusicology, method (as actualized in "pieces of research") bears no coherent relation to a shared theory. Third, we believe that fieldwork, particularly "intensive work with small numbers of individual informants," is an indispensable method, even in the absence of any theory that it might test. If theory and method seem unlinked or incoherent in the second aspect of the credo, in the third aspect theory disappears altogether, although, to be fair, this belief in extended fieldwork should probably be linked to the theory that music is a part of culture. Fourth, "we believe that we must study all the world's music."

Two theories support Nettl's credo. The first states that music derives its value as an object of study not from the complexity of its formal properties or its association with privileged social and historical groups, but by virtue of being a human activity—and all humans and all their behaviors are properly the object of scholarly inquiry. The second theory states that any claims about music that pretend to be universally true, or even true for a particular culture, have to account for all music, whether considered globally in broadly comparative studies or locally in characterizations of musical practice in a single culture. These two theories require methods that capture and consider all music within a culture and in the world, rather than methods designed to assess the relative value of particular genres, works, or musicians.

So what does ethnomusicology as a unified discipline, with its associated fieldwork methods, look like from the perspective of this credo? First, we need methods to collect and study all the world's (and a culture's) music so that we can make general, even universal, claims about the nature of music. We need methods to distinguish the typical from the idiosyncratic in the music we collect, presumably so that our comparative statements and universal claims have some statistical relevance. The methods we use during our extended, intensive fieldwork in one place, presumably to explain our theory that music is a part of culture, are apparently so disparate that they must be excluded from a shared credo. In fact, it may be possible to understand this relationship between music and culture in the absence of method, just by being there. If none of these theories appeal, then ethnomusicologists just churn out "pieces of research" in the absence of theory, and probably method as well. Read this way, Nettl's credo has the advantage of catholicity, but it returns us, ironically through shared beliefs, to a polyphonic understanding—and possibly an accurate one at that—of ethnomusicology without much shared method to go along with three shared theories. The one method we do share, extended fieldwork in one place, exists, according to this credo, unconnected to any particular theory.

In the 1990s, a case for a view of ethnomusicology as a unified discipline would probably be built around Nettl's credo that music is a part of culture (or is culture) but with the explicit continuation that fieldwork methods, including extended, intensive work in one place, exist or must be developed to demonstrate that relationship. This theory, that music is a part of culture, necessarily rests on a theory or theories of culture imported primarily from anthropology.

Anthropologists have "vexed" each other, to use Geertz's telling phrase, over the proper definition of culture, how it is manifested, and how it can best be observed and studied. At least three concepts seem in some sense primordial to the culture concept, though even these features have not escaped critique. First, culture, however defined, has to do with what is shared among a people. Second, cultures are bounded in space and often in time by the "ethnographic present"; we speak routinely and metaphorically of cultural boundaries that apparently block easy intercultural understanding. Third, bounded cultures contain insiders in relation to which the researcher, whether anthropologist or ethnomusicologist, is an outsider. Attempts to understand music as a part of culture involve specifying methods for border crossings in order to live and work among insiders long enough to apply other methods designed to elicit the shared musical, speech, and other behaviors that would demonstrate this music-as-culture theory. It is probably not too bold to claim that the most frequently cited research in ethnomusicology since the late 1970s has attempted to define and apply methods designed to work out the implications of this theory.

The Field

In this review of the role of methods in relation to theory in ethnomusicology, the field emerges as the place where data are collected to test theories. It is a bounded place filled with insiders who share views about music, musical practices, and a host of other things. It is the place where we outsiders must go to encounter these insiders and their culture, and explain to other outsiders the relationship between music and culture posited by our theories. It is, above all, the primary place of knowing in ethnomusicology, a place privileged epistemologically by the theory that constructs it as the locus where methods will be applied to demonstrate the truth of our theory that music is a part of culture.

However, in this review of theory and method there was a suggestive alternative to this epistemological vision of fieldwork, an alternative that seemed unconnected to theory, that by implication left method behind. It was the third aspect of Nettl's credo: We believe in fieldwork. Fieldwork for what? Not apparently as a place to test and work out theory, an experimental place in other words, but a place to become an ethnomusicologist, an experiential place. This third aspect implies the belief that the experience of fieldwork, whatever its methods or even in the absence of methods, constitutes the sine qua non of the state of being an ethnomusicologist. In this credo we have the privileging of ontology (being there) over epistemology (knowing that), and the beginning of a potentially fruitful turn away from fieldwork methods toward fieldwork experience. According to this credo, sometime during or after fieldwork, one becomes an ethnomusicologist. In effect, the self is transformed and reconfigured in the act of understanding one's own or another culture.

The view outlined here that the field is a place of experiment and that fieldwork is an epistemological process exists in parallel and unconnected to the view that the field is a place of experience and that fieldwork is an ontological condition. It would be easy and tempting to demand that we choose one or another of these views; indeed, both sides could and have been the subjects of merciless critiques. But instead of choosing between the two positions, it may be more profitable to attempt a mediation between them. Could, for example, the transformative moment in one's "being-in-the-world"—in one's self, as it were—from nonethnomusicologist to ethnomusicologist be understood as a particular example of more general transformative experiences during fieldwork that lead to new understandings? If the self rather than method were the locus of explanation and understanding (not, by the way, the solipsistic object of understanding), might this realignment contribute to the reformulation of theory and method? On the other hand, could theory and method, which take for granted a fixed and timeless ontological distinction between insider and outsider, be reordered within an ontology that understands both researching and researched selves as potentially interchangeable and as capable of change through time, during the dialogues that typify the fieldwork experience? Although such a mediation may be too ambitious for this chapter, it is on the horizon both of this chapter and of this volume.

Work

The emphasis on theory and its accompanying epistemological problems helps to account for the term "work" in our hypothetical course title, "fieldwork methods." Aside from the way "work" valorizes the enterprise as possessing at least the potential for generating both symbolic and economic capital within our own social and economic system (Bourdieu 1991), work must surely be necessary if an outsider is to cross cultural boundaries and enter a conceptually distant field—this last metaphor itself configures a place of unremitting physical drudgery—filled with another category of beings, insiders, whose workings with music as culture must be explained. But if fieldwork is reconceptualized as an ontological project, would the term "work" still be appropriate? When one *is* in the field, isn't existence also fun and playful, at least from time to time? And don't we, as human beings, enter into caring, as well as working, relationships with other human beings while in the field, even as we do our research, apply our methods, and test our theories? Could we not search for another mediation, along the lines of the one suggested earlier, between the epistemological, methodological work of explanation in the field and the ontological understandings of human and musical experience in the field? Would we whimsically retitle our course, "life-experience understandings in ethnomusicology"?

Playing, Caring, Experience, and the Understanding of Bulgarian Music

At Home in the Field

My own sense that concepts such as the insider–outsider dichotomy, the impermeability of cultural boundaries, and even the field as the privileged place of ethnomusicological understanding might need rethinking began not with reflections on theories and methods like those above but with various attempts to understand Bulgarian music, both in and outside what ethnomusicology traditionally defines as the field. The most important event that led me to rethink these ethnomusicological givens occurred when, after a long and unsuccessful period of trying to learn to play the Bulgarian bagpipe (*gaida*) from one of Bulgaria's finest pipers,

Kostadin Varimezov, I suddenly understood the basic kinesthetic principles that would allow me to play somewhat adequately in what I think is fair to call a virtuosic instrumental tradition (Rice 1985, 1994, 1995).

As part of my research on Bulgarian music, I decided that I should learn to play a traditional wind instrument, either the *kaval* (an end-blown, rim-blown flute) or the *gaida* (a mouth-blown bagpipe with one melody and one drone pipe). When I began this project, I was working on a dissertation topic; one of my goals was to discover native terminology used by women to describe their polyphonic musical practice (Rice 1977, 1980, 1988). I was distanced by gender and methodological stance from participating in what was essentially a women's singing tradition. In learning to play an instrument, I had no particular research questions I was asking, but as a musician I wanted to learn to play and participate in this tradition. In retrospect, I realize that I separated fieldwork from fieldplay at this early stage of my career in a rather unprofitable way. Epistemological methods and questions were associated with the former, and the ontological process of becoming a musician was the goal of the latter. At the time I gave no thought to whether and how these two positions might be linked or mediated.

Some years later I was able to invite Kostadin to come to the University of Toronto, where I was teaching at the time, as an artist-in-residence for the academic year. During this period we, along with his wife Todora, co-created a "field" in which collecting and interviewing work and learning to play were conjoined. I recorded their repertoire of instrumental music, song, and dance in the manner of epistemologically oriented fieldwork, and continued to learn to play, dance, and to a lesser extent sing in Todora's monophonic tradition, which was open to male performance. Even though I acted methodologically in the collection process, I didn't know where it would lead me theoretically, since I was more interested in music-as-culture questions than in music as sound fact, and I couldn't really observe music in Bulgarian culture in Toronto. In fact, I collected for two existential reasons. First, I imagined that the items I recorded would provide the repertoire for my existence as a musician, which it did. Second, I worried that, far from their close-knit, extended family, time would weigh heavily on them. I reasoned that spending time with me recording their repertoire and their life stories would make their stay more pleasant, which it did. My collecting in this case resulted from caring for them, not from theory or method. In retrospect, I would say that I had created a fieldwork situation that was structured ontologically rather than epistemologically, and with no particular expectation of a connection or a productive mediation between the two positions. It is probably unnecessary to add that even in the more typical situation of fieldwork far from home, there is no field there; the field is the metaphorical creation of the researcher.

The oddness, as fieldwork, of my research in Toronto only increased when the Varimezovs returned to Bulgaria and left me alone to continue on the path of becoming a musician in this tradition. (In Bulgaria, at least before World War II, little boys who would be musicians were sent to a real field to learn on their own, out of hearing range of adults; I was, at home, metaphorically in just such a field, one rather different from the one constructed by ethnomusicologists.) Under Kostadin's supervision I had mastered certain aspects of the playing technique; I could play melodies in a number of different pentachordal modes and in the famous Bulgarian asymmetric meters (5/8, 7/8, 11/8, etc.), and I could separate melody notes one from another by creating low-pitched "crossing noises," to use the pejorative Scottish bagpiping expression, with the appropriate closed-fingering technique. (These noises are necessary because the bagpipe's sound cannot be stopped with the tongue, as on most wind instruments.) However, I had failed to understand how to create the characteristic high-pitched ornaments that seemed so crucial to the bagpipe's style. Kostadin could not explain them to me in words, gestures, or musical notation the way he could melody, rhythm, and articulation, and, whenever I tried to insert them by lifting my thumb before the melody note, he would complain that I had "lost the style" and that I didn't yet have "bagpiper's fingers" [*gaidarski prŭsti*].

If I wanted to *become* a musician, I now had to so in the presence of the tradition in what I would now call its textualized form—as both recordings of Kostadin and my memories of lessons with Kostadin—rather than in the presence of informants and insiders. Again in retrospect, I would argue that this apparent liability, as understood from the perspective of traditional fieldwork, imitates, in fact, one of the experiences of acquiring culture generally. All of us who grow up in culture and acquire its traditions do so only partly as a result of direct, pedagogical intervention of the sort commonly associated with scolding by parents, teaching by teachers, or informing by informants; culture and its traditions are also acquired by observing, mimicking, and embodying shared practices (Bourdieu 1977) and by appropriating, understanding, and interpreting shared, symbolic actions (Ricoeur 1981c) without the direct intervention of parents, teachers, informants, and insiders.

Without Kostadin, but still determined to learn to play the *gaida* adequately, I analyzed the recordings by slowing the tape down, only to discover that the high-pitched ornaments were richer and more varied than I had imagined. Moreover, I realized that my mental image of how to move the thumb and forefinger of my top hand could not under any circumstances produce this dense ornamentation. Still, I struggled gamely on, trying to play with some, if not all, the ornamentation and to approach the speed with which Kostadin and other Bulgarian musicians played. Then, one day I began to think about one of what I now call the "textualized traces" of Kostadin's attempt to teach me to play. He had told me that the key to the ornamentation was in the *razsvirvane* (the "playing around"), a series of melodic phrases as the bagpiper fills the bag with air and starts the reeds of the melody and drone pipes. Each phrase begins with a long note on the highest pitch of the *gaida*, followed by an ornamented descent. To play the long note, the player lifts simultaneously the thumb and two or three fingers of the top hand off the instrument. It suddenly dawned on me that if I did the same when I played the ornamentation, that is, if I lifted all my fingers simultaneously rather than, as I had been doing, the thumb first followed by the fingers necessary to produce the melody note, then I could produce the complexity and variety of ornaments that had proved so perplexing. This new kinesthetic understanding allowed me to play faster and more relaxed, and include more ornaments, than I ever had before. It sounded to me as if I had found "the style" I previously had "lost," acquired the elusive "bagpiper's fingers," and solved *le mystère des doigts bulgares.*

Between Insider and Outsider

It was this learning experience, at home in the Bulgarian version of the field to which children are sent to become instrumentalists, that caused me to reflect on some of the basic tenets of ethnomusicological theory and method. One of the most troubling questions was simple: Where was I? And I didn't mean the question just in spatial terms, that is, where is the field? Where was I in relation to ethnomusicological theory? And where was "I" in the temporal trajectory of myself becoming an ethnomusicologist and musician?

Until I found "*gaida* player's fingers" in the early 1980s, I had been strongly influenced by the methods provided by cognitive anthropology to develop a theory of culture as mental activity. Cognitive anthropology uses the elicitation of language terms to make inferences about internal rules, categories, and distinctions that "natives" employ when acting culturally and socially. Its positing of a contrast between "etic" (from phonetic) and "emic" (from phonemic) analyses seemed particularly attractive to me and other ethnomusicologists, who feared that Western-style (etic) analyses might ignore, misunderstand, or even violate important (emic) principles operating within a culture. Given that ethnomusicologists think and talk a lot about music, it seemed an attractive way to discover how natives think and talk about music, and thus gain insight into a supposed insider's perspective on musical and other forms of cultural practice. When I distanced myself from music making and tried to understand the Bulgarian insider perspective through words about music, I was happy with the results and felt that they represented significant advances over an outsider's etic analysis (Rice 1980, 1988), but when I fully engaged with the music, overcame my scholarly distantiation, and attempted to appropriate the style to the point where I could not just talk about it but play it as well, I ran into the limits of this language-based method and its associated theory of culture. I encountered precisely the "linguocentric predicament" that Charles Seeger (1977:47) would have predicted for me.

Starting with etic musical analysis and working with a native musician whose vocabulary for talking about music was limited, I had approached an understanding of the tradition, but there still was a significant gap between where I was as an outsider to the tradition and where insider instrumentalists were. They knew it, and worst of all I knew it, too. Bulgarians have a theory to explain this gap: How could I ever really understand their tradition when it wasn't "in my blood"? And some ethnomusicologists have a comparable theory; outsiders are forever doomed to partial understandings compared to insiders, never mind that most Bulgarians can't play the *gaida* either.

When I finally solved the mystery of bagpiper's fingers, I did so in dialogue with Kostadin's tradition of playing, preserved in recordings, after my conversations with him had ended. In the process, I believe I moved to a place untheorized by the insider–outsider distinction so crucial to much ethnomusicological thinking. After talking to a cultural insider, which took me in the direction of an emic understanding of the tradition but not all the way there, I confronted the tradition directly as a sound form and kinesthetic activity, and made it my own in an act of appropriation that transformed me, my self, into something I hadn't been before, a person capable of playing in this tradition with at least minimal competence. This transformation did not, however, make me into a cultural insider; I was not, at least it seemed to me, a Bulgarian. While Kostadin couldn't explain his ornamentation to me in enough detail to make me understand it, I came to be able to explain it to myself and to others; I now understood the finger movements and other mental processes necessary to produce the *gaida*'s characteristic ornamentation. My understanding was neither precisely that of an outsider nor that of an insider. Although the linguistic methods of cognitive anthropology had helped me narrow the gap between emic and etic perspectives, I could not in the end close that gap completely. When, on the other hand, I abandoned those methods and acted musically, it seemed as if I fell right into the gap between insider and outsider, into a theoretical "no place" that felt very exciting, if not exactly like a utopia. I was neither an insider nor an outsider.

The perspective I had acquired in the process of learning to play competently (not necessarily well) was neither emic nor etic. It was my own. I could now supply from my own self-understanding verbal explanations of the complex mental processes necessary to generate this music, explanations that at least one insider, Kostadin, had been unable to supply. If emic understandings are located in other people's heads and given to us in their language reports, then my understanding wasn't emic. On the other hand, if etic understanding involves applying objective analytic methods to sounds without regard for their cultural salience, then my understanding wasn't etic either. I felt as if I had achieved a mediation between these two theoretical categories, these two ontological conditions, and that this mediation challenged fundamentally one of the most important theoretical foundations of our discipline. If I was right, I would eventually need to search for new foundations. But before doing that, I needed to return to Bulgaria and put my new understanding to the test by playing for Bulgarians.

Playing in a Field of Expanding Horizons

When I returned in the mid-1980s to Bulgaria, the ethnomusicological version of the field to which outsiders are sent to become experts, I was delighted when

Kostadin and others confirmed my self-assessment of my understanding in a number of direct and indirect ways. He stopped asking me to leave out the high-pitched ornaments, and we worked on inserting them into all the necessary places. He could now show me where in the melody to use them by gesturing in midair with his "bagpiper's fingers" as I played—and I understood what he meant. One of his sons, an amateur player himself, noticed that the first finger of my top hand, crucial to the ornamentation, moved just like his father's, that is, he saw as much as he heard one of my "bagpiper's fingers," which I had acquired not from observation of his father's finger but in a metaphorical dialogue with his father's recordings. A younger bagpiper, who had also learned, as I had, by listening to Kostadin's recordings rather than by being taught and informed directly by him, recognized in my playing Kostadin's ornamental style: "It is as if you are listening to Varimezov."

I was, of course, pleased and excited by their comments, but one of the most touching moments for me occurred at a celebratory gathering of their extended family in a village near Burgas in the foothills of the Strandzha Mountains, the area where Kostadin and Todora came from and in which their tradition flourished. We sat outside under a grape arbor on either side of the traditional *dülga trapeza* [long table] that provides the locus of all Bulgarian celebratory meals. As we ate and drank, Kostadin played the *gaida* and Todora and a younger woman sang songs. During the evening an elderly neighbor, with an impressive mustache of the type worn mainly by older villagers, approached and sat down across from me. Kostadin introduced me as the professor who had invited him to Canada for a year, and told the man that I played the *gaida*. "Hah, an American plays the *gaida*," he almost spat out in surprise and disbelief. He then turned to me and ordered, "Play, and I will tell you whether you are a *gaidar* [bagpiper]." I thought, "Oh brother, there is no way I can satisfy this guy," particularly since my playing usually went to pot when I was nervous, as he had made me. Kostadin handed me his *gaida*, and I reluctantly began playing. When I stopped, to my surprise he smiled, seemed pleased, and said, "You are a *gaidar*."

In their comments and actions, these Bulgarians confirmed that my self-understanding was now leading to recognizably Bulgarian musical behavior. Although I wasn't a Bulgarian, I could act like a Bulgarian in the production of a complicated musical form, and when I acted like a Bulgarian in this particular way, they did too; that is, if the occasion were right, they danced. I could now enter into a dialogue with Bulgarians not just in their language but in their music and dance forms as well. Although I was no doubt an outsider ethnically, weren't they accepting me as something like an insider musically and therefore culturally? (After all, music is culture, according to one ethnomusicological metaphor.) Actually, one Bulgarian took this connection between cultural performance and ethnicity further than I was willing to. During a village fair in 1973, a man, whom I had noticed scrutinizing me intently as I talked and danced but whom I didn't know, called me over and demanded to know where I was from and why I was there. (I worried that he was a member of the state security apparatus, with whom I had had a number of unpleasant run-ins.) I explained that I was an American living in Bulgaria for a year or so "on a specialization" to study its folk music. "Hah," he said, "you lie! You speak Bulgarian, and you dance Bulgarian dances. Therefore, you are a Bulgarian."

These sorts of interactions "in the field" suggest that categories of insider and outsider may not be particularly helpful terms to describe the kind of dialogic relationships in language, music, and dance that develop between people who perform and appreciate traditions they have each made their own in varying degrees. Just as I had tried to enter into the horizons of their tradition, they now seemed to accept and include at least some of my actions within the horizons of their understanding of that tradition. Perhaps, I thought, now was the time to begin in earnest the search for new theoretical and even philosophical foundations for ethnomusicology.

Field-Play Understandings: Ontological Solutions to an Epistemological Problem?

Remnants of Romantic Hermeneutics in Ethnomusicology

The recognition of a distinction between the knowledge of insiders to a culture and the knowledge of outsiders to that culture has been, since the early 1970s, an important, perhaps even central, aspect of method in, and a fundamental epistemological problem for, ethnomusicology. The distinction is usually traced to a book published in 1954 by the linguist Kenneth Pike, who distinguished between what he called etic accounts of language and culture, which were based on the categories of scientifically trained observers, and emic accounts, which sought to understand the categories and meaningful distinctions of native speakers and cultural insiders. Cultural anthropologists in the late 1950s and 1960s found the distinction useful, and it spawned a number of new research paradigms variously labeled ethnoscience, cognitive anthropology, and the ethnography of speaking. It was these trends that influenced a new stream of ethnomusicological research in the 1970s and 1980s, including my own.

Nearly forty years after Pike's work, ethnomusicologists continue to discuss it, reinterpret it, define research projects and methods in terms of it, and criticize the limitations of the work based on it. A panel at the 1992 SEM annual meeting took it up, and in 1993 the journal *The World of Music* devoted an issue to it. At some level the distinction seems axiomatic; after all, it is rooted in the very concept of culture and the concomitant notion of cultural boundaries. It is cultures with boundaries that define the positioning of insiders and outsiders. On the other hand, when we start analyzing this supposedly axiomatic distinction, we bore each other with questions and doubts. Isn't etic really a particular kind of emic? Is it a dichotomy or a continuum? Have we misinterpreted Pike's original idea? And on and on.

Pike's distinction has its roots in a philosophical tradition begun by René

Descartes inquiring into the epistemological foundations of knowledge. Descartes felt that, only by doubting being, both in its supernatural form as defined in the religious tradition of the day and in its natural form as the perceptible world, could he understand the conditions limiting human knowledge. His radical doubt of supernatural and natural being led him to conclude that only ego could be known to exist without doubt; his argument, *cogito ergo sum*, might be glossed, "I doubt therefore I am." Descartes' doubt of the possibility of knowing anything about the world set in motion the long history of Western Enlightenment philosophy devoted to the epistemological questions "what do we know" and "how do we know it." This stream of Western philosophy spawned a seemingly necessary set of distinctions between the ego and the Other, subject and object, objective knowledge of observed behavior and subjective knowledge of inner experience, mind and body, the natural and social sciences, and insiders and outsiders. In this Enlightenment view, knowledge of the world is dependent on methodologically precise, objective observation. In turn, the limitations of these methods prevent us from examining inner experience and the intentions and meanings of others—at least without experiencing what might be called methodological embarrassment.

I undertook my search for alternatives to the Enlightenment position that privileged epistemological problems while doubting being and the existence of a world as the result of my fieldwork experiences. But I came to realize that such a search had already been started by nineteenth-century Romantics, who were desperately interested in understanding the intentions, abilities, inner experience, and motivations of Others, especially those Others they believed to be geniuses. A theologian, Friedrich Schliermacher (1977), and a philosopher, Wilhelm Dilthey (1989), are usually credited with founding Romantic hermeneutics to interpret and understand the works of genius produced by Others. But in keeping with the Enlightenment and the scientific revolution for which it provided the philosophical foundations, Dilthey in particular suggested that one would have to understand the Other by analyzing directly observable behavior. Today much work in the social sciences, including ethnomusicology, relies in large part on this Romantic hermeneutic tradition, where the Other is now not the genius of Romanticism but the exoticized Other, the insider, of fieldwork methods. This work is simultaneously reluctant to give up on the possibility of objectivity, and possesses a new confidence that formal methods, like those of ethnoscience—a telling label, by the way, ethno*science*—can be applied to knowing something about the Other.

Although the Romantic hermeneutic tradition, which continues to influence much of the social sciences and ethnomusicology, fosters objective methods, much of twentieth-century philosophy, social sciences, and natural sciences, the last in the wake of the theory of relativity, has made us skeptical of even this much recourse to objectivity. It is now common to point out that the outsider stance is not objective but a particular kind of emic perspective with the backing of powerful institutions in powerful countries. But the opposite is also true, that is, we often continue to insist that claims to an emic perspective and to understanding the meanings assigned to behavior by insiders must be subjected to the same standards of validity and verifiability as objective inquiry. So, although many of us believe in something like multiple subjectivities and have abandoned the search for objective knowledge, we still tend to demand and trust in objective methods to demonstrate to colleagues our understandings of the other's intentions, feelings, perceptions, distinctions, and rules. It is at this contradiction that we really have to seek a new philosophical foundation for our ethnomusicology and our social sciences and to try to mediate the dichotomies we have inherited from the Western Enlightenment and pre-modern scientific traditions.

Phenomenological Hermeneutics as a Foundation for Ethnomusicology

The philosophical tradition that I have found most helpful in reinventing myself as an ethnomusicologist, because it seems to possess the potential for just such a productive mediation between experimental, objectivist strategies of observation and experiential, subjective knowledge of the force of meanings and intentions, goes by the name of phenomenological hermeneutics. It represents both a continuation and a break with the tradition of Romantic hermeneutics, which, in the work of Dilthey, has been so influential in the social sciences. The main thinkers and their works that have influenced me are Martin Heidegger's *Being and Time* (1978), Hans-Georg Gadamer's *Truth and Method* (1992[1975]), and Paul Ricoeur's *Hermeneutics and the Human Sciences* (1981c). Clifford Geertz's (1973a, 1983) interpretive anthropology also participates in this philosophical project. I am going to review some of the main claims of this philosophical tradition, particularly those that radically challenge the Enlightenment tradition, which provides the foundation for so much of contemporary ethnomusicology. As I do so, the sources for some of the language in the previous two sections should become clear.

In phenomenological hermeneutics, the world, far from being doubted by the subjective ego, is restored to its ontological and temporal priority over the ego or subject. The world—or in our terms, the culture or the tradition—exists and the subject/ego is "thrown" into it. According to Heidegger, "being-in-the-world" is the ego's ontological condition before knowing, understanding, interpreting, and explaining. What the ego/subject comes to understand and manipulate are culturally and historically constructed symbolic forms such as language, dress, social behavior, and music. In hermeneutic jargon, the unbridgeable gulf between subject and object is mediated as the subject becomes a self through temporal arcs of understanding and experience in the world. The self, whether as a member of a culture or a student of culture, understands the world by placing itself "in front of" cultural works. This sense of understanding a world is rather different from the notion that the outsider as subject must, through the application of ethnoscientific methods, get behind the work to understand another subject's (the insider's) intentions in producing the work. In the hermeneutic view, the subject, supposedly freed from prejudice by method, is replaced by the self, who inevitably interprets and understands the world before any attempt to explain it can proceed. Understanding, in this tradition, precedes explanation rather being the product of it, as it is in the Enlightenment tradition. This idea should be immediately attractive to ethnomusicologists, who have frequent opportunities to observe that highly sophisticated nonverbal musical understanding often exists in the absence of verbal explanations of it—precisely the case with Kostadin's knowledge of high-pitched ornamentation.

Since, according to this philosophical tradition, we understand our world in terms of pre-existing symbols, like language, before we explain it, our explanations are always conditioned by pre-conceptions and pre-understandings given to us by those symbols. The self-conscious task of bringing that understanding to language involves what Ricoeur (1981c:164) calls a "hermeneutic arc." If we take music to be one such symbol system, we can say that the arc begins with pre-understandings of music, either as a performer or as a listener who finds it coherent, and passes through a structural explanation of music as sound, behavior, and cognition, to arrive at an interpretation and new understanding of the world or culture referenced by music acting as a symbol. Phenomenological hermeneutics thus helps to recast the problem of understanding the experience of musical symbols from a fruitless and methodologically unsound search for an unknowable, subjective, psychological inner quality in the subject or the Other to an interpretation of the world that music references by a self operating within finite but expandable horizons.

The metaphor of horizons, which we use routinely in our pedagogical work ("Let's study this music to expand our horizons") but often replace with boundaries in our scholarly analyses of cultures, has been theorized anew by Gadamer. Rather than cultures with boundaries, Gadamer explores the metaphor of a world with horizons. Like the physical world, the horizons of an individual's social and cultural world change as he or she moves through space and time. Whereas Enlightenment philosophy leaves us with a certain confidence in a rational and fixed subject moving through the world, analyzing and in some sense controlling it while keeping it at a distance, hermeneutics suggests that the subject becomes a self in the encounter with the world of symbols. In other words, I became a *gaidar* (and an ethnomusicologist) in the encounter with Bulgarian music and musicians. The notion of the subject as constant and above the world, as "reigning over objectivity," is an illusion (Ricoeur 1981c:190). It follows that, if such an independent subject existed, it would impose its interpretation on the world. In Ricoeur's view, on the other hand, the ego constructs itself as a self by being thrown into a world. In his view, appropriation, or "the act of making one's own that which was previously alien, . . . ceases to appear as a kind of possession, as a way of taking hold of." Rather, appropriation "implies instead a moment of dispossession of the narcissistic ego." Ricoeur continues, "By the expression self-understanding, I should like to contrast the self which emerges from the understanding of [symbols and symbolic action] to the ego which claims to precede this understanding. It is cultural works, with their universal power of unveiling, which give a self to the ego" (Ricoeur 1981c:192–93.)

My appropriation of Bulgarian bagpipe performance, although it began as a selfish desire to learn the tradition for myself and what it could do for me in the American world of scholarship and amateur performance of Balkan music, went as far as it did because I cared for Kostadin. He in turn began to pressure me to appropriate the tradition completely, that is, to transform myself into a *gaidar*, for himself. My self-transformation had become meaningful and important to him and his self-definition and self-regard. He did not remain the inveterate insider, but transformed himself and expanded his horizons in his encounter with me and my world.

Marcia Herndon, in her 1993 article in *The World of Music* issue devoted to the emic/etic dichotomy, wrote "I speak as myself; neither fully insider nor outsider, neither fully emic nor fully etic" (1993:77). I believe that I got to this place vis-à-vis Bulgarian culture, but by a different route. Herndon attributed her ontological condition to "my mixed-blood status with Cherokee coming from both sides of my family" (1993:77). In hermeneutic terms, however, all those who place themselves "in front of" recorded or performed musical works, whether or not they can claim any genetic relation to those who produced them, may be able to make this claim: I am neither insider nor outsider; I speak as myself, a self formed, reconfigured, and changed by my encounters with and understandings of Bulgarian, and indeed all kinds of other, musical works and performances.

For Ricoeur, appropriation is the process by which a scholar, or anyone thrown into a world, "struggle[s] against cultural distance and historical alienation." Since, in this starkly un-Romantic view, access to the inner experience of the Other is neither attainable nor sought after, one is left to interpret symbols and symbolic behavior in terms of the world or worlds they potentially reference, an understanding that is finite, changeable, multidimensional, forced to compete with other interpretations, and limited by the expandable horizons of the individual. As Ricoeur puts it, "It is because absolute knowledge is impossible that the conflict of interpretations is insurmountable and inescapable. Between absolute knowledge and hermeneutics, it is necessary to choose" (1981c:193).

When, as in ethnomusicological research, a new world of music is encountered, new understanding results when the horizons of the researcher's world are expanded to include at least part of the world that the new music symbolically references. From this perspective, the researcher seeks to understand not so much the inner experience of people from another culture, but rather the world suggested by music sounds, performances, and contexts. Because ethnomusicologists often find themselves at some cultural or historical distance from the traditions they study, appropriation is the dialectical counterpart of that initial distanciation. Even so-called insider ethnomusicologists, those born into the traditions they study, undergo a productive distantiation necessary for the explanation and critical understanding of their own cultures. Rather than there being insider and outsider ways of knowing, all who place themselves "in front of" a tradition use the hermeneutic arc to move from pre-understandings to explanation to new understandings. Even an insider faced with a particular cultural work or performance may not interpret it in the same way as the insider who produced it and was "behind" it. In other words, not just scholars follow this hermeneutical arc. All individuals operating within tradition continually reappropriate their cultural practices, give them new meanings, and in that process create a continually evolving sense of self, of identity, of community, and of "being in the world."

More Field Experience and Dialectical Strategies

Ricoeur is a master of dialectical thinking. First of all, he identifies seemingly irreconcilable oppositions, like the one between objectivity and subjectivity (or, in another essay, between history and fiction), demonstrates how each side partakes of qualities of the other, and then finds a way to mediate the opposition by resetting the terms in which the opposition was proposed and seemed so primordial. If ethnomusicologists adopt his philosophical stance, then we will be forced into such dialectical strategies. We will no longer be satisfied with identifying and then choosing between the oppositions we generate. Just such a mediation between insider and outsider was what I attempted in the previous sections.

Other oppositions await mediation as well. For example, the experience that I described earlier of becoming a musician through an encounter with the Bulgarian tradition suspiciously echoes Mantle Hood's 1960 call for acquiring "bi-musicality." In the 1960s Mantle Hood and his students often seemed to acquire this "bi-musicality" in order to study and report on music "in its own terms" and for its own sake, with culture and history providing little more than a "context" in which music was made. Alan Merriam and his disciples, on the other hand, were calling for a study of music as culture that often seemed to ignore "the music sound itself" and to challenge the respectability, and certainly the relevance to music-as-culture studies, of the knowledge gained through "bi-musicality." As I mentioned, I was mainly interested in the music-as-culture metaphor when I began my study of the *gaida*. In touting the scholarly benefits of becoming a musician in a tradition I wish to understand, have I entered a vicious circle? Am I merely reproducing the oppositions of thirty years ago? I don't think so.

One payoff of my self-transformation into a *gaidar* superficially resembles Hood's emphasis on music in its own terms, and that is my ability to explain aspects of the sound structure of the music from the perspective of a performer using the language of Western music theory and notation. Some of the description in the second part of this essay was devoted to such explanations, but my emphasis on the state of "being-in-the-world" with Bulgarian musicians also refocuses questions of music as culture beyond notions of the analogies and homologies that musical performances and other cultural actions possess to questions of the social and cultural relationships generated between the selves who make music in culture. When the field researcher begins to participate in meaningful cultural action, then the pragmatics of music and culture, that is, the study of the conditions underlying specific musical and cultural utterances, becomes the focus of investigation. When the field researcher engages in acts of musical interlocution, as I did, then the ontological condition of the self and other agents seems to compete with the ontological priority normally given to observable music and language behaviors and events in epistemologically driven ethnomusicological theory and method.

It was when I began to participate, even at my limited level, in musical conversations with Bulgarian musicians during field trips in the late 1980s, that I came to understand how Bulgarians, operating from a variety of social positions, interpreted the structures of musical utterances as referencing a world. Bulgaria in the 1980s experienced the death throes of communism. As the society divided itself along political and ethnic lines (the latter in the form of severe government-imposed sanctions against the Turkish and Gypsy Muslim minorities), musical practice participated in the contestation. Where the Communist Party had once dictated the public forms of musical production, during the 1980s those in opposition to the Party sought new musical forms to express their distaste for the Party's policies, practices, ideology, and aesthetics. Musicians played and listeners heard enormous variations in musical style, and often seemed to make aesthetic choices based on political preferences. It was in this political context that Todora said to me, as we listened to an outstanding *kaval* player on the radio, "May it fill your soul." There are a number of questions that her expression of enthusiasm raised for me. Why is the soul the locus of aesthetic pleasure? What in music filled her soul? Why did that performance fill her soul?

I can't yet answer the question of why the soul is the locus of aesthetic pleasure, except with the rather banal suggestion that it may have something to do with self-identity as Orthodox Christian Slavs (even when people like Kostadin and Todora are not particularly "religious"), but in musical conversation I began to get an inkling of the what and why of soul-filling performances. The precise pitch and presence or absence of the barely audible ornaments and "noises" between melody notes in instrumental performances, which had presented me with so many technical and musical problems, turned out to be crucial to the identity of the player and the playing style. And questions of identity—whether one was Bulgarian, communist, anticommunist, Muslim, Gypsy, Turkish, Western-looking, or backward-looking—were what was at stake for most Bulgarians in the late 1980s. Kostadin's way of playing the ornaments was "Bulgarian" and even regionally distinctive, a marker of "authenticity." Muslim Gypsy musicians, on the other hand, used a slightly different style of ornamentation, and some younger *gaida* players tried to imitate it, primarily because it was flashy and fashionable, even when they didn't care to link it to its possible political references. I learned to play one such tune "in conversation" with Kostadin's nephew, who for the most part followed Kostadin's example, but when I played this tune for Kostadin he insisted that I replace an ornament his nephew had played below the melody with one above it. The way his nephew and I played the phrase was "empty," according to Kostadin. Though the quantity of ornaments didn't change, one version created for Kostadin an aesthetically empty response whereas the other one was capable of filling his soul. Fieldwork in Bulgaria had taught me that his preferred way of playing was filling because it referenced a familiar, comfortable world of previous experience, a world dominated by Bulgarians and the progress and security provided by the Communist Party. His nephew's way was empty aesthetically because it referenced a world of change, threat, and potential instability. Without that participatory experience of music making and living in Bulgaria, the explanation of what at first glance seemed a rather mystical link between aesthetics and metaphysics—"May it fill your soul."—would be impossible. That nearly imperceptible ornamental tone was not just a feature of musical style but a source of soul-filling (or empty) aesthetic experience and, through its capacity to reference a world, of social and political experience.

Throughout this chapter I have exposed a number of oppositions: studies of music "in its own terms" versus music as culture; explanations based on methods versus understandings based on experience; and insiders and outsiders. I have held out the hope for some sort of mediation, rather than a choice, between them. This study follows the temporality of my experiences with Bulgarian music and with ethnomusicology, and in so doing reveals that it is almost surely in the temporal dimension that the mediation between these oppositions will occur. Heidegger's insight that the fundamental ontological condition of "being-in-the-world" was its temporality is probably also the place to seek the kinds of mediations demanded by these oppositions. An initial understanding of musical style and production became the ground on which I in time built an understanding of music as culture. Instead of bracketing experience while focusing on experiment as our methods require—or glorifying experience while abandoning method as our dissatisfaction with positivism grows—Ricoeur's phenomenological hermeneutics suggests bringing experiment within the framework created by experience. Instead of explanation for the natural sciences and experience for the human ones as Dilthey suggests, Ricoeur brings explanation within the framework of experience in his "hermeneutical arc." Instead of immutable outsiders, the "hermeneutical" arc may provide a pathway from the outside, with its cultural alienation, toward the inside by means of appropriation and understanding. Instead of generalized insiders, the "hermeneutical" arc may provide another path from the inside, with its cultural engrossment, toward the outside by means of distanciation and explanation.

In this chapter I illustrate two "hermeneutical" arcs that mediate between method and experience and between explanation and understanding by moving through time. The first began with my understanding of many elements of Bulgarian musical style as well as an understanding of the limits of that understanding as far as ornamentation was concerned. Further attempts to appropriate the tradition led to an explicit, verbalized explanation of how those ornaments must be produced and to corresponding problems of the appropriate methods to use in their description. The arc ended, "for the time being," when explanations led back to an understanding of how to play the instrument to produce sounds that were understood by me and interpreted by Bulgarians as adequate representations of Bulgarian musical style. The second arc began with this new understanding of musical style, moved through an explanation of the locus where musical style accounted for aesthetic satisfaction (the exact position of particular ornamental notes), and ended, again for the time being, with an understanding and interpretation of how and why this musical style references the politically charged Bulgarian world of the 1980s. These temporal arcs from understanding through explanation to new understandings contain the possibility for the mediation between field methods and field experience posited at the beginning of this chapter.

What's the Difference?

Reflections on Gender and Research in Village India

In 1974, coincidently about a year before I first heard of a field called ethnomusicology, Edward Ives wrote the following in a manual on field research. About setting up the initial interview, he said, "There are two questions that students often ask at about this point. The first, and by far the more common, frequently comes out something like this: 'Do you think it's going to make a difference that I'm a girl when I go talk to Mr. Bilodeau about lumbering?' My answer is usually, 'Of course it's going to make a difference, but I can't tell you what kind of difference.'" Ives goes on to say a bit later, "Just about every time I have predicted how the man/woman of it would work out in some particular case, I have been wrong, which means that I have stopped predicting" (1980:37). This may be the wisest statement that I've come across concerning the difference that gender makes in field research, although it probably wasn't the answer the student was looking for.

This chapter concerns the differences that gender, or more precisely gender identity, may have made in my own research in village India.[1] I say may have made because even in hindsight we can't always tell. I'm considering the issue with respect to two rather different field research projects. The first was field research for my dissertation, carried out for five months in 1981 and another thirteen in 1983–1984 in villages in the southernmost region of Bihar, an area of mixed Hindu and aboriginal (the preferred English term there is "tribal") population. This is research that exists now only as recollections of various sorts. There are my journal notes, in which the roles and identities discussed here (researcher, writer, female, musician) are freely intermingled and undifferentiated; there are moments, musical and otherwise, frozen in tape recordings and still photos; and then there is that very particular distillation of recollections, the dissertation. The second field project to be considered here is one that, at the time of this writing, was yet to be—a research project eventually carried out during spring and summer 1993 concerning a predominantly Hindu performance tradition in the same area. When this chapter was originally written in November 1992 this was research that was yet only imagined, but very actively imagined, and so in some ways more real than the earlier.

The two projects are quite different in their subject matter. In the first, I was interested in the musical exchange between two groups of people, the tribal Muṇḍas and their Hindu (Nāgpuri-speaking) neighbors. I was interested in concepts of culture and ethnicity, and constructions of otherness, from a Muṇḍāri point of view. In the course of my field research for this first project, I became acquainted with a few women within the Hindu community who sang and danced professionally at village weddings and festivals, and who are also what we might call concubines, courtesans, or in some cases prostitutes. These women, called *nacnis*, and their performance tradition were the focus of the 1993 research that was in its planning stage at the time of this writing. The issues I'm confronting in this second research project specifically concern gender identity and the female musician in India.

It was the subject matter of my second research project that prompted these reflections about the impact of a researcher's gender roles and identities on her work, not simply in "the field" but also in the translation of that field experience into a written form. I became particularly interested in the issue as I set out to do fieldwork again in India in 1993 because of the intense disjuncture I experienced in the earlier project between the experience *there* and the writing that followed, *here*.[2] Clifford Geertz and other anthropologists reassessing the relationship between fieldwork and ethnography have noted the difficulty of this enterprise, "the oddity of constructing texts ostensibly scientific out of experiences broadly biographical" as Geertz has put it (1988:10).

In my own case, I think I speak of field research and writing as separate activities, at least in the earlier project, because that was my expectation going in. This is often the case for those of us who do research outside North America. Our field research is clearly bounded by time, space, "culture," and language. We experience a very real dislocation when we go to "the field." We know that our time there is finite, and it will be difficult to return once we leave. Every moment should be spent doing research, attending events, talking to people, and making music, rather than writing. What's more, when I work in villages in India, I am also relocated ouside the academic world. My friends and research partners there don't spend their time sitting alone, reading and writing. Such activity is downright antisocial. And everyone knows you can't learn music or dance by reading and writing about them. The physical circumstances of my research and the very nature of living in village India certainly contributed to the disjuncture I experienced in making the transition back to academic life upon my return.

One could argue that such disjuncture between the research experience and the writing are common among anthropologists and ethnomusicologists, regardless of the gender factor. As Mark Slobin put it in a recent article in *Ethnomusicology*, we all grapple with the "problem of welding the disparate strips of observation into a finished work of analysis" (Slobin 1992b). An aspect of that problem is our imperative to spin generalized analyses of culture and traditions out of intense, particular experiences with only a few individuals.

Still, I think that the differences in my gender identities, both chosen and assigned, within my academic world here and in "the field" in India were also a factor. The disjuncture was particularly intense because central aspects of the experience—related to my roles and identities as female and as musician and dancer—were left out of the writing (or, you might agree by the end of this chapter, were deeply buried in it). I should note that it was never a matter of consciously suppressing or editing out the experiential in the writing. But I knew as it developed that the written report was much more distant from the experience than I would have liked it to be. Not incidently, those buried experiences were also the most emotional, sensual, and physical aspects of my being in India. I don't want to simply rechew old experiences here. I am interested in the implications of such a distillation of the experience in the writing as I proceed with the second research project, one that explicitly concerns issues of women (including myself) as musicians and dancers. Can I avoid the same disjuncture? Should I?

The Ungendered Researcher

Although it isn't my central purpose here to examine why I feel that these aspects of my experience—as female, musician—were suppressed in the first project when it came to writing the ethnography, I will digress for a moment and offer a bit of speculation. It concerns gender identity in the American academic world.

In my academic studies, somewhere along the way, I developed a conceptualization of the scholar (researcher, writer) as ungendered, or gender neutral. The idea was reinforced by both personal experiences and institutional paradigms. In graduate school, first at the University of Minnesota and then at the University of Illinois, some professors questioned the ability of female students to do field "work" (lacking the necessary physical strength) or even to pursue a career (distracted as they were by marriage and children). My female classmates and I came to understand that being female was risky in this environment, so we often chose not to expose our gender. We were working hard to enter an obviously male-oriented profession, and we wanted to be perceived as no different from the male students. Gender-neutral scholarship, we thought, worked to our favor.

Our perception of the gender-neutral scholar was reinforced by official discourse in ethnomusicology. In my student days, gender was discussed sparingly, if at all, in textbooks and courses on fieldwork. Edward Ives notwithstanding, most of our written guides to doing field research—Hood, Nettl, Merriam, Goldstein, Karpeles—did not mention gender at all.[3] In some of my courses, the gender of the researcher *was* discussed in terms of access, rapport, and role expectations.[4] We were encouraged to be flexible and sensitive to the impact of our gender, but the field methods and techniques themselves were universally applicable and ungen-dered, as were the models for writing.[5] After all, we were all after the same informa-tion, the same knowledge. Managing gender relations in the field was a personal, private matter. Those aspects of doing field research that were most closely related to the experience of being female in the field were, and to a large extent still are, discussed not in the official discourse about field research but in a sort of unoffi-cial, underground discourse in which women (and sometimes men) shared experi-ences and advice about managing sexual miscommunication and harrassment, conflicting role expectations, gender relations, female hygiene, and sexual relations in the field. To some degree I think this was and is our choice; we still have a stake in maintaining the illusion of the ungendered scholar.[6]

The paradigm of the ungendered scholar has been sustained almost uniformly in our models for the written ethnography. In many of the classic ethnographies of music-culture, the subjects themselves (the 'Others') are unmarked for gender, though most often, in reality, they are male. And even when the subject *is* gender, the author's gender typically is not part of the text. Like her male counterparts, she's an omniscient voice, an ungendered observer, reporter, and interpreter.[7] Although intense participant-observer-based ethnography was once regarded among femi-nists (sociologists, notably) as a qualitative, "feminine" alternative to more positivist, abstract, "masculine" methods, the social science paradigm for written ethnography has remained unchallenged until recently, when it has come under attack by femi-nist scholars such as Lorraine Code (1991), Katherine Borland (1991), and Judith Stacey (1991). As they see it, the paradigm, with its objectification of experience, "denigration" of emotion, potentially exploitative methodologies, unidirectional flow of information (source to scholar to academic audience), and imperative to 'take a stand and defend it' is not gender neutral at all, but inherently androcentric.

Well, probably so. It *is* the paradigm, modified a bit, upon which much of my dissertation, my written distillation of those field experiences of 1981 and 1983–1984, is based. In an effort to avoid the appearance of writing the "truth," I contextualized my very particular interpretations of Muṇḍāri and Nāgpuri musical interaction within my own experience in an account of fieldwork that conventionally prefaces the body of the work as a long section of personal, reflective remarks; the remainder of the dissertation is punctuated occasionally with vignettes that remind the reader that "I was there." Throughout most of the text, however, the ungendered scholar prevails. This is not to say that it does not represent something of my research expe-rience or that it is somehow dishonest or invalid. A written account of field research can be nothing more than a sorted and sifted reconstruction of that experience. In fact, the dissertation passed several "validity" tests: it rang true to my Muṇḍāri men-tor, Dr. Ram Dayal Munda's own interpretations, it did not offend or embarrass anyone, and it met the expectations of research partners and scholars in India whose support I value. Leaders of local political parties and tribal youth organizations now quote from it to support and validate their struggle for cultural identity and auton-omy. But because of its bow to the social science paradigm, it exists quite separately from the field research in my recollections, particularly with respect to my experi-ences in Bihar as female and as musician and dancer.

Gender in the Field Experience

To consider how gender identities shaped my previous field experience in villages in Bihar in 1981 and 1983–1984—and to let the reader in on what was left out of the written work and why—I'd like to quote from the introduction to the dissertation. I've chosen one of the more personal, reflective statements, one that tells the reader something of the nature of my interaction with Muṇḍas (an aboriginal or "tribal" group) on the one hand and Nāgpuri-speakers (predominantly Hindu) on the other. In this passage I describe a party thrown by myself and the three tribal women with whom I lived in a rented, tin-roofed, bug-infested house in Ranchi city. The house was a duplex, with separate entrances to each side, and two rooms per side. This was a sort of farewell party, as I was approaching the end of my stay. We had invited many of the people with whom I had worked during the year, Muṇḍāri and Nāgpuri, and a few other friends.

> The way in which our guests arranged themselves on the night of that farewell party revealed much about the nature of my field experience of the previous thir-teen months. Nearly all of our *ādivāsi* [tribal] guests, most of them Muṇḍas in roughly equal numbers of men and women, gathered on the side of the house in which Charia, Madhu and Asrita had their rooms. The Nāgpuri and Bengāli guests, mostly men, as well as our Nigerian friend [also a man], gathered in the music room, next to my room. On one side, then, was a socially homogeneous group, nearly all Muṇḍas, all of the same status, belonging to one endogamous social group, speaking the same language, but of mixed gender; in its make-up it was a group typical of Muṇḍāri social gatherings. On the other side, not coinci-dentally my side, was a predominantly male but socially heterogeneous group of people of different statuses and occupations, different endogamous groups, and different native languages, conversing with each other in two common languages, Nāgpuri and Hindi. At some point, as the night progressed, the guests on both sides of the house began making music. There was Muṇḍāri drumming and group singing and dancing by the *ādivāsis* (Muṇḍas and a few Oraons) on the one side, and Nāgpuri drumming and solo singing, without dance, by individual Nāgpuri men, most of them specialists in stage performance, on the other. (Babiracki 1991:7–8)

The description of the party continues a bit later:

> Throughout the night of the farewell party, I moved back and forth between the two sides of the house, trying to distribute my time and attention equally between

these two different social and musical groups, as I had during the course of my research. Even more interesting, those individuals who had been most closely associated with me as research companions and assistants—Mukund Nayak [a popular Nāgpuri stage musician] and the three women with whom I lived—likewise moved between the Muṇḍāri and Nāgpuri sides of the house. Mukund and Madhu [one of my Muṇḍāri housemates] even made attempts to participate in one another's music making, just as I had been doing during the last thirteen months. For the most part, though, those who "crossed over" simply observed the music making of the other side. My participation in both was more complete, as it had been throughout my research. (Babiracki 1991:9)

The excerpt tells you a good deal about what I perceived to be differences in male and female roles in Muṇḍāri and Nāgpuri music-cultures. It represents Muṇḍāri music-culture as unsegregated by gender, and communal and egalitarian in participation, and Nāgpuri music-culture as segregated by gender, and dominated by male instrumentalists and soloists. It is an accurate representation of what I still consider the significant differences between these two music-cultures, and also of what was my very different participation in and experience of each, but it tells you nothing about how my personal, gendered experiences and my various gender identities may have shaped my perceptions in the first place.

By gender identity (as opposed to biological, sex identity), I mean the particular constructions of female, male, and things in-between that one chooses and/or is assigned in particular situations. As you will see, the identity I chose for myself and the identity others thought I had chosen were not always the same (or so I think now). I also want to add that gender was only one of many factors that shaped my experience. Age, status, race, language, education, physical appearance, political ideology, concepts of individual and group, and many other factors, all of them interconnected, contributed.

Several months into my field research in 1981, Mukund Nayak, a Nāgpuri friend and research partner, confessed to me that when they (my new Muṇḍāri and Nāgpuri friends) first met me, they had concluded that, since I was apparently unattached, not "going with" any man *or* woman, I must be "neutral" (he used the English term). Looking back on it now, I see that I eventually established my humanness among Muṇḍas and Nāgpuris in very different ways, in both cases through gendered, personal relationships involving active participation in music and dance.

Among Muṇḍas

Muṇḍas establish new relationships with each other and with "outsiders" (a loose translation of their word *diku*) on the basis of existing relations. I was first introduced to the women who became my housemates by Dr. Ram Dayal Munda, a linguistics professor with whom I had studied at the University of Minnesota and who became the head of a department and for a time Vice-Chancellor of Ranchi University. Dr. Munda introduced me as his sister-in-law, the "sister" in a fictive or extended sense of his American wife at the time.[8] My extended kinship relations with my housemates, and through them with every other Muṇḍa I met, were all determined by that first introduction, and from then on kin relations determined with whom I could talk or joke, those I had to avoid, and those I could count on for help—in other words, those to whom I had access for research purposes. After Dr. Munda introduced me to my housemates, he had little to do with the day-to-day activities of my research, though he continued to guide my interpretations. In village situations in which I felt I could not fulfill the expectations of my assigned, female roles and still accomplish my research objectives, my housemates, who traveled to villages with me, became mediators, explaining me and my work to others, and sometimes even taking on my expected household roles themselves.

Maintaining my assigned, female identity while documenting and participating in Muṇḍāri communal song and dance events proved more difficult. At times their expectations of me and my behavior conflicted with my need to be a researcher. These dance occasions are highly gendered events. In the dancing ground the roles of men and women are clearly defined—men play instruments, dance in a sort of freestyle, and introduce songs; women dance a repeated step pattern together in a tight line and respond to songs—and there is a very specific etiquette of coded male–female behavior. One of the purposes of communal singing and dancing is to bring together potential marriage partners at periodic festivals to give them an opportunity to get to know each other. I was expected to join the women's line, usually somewhere near the head, and eventually to take my turn at leading. It was a role I gladly accepted and thoroughly enjoyed, but one that precluded documentation of the event or conversation with others—particularly men—in attendance. My solution was to document as much of an event as I could early in the event, before my age and gender identities were clearly established and understood. With tape recorder in one hand and microphones in the other, I positioned myself between the head of the women's line and the group of men dancing in front of them, then simply moved around the circle with the flow of the dance, neither male nor female—the ungendered researcher. Once I put my equipment away and joined the line, in effect declaring myself female after all, there was often no going back. The women usually refused to let me leave the line or pick up my tape recorder again for any length of time.

My research methodology among the Muṇḍas was also defined by the ethnographer's imperative, a desire and need to understand all aspects of their music-culture. It is probably in the ethnographer's attempt to fulfill this directive that his or her gender has its most noticeable impact on the final representation, although that impact often goes unacknowledged.

I had already played with assuming both male and female roles in Muṇḍāri music making long before my first research trip, as a member of a Minneapolis-

based music and dance troupe established by Dr. Munda to present stage performances of the songs and dances of his people in performances throughout the
Midwest. I alternated female and male roles in those performances: singing and
dancing with the women in one half, and playing flute and dancing with the men
in the other. Dr. Munda insisted, for the recreation to be authentic, that I must take
on the role of a man completely when playing the flute. I dressed in a *dhoti* and
kurtā, with my hair in a topknot, and shadowed his dance movements until I could
move like a man. Troupe members dubbed me "Little Munda." Once in India, with
Dr. Munda's encouragement, I continued to play Muṇḍāri songs on the flute in
stage programs and with small gatherings of men in his village. And I learned to
play the large kettledrum (*nagāṛā*), like the flute a male instrument. There was no
taboo against women playing these instruments, and no penalty for doing so, but
women normally didn't. Dancing as part of the group of men in the dancing
ground would close off the kind of playful interaction with men that women seek
in the dance. My housemates were intrigued by my "boldness," my crossing of gender roles in this way. Eventually each one tried her hand at playing the flute. Only
one continued to play after I left, and then seldom in public. Only in Dr. Munda's
native village did I feel free to play the flute and kettledrum in the dancing ground,
dancing with and like the men, though without my earlier change of costume. The
men seemed amused and accommodating.

It occurs to me now that my crossing of gender boundaries, mixing of gender
roles, and creation of new roles (the ungendered researcher) may have contributed
to my perceptions of the equality of men and women in the Muṇḍāri communal
dancing ground. This characterization of Muṇḍāri music-culture as egalitarian was
also influenced by Dr. Munda's own representation of his society. His desire, in
light of current political movements, to represent it as egalitarian is a way of distinguishing it clearly from hegemonic Hindu society. The fact that my play with roles
was acceptable, albeit unusual, to other Muṇḍas lent validity to his interpretation. I
accepted readily the illusion, created in part by Dr. Munda, that I had participated
in both male and female aspects of Muṇḍāri music-culture. In reality, I am sure
that Muṇḍāri experiences of the dancing ground, whether as men or women, are to
a great extent individual and situational, as were my own.

Among Nāgpuris

The picture of Nāgpuri music-culture I presented in the excerpt from the beginning of my dissertation, that of a music-culture segregated by gender and dominated by male solo performers, in its own way reflects the nature of my gendered
experience of that music-culture and my relationships with Nāgpuri musicians. It
represents only that part of Nāgpuri music-culture in which I most actively participated: public stage performances, dominated by men. My role among these musicians was mediated by one man, a musician named Mukund Nayak, who is one of

the stars of the Nāgpuri stage. Mukund is a singer, poet, drummer, and dancer—and a Ghāsi, a member of the traditional village musician caste. It was my close, romantic friendship with Mukund that probably first made me human in the opinions of my Nāgpuri acquaintances.

Mukund and I met during my first, "preliminary" research trip of 1981 . I say preliminary because I thought I was only looking around, not doing "serious" research; as it turns out, much of the dissertation was based on events documented and impressions formed during that first trip. Mukund quickly pulled me into his stage troupe, a group consisting for the most part of Ghāsi men, and I subsequently traveled throughout the area performing Nāgpuri songs on bamboo flute with them in village stage performances. Consequently, although I am aware of the village world and music of Nāgpuri women and occasionally participated in it, I do not have the intensely familiar experiences to draw upon in developing an understanding of them that I do in the case of Muṇḍāri women's culture. My perceptions of Nāgpuri music-culture were colored by Mukund's own representation and interpretation, just as my perceptions of Muṇḍāri music-culture were influenced most by the interpretations of Dr. Munda and my housemates.

During my first research trip to the area in 1981, the nature of my friendship with Mukund had remained private, or so I thought at the time. After five months, I returned to the University of Illinois to finish coursework and preliminary exams, write a dissertation proposal, and apply for a grant. In short, I settled back into my academic persona. When I returned to Bihar in 1983, I seriously considered breaking off my relationship with Mukund. I knew that if the relationship were to continue, it would have to become public knowledge, and I had some vague notion that such a relationship was a breach of ethics. I feared that some Muṇḍas might not approve. And I think I sensed intuitively that such a relationship would be incompatible with the role I had now embraced as "serious" researcher. The paradigm of the ungendered researcher, untainted by the female musician, had reasserted itself with determination. It didn't take long for me to realize, with Mukund's help, that to break off my relationship with him would not only sadden us both, but would betray the trust and expectations we had established during my first trip. Humanism won out; our friendship continued.

It did indeed become public knowledge, although it remained unofficial, that is, without public acknowledgement. Our friendship determined my further relationships with Nāgpuris, particularly musicians, as well as my own experience and understanding of Nāgpuri music-culture. Because Ghāsis, people of Mukund's caste, are considered by others to occupy the lowest rung in the caste hierarchy, my access to many Nāgpuris of high caste was effectively closed or constrained. To pursue close relations with them would have been taken as an insult by Mukund and many of our friends. My friendship with Mukund also established an avoidance relationship between me and his "older brothers" in an extended sense. But the younger men who performed and traveled with Mukund and learned music from him became my "younger brothers" too. Not only did they stop soliciting my romantic attention, but they honored their kinship obligations to me of assistance and protection with amazing generosity. Muṇḍas, as it turned out, seemed little concerned by our relationship (with one exception). They had never considered me a potential partner for Muṇḍāri men to begin with, due to their strong ideas of tribal endogamy. I was a *diku* no matter what I did.

My travels with Mukund and the troupe were a source of great pleasure. Although I was still busy documenting, observing, asking questions, and so forth on these jaunts, I looked forward to them as a kind of break from my research. Mukund was the only person I saw regularly who spoke English, and my participation as a soloist in Nāgpuri stage performances was comfortable, more consistent with my self-identity as a musician here in the United States than was my participation in the Muṇḍāri communal dances. Although I took joy in singing and dancing with Muṇḍas, my travels with the Nāgpuri troupe offered me a release from the stress of adapting to the Muṇḍas' intense communalism and their censorship of behavior that calls attention to oneself as an individual. Although few other women participated in these Nāgpuri stage programs, aside from a few *nacnis* (professional village entertainers) or former *nacnis*, I rarely felt uncomfortable with this. Instead, I followed Mukund's cue, concluding that my identity as an educated white woman somehow lent respectability to my otherwise questionable behavior as a female entertainer.

My relationship with Mukund also gave me a unique insight into Nāgpuri music-culture, an insight that, like the other experiential aspects of my research, is only suggested in the dissertation. In 1981, shortly after we met, Mukund began composing songs inspired by our friendship. By the time I returned to the United States in 1984, he had composed eleven of these. Since then he has composed several more, so there are perhaps fourteen or fifteen altogether. By composed I mean that he set new stanzas of words to traditional seasonal tune types. All of these songs could be considered part of a larger tradition of songs of love in separation or unattainable love, a tradition related to and perhaps derived from Vaiṣṇava devotional poetry, in which the unrequited longing for the beloved is a metaphor for the devotee's longing for union with the divine. For Nāgpuri poets, the ostensibly devotional tradition is simultaneously, even primarily, a vehicle for the expression of sentiments that cannot otherwise be made public.

Mukund composed the first of these songs, "*piyo mainā*" (blue and yellow maina-bird), in September 1991 as I was leaving Ranchi city for a week-long stay in a Muṇḍāri village. The song is about the poet's loss of his beloved *piyo mainā*. In the song, Mukund is also invoking my eventual return to the United States, which we both knew was coming:

bahute jatana karī re   Taking great care
posalō mōe piyo mainā   I kept a piyo maina.

kāle re piyo mainā,	Why did piyo maina,
piyo mainā uṛi bana jāe	Piyo maina fly away to the forest?
bana jhāra chāin delō re	I searched every corner of the forest,
gach khuṭ se pūich lelō	I asked all the trees and stumps,
kāle re piyo mainā	Why is piyo maina,
piyo mainā nahī to bhẹtāe	Piyo maina not found?
nita dina khojī lorhī re	Night and day, searching and gathering,
khudī cunī ṭhurāe rahō	I collected bits of grain.
kāle re piyo mainā	Why did piyo maina,
piyo mainā gele bisurāe	Piyo maina forget?
tana ke pījarā mānī re	Thinking my body a cage,
man mē basāe rahō	I kept [piyo maina] in my mind.
kāle re piyo mainā	Why did piyo maina,
piyo mainā karejā bīdh jāe	Piyo maina shoot my heart [with an arrow]?
mukund binu pākhī re	Mukund, without wings,
guni guni prāṇ taij delō	Thinking and thinking, lost his life-breath.
tabe re piyo mainā	Just then, piyo maina,
piyo mainā ghurī pachatāe	Piyo maina came back and was full of remorse.

(Translation by M. Nayak and C. Babiracki)

The song became a hit in village stage performances and even inspired several parodies. Each of Mukund's songs that followed "*piyo mainā*" either related to a specific event in our friendship or reflected Mukund's state of mind at a particular moment. Significantly, there is no mention of these songs in the dissertation.

Identity Conflicts

The theme of love and longing in separation also characterizes the Vaiṣṇava songs sung by the *nacni*s, the professional female singers and dancers with unorthodox lifestyles who are the subject of the second research project considered here. *Nacni*s are non-"social" women of lower status, who are "kept" by men of higher status as professional entertainers. They live outside the conventions, restrictions, privileges, and protection of socially sanctioned married life. At the same time, each is Radha incarnate, free to experience and enact fully the goddess' passion of pure love and devotion. A *nacni* often sings in the voice of Radha longing for her beloved, Krishna. She herself is regarded as an unattainable object of desire, particularly when she is performing. It is her singing and dancing that make her attractive, just as it is Krishna's flute and dance that attract Radha, and Radha's dance in turn that attracts him. A *nacni*'s songs are simultaneously interpreted as secular, sensual and divine, and her performances are valued as a manifestation of the relationship of Radha with Krishna. The *nacni* and her partner (who may or may not be her "keeper") are hired as auspicious performers at village weddings and festivals. Yet for all her cultural value, the *nacni* herself is degraded socially for her unorthodox life-style, for her flaunting of societal norms, and for singing and dancing in public.

During my research trip of 1983–1984 and for some time after, I thought that I had created a unique identity for myself as a female musician within Nāgpuri music-culture, or at the very least, that I had succeeded somehow in changing Nāgpuri ideas about the impropriety of a woman performing in public. I continually ascribed a gender identity to my role on the Nāgpuri stage based on my identity as a female musician in my own country, and Mukund reinforced this notion. He believed so strongly in the power of my respectability that he persuaded me to work with him to reintroduce group dancing to Nāgpuri stage programs. We began with brief interludes of dance performed on the tiny stage by a handful of musicians. Other female singers sometimes joined me in the women's line, ironically with the exception of a former *nacni*, who was trying to establish herself as a respectable stage singer. By the time I left in 1984, we were ending our all-night performances with communal dancing at dawn in a makeshift dancing ground among the audience.

Nevertheless there were moments when I was jolted out of my comfortable perceptions of myself as a female musician among Nāgpuri musicians, moments when I realized that the people around me weren't perceiving me in quite the way that I would have liked. At a village festival in 1984, late in the night, Mukund coaxed me out of a Nāgpuri women's dance celebration (segregated from the men) to observe a group of men, in another part of the village, dancing *mardānā jhumar*, a genre they usually performed with a *nacni*, though none was present at this event. I positioned myself among them with my tape recorder, moving with the flow of the dance, once again the ungendered observer. At some point I became aware of the fact that I was the only woman in this dancing ground, and that the men seemed to be singing with and to me—not to the tape recorder, but to me. I had the sudden and uncomfortable realization that perhaps they thought I was the *nacni* in this dance. I immediately began suppressing my own response to the music and avoiding eye contact in an attempt to reassert my researcher's identity. Although the ploy worked for me, I wonder now if it produced any shift in the identity they ascribed to me.

At the end of my stay, after many attempts to arrange an interview with a member of the lineage of the Mahārāja of Choṭanāgpur about his family's patronage of Nāgpuri music, I finally got the opportunity following a stage program in his village. The interview was a model of cross purposes. The rāja was rather drunk, insisted that I drink rum with him, and became increasingly aggressive in his flirting; his wife scowled at me in open hostility from across the compound; and I relentlessly, futilely, tried to invoke my neutral, ungendered researcher identity. I realized too late that this rāja—and his wife—had both regarded me, in their own gendered ways, as they would a *nacni*. This was later confirmed by Mukund, who was there but had assumed a traditional role of court musician and so did not want to intervene.

It is quite possible that, while I thought I was constructing a new identity for the Nāgpuri female performer, one that Mukund felt would serve the advancement of Nāgpuri music, many people had in fact simply assigned to me a familiar female identity, that of the *nacni*. I must admit that the thought did cross my mind more than once while I was there, and I greeted it with ambivalence. I valued and admired the *nacnis* as musicians and performers, and their life-styles and performances resonated with some of my own ideals: behavioral freedom, individuality, economic independence, and artistic achievement. On the other hand, I was and am mindful of the disdain that most Muṇḍas and Nāgpuris (nonmusicians) I knew had for the *nacnis* as individual women. My Muṇḍāri acquaintances, particularly, see the *nacni* tradition as the legacy of a patriarchal feudal system that degrades and exploits women. The scorn was clear in the voice of Gandharva Munda, Ram Dayal Munda's father, as he responded to my question about who becomes a *nacni*:

> "Who becomes a *nacni*? Those who have no shame, who don't respect anybody. *Nacnis* are spreading. [something unintelligible] They become them all by themselves. They absorb it. They don't have any training. They won't make an [artistic] impression."
>
> Then he stopped and looked at me, "Okay, you'll become one. You could easily become one" (Field notes, Diuri village, 9 Dec. 1984. Translation by Carol Babiracki).

He could speak to me in this way, because he was like a "father" to me, but I *was* taken aback. Once again, the identity I had constructed for myself had run up against one assigned to me.

Implications for Future Field Research

My past acquaintance with the *nacnis* and their performances has moved me to research them and their tradition further. I was fascinated and probably a little flattered during those past research trips to find that the *nacnis* themselves were drawn to me, though in retrospect I have a better understanding of why. I am intrigued by the ambiguity of their status, the multilayered interpretations suggested by their performances, and my own ambiguous responses to them. *Nacnis* were the site of conflict in my past research between identities of female and musician chosen by me and those assigned to me, and as promised, they became the site of conflict between my models and ideologies of musician, female, and the gender-neutral social scientist in my new research project of 1993, which was anticipated at the time of this writing.

I am also intrigued by the possibilities this new project offers for exploring research methodologies and writing strategies that attempt to bridge the chasm between the field experience and writing about it. This new research presents an opportunity to put the female musician back into the ethnographer.

The paradigms outlined by feminist scholars of oral history, psychology, sociology and other disciplines seem at first glance to be promising alternatives to the social science paradigm of ethnographic research. They are also familiar to those of us who know them in their incarnation as postmodernist ethnographic methods (e.g., Clifford and Marcus 1986; Clifford 1988a). These paradigms shift the object of representation from culture or a people to "fleeting" moments of discourse (Salazar 1991). They favor dialogic forms of representation that place multiple voices and interpretations into the written work and that reflect the dissonance of the research process itself (Stacey 1991). They propose interview strategies based on models of women's natural conversation, especially small-group conversations in which everyone participates simultaneously and nobody holds the floor (a nightmare to transcribe!), in an effort to shift the focus away from activities and facts (information) and "attention-getting, well-polished monologic narratives" (Minister 1991). And they teach us to extend the conversation (as opposed to the interview) between researcher and subject into the later stages of interpretation in a process of collaborative story making (Borland 1991).

These strategies are enticing but are not without their own shortcomings. The intersubjective and self-reflexive approaches tend to place the researcher herself in the center of the story, potentially marginalizing the subject and subordinating her story to the method itself. Some feminists argue that dialogic, self-reflexive approaches tend to privilege the researchers' ideologies and agendas over those of the subjects (Hale 1991; Borland 1991). And, of course, the intersubjective interview strategies that I mentioned earlier are based on observations of women's communication in North America, in the English language.

Dialogic interview strategies can create what Judith Stacey has called a delusion of alliance, a search for the self in the other, based on assumptions about the unity of women that the subject may not share with the researcher. Stacey concludes that, in her experience, the more intimate, intersubjective methods actually place subjects at greater risk of exploitation and manipulation than the more positivist research methods. She argues that ethical questions of authority, exploitation, and the inherently unequal relationship between researcher and informant/subject are not eliminated, or even minimized, by the postmodern ethnographic strategies, but simply acknowledged by them (Stacey 1991).

My difficulties in writing this chapter only underscore the concerns voiced by these scholars about the risks inherent in intersubjective, self-reflexive methodologies. I suspect that my Muṇḍāri and Nāgpuri friends in Bihar would neither understand nor applaud my self-absorbed musings, and they certainly wouldn't find that I had served *their* needs.[9] The subjective, reflective paradigms of writing may better represent *our* experience as researchers, but for my Muṇḍāri and Nāgpuri research partners, representing the *memsāhab*'s experience was not the objective. In their view, my research was about their people and traditions. They were and are keenly interested in *how* I represent them and their traditions, that my representations are consistent with their self-image, and that they serve their personal and political aims.

It is no accident that I have chosen not to write about my more personal encounters with Muṇḍāri and Nāgpuri music and musicians before this; I did not want the writing to impinge on or trivialize my remembrance of the experiences themselves, and of course it has. I struggled with the ethics of discussing my personal relationship with Mukund in this public way. On my return to Ranchi in 1993, Mukund gave his approval of the discussion here, with some pride, although he found my asking for it rather ridiculous. Our friendship *is* public knowledge over there, after all.

What we must strive for, I think, is a keener awareness and acknowledgment of the objectives and audiences of our writing and a set of paradigms from which we may choose the most appropriate. This, too, has implications for our field research. Can one, for instance, produce intersubjective *and* paradigmatic social scientific works based on the same field research?

Just as I approached my new research project in 1993 with an assortment of paradoxical, ambiguous interpretations of the *nacnis* and their performances and a willingness to add more, I also carried a collection of possible research strategies and a willingness to be flexible.[10] But my plans and expectations were tempered with the hard-won wisdom that choices would be made for me and that what is probably most interesting about the "man/woman of it" is its unpredictability.

Notes

1. This chapter was originally written in November 1992 for presentation at a colloquium on Fieldwork in Contemporary Ethnomusicology organized by the graduate students in ethnomusicology at Brown University.

2. I want to make it clear that I see both my research experiences in India and the writing of them back in the United States as facets of my life as a scholar. Both *are* scholarship. But qualitatively they are vastly different, hence the disjuncture. Paradigms of academia, including that of the ungendered researcher, encourage such a false dichotomy between scholarship and life.

3. Thankfully, this is no longer the case. Notable collections on gender and the field research experience include Whitehead and Conaway's *Self, Sex, and Gender in Cross-Cultural Fieldwork* (1986); Gluck and Patai's *Women's Words: The Feminist Practice of Oral History* (1991); and Bell et al.'s *Gendered Fields: Women, Men and Ethnography* (1993).

4. This was particularly true in my first formal courses in field research with the folklorist Dr. Ellen Stekert at the University of Minnesota.

5. See also the growing literature exploring a feminist approach to writing, all of which have implications for ethnographic writing (Caws 1986; Cixous 1991; Finke 1992; Heilbrun 1988).

6. In the fall of 1992, I was asked to write a recommendation for a student who was competing for an AMS50 grant from the American Musicological Society. I was admonished

to make no reference to the applicant's gender, race, or origins in my letter. In grappling with such an awkward task, I found that, in the end, I had also left out any indication of my own gender. We are all ungendered in the academy.

7. As examples, see any of the essays in Ellen Koskoff's collection *Women and Music in Cross-Cultural Perspective* (1989).

8. Mundas do make a conceptual distinction between fictive and blood kin, although that distinction is not revealed in the terminology they use.

9. This has since been confirmed by the reaction of my friend and coresearcher Mukund Nayak to this chapter. He found it acceptable, but not very interesting or useful.

10. After this chapter was written in 1992, I did indeed undertake seven months of field research in 1993 on the new project anticipated here, a study of ideologies of gender, religion, and music among village *nacnis* of Chotanagpur with my coresearcher Mukund Nayak. Just as the on- and off-stage personas of the *nacni* and her partner are seemlessly and simultaneously intertwined, so were Mukund and my identities as partners in daily life, stage performance, and research. The flow of our research included a continual "off-stage" dialogue about whether and how I was—and wasn't—like a *nacni*. A full exploration of the play of gender in that research properly requires a separate chapter, which might address the problems of integration of the identities of female, musician, and ethnographer for the researcher (neither an easy or natural process, even when consciously sought); the consequences of privileging gender over other social identities; the benefits and constraints of cross-gender collaborative research; and the ethical questions raised by intersubjective, individual-centered research. It is rich ground for future consideration.

PART III

The Ethnomusicological Past, Present, and Future

Fieldwork in the Ethnomusicological Past

Even this idyllic scene, though, isn't innocent of history.

Eva Hoffman, *Exit into History* (1993):333

On the Boundaries between Past and Present

The Jewish communities of the *shevah kehillot*, the Seven Holy Cities, of Burgenland constituted, until the 1930s, a boundary region between Central Europe and Eastern Europe. The villages and small cities of the *shevah kehillot* and the areas of previously intensive Jewish settlement in this border region attract relatively little attention today. Most of them are unknown outside of Austria, although a few claim a bit of fame from famous musicians who once lived there: Franz Joseph Haydn and Fred Astaire in Eisenstadt, Karl Goldmark in Deutschkreuz, and Joseph Joachim in Kittsee. Some physical evidence of the Jewish past from the Seven Holy Cities survives: the synagogue in Kobersdorf; cemeteries, or at least the stones of cemeteries, rescued from the ravages of neglect; and streets and walls intended to bound the Jewish quarters of a town. Human evidence did not survive to the present quite so well; there are reputed to be three Jewish families still living in the Seven Holy Cities today, but no one knows who they are, and they do not identify themselves (Gold 1970).[1]

The most ethnically diverse province in Austria, with modern ethnicity consciously historicizing the diverse musical life of the past,[2] Burgenland witnesses virtually no Jewish music today.[3] Jewish musical life, for all intents and purposes, does not exist in Burgenland at the end of the twentieth century. Nonetheless, it was the Jewish musical life of Burgenland that led me to this borderland between Central and Eastern Europe, this field located between the past and the present. The Seven Holy Cities were in many ways emblematic of Jewish musical life in Europe: a mixture of traditional and modern repertories; complex and contested practices; and a music history shaped by movement both toward and away from the conscious expression of Jewishness. This chapter examines why I chose fieldwork to draw me closer to the Jewish musical life of a past that no longer existed in the present.

The emergence of fieldwork as a research method in the social sciences has resulted to a large degree from its capacity to bring the scholar into contact with the present. The fieldworker not only makes observations in the present, but the present provides diverse frameworks for the several narratives reported by the fieldworker, through fieldnotes, accounts of participant-observation, or full-blown ethnographies. As a lived experience, fieldwork's encounter with the present is an uneasy paradox. On one hand, fieldwork takes place as an excursion into the culture of the Other. In contrast, however, fieldwork must account for everyday practices. The paradoxes proliferate as we attempt to connect the different elements in these statements. "Everyday" and "Other" seem counterpoised at opposite extremes; "culture" and "practice" exhibit no less disjuncture. Temporal considerations sharpen the paradox. Whereas the everyday and its practices would seem to unfold within the present, the culture of the Other requires a systematization, even ossification, of moments gone by. The present, therefore, is ongoing, but once inscribed in ethnography, it is marked by the syntax of pastness. The past, in contrast, is frozen in a timelessness, from which it must be wrenched to be synthesized into the presentness of history. The disjuncture between past and present makes it increasingly difficult for fieldwork to examine either, but necessary to examine both.[4]

I take the paradox and disjuncture of fieldwork as givens in this chapter. I do not try to resolve them; rather, I try to identify an ethnographic and historical space that they open. It is a discursive space of boundaries, not boundaries between cultures, instead a space within which cultures locate themselves. These boundary spaces undo many of the categories that ethnomusicologists and those engaged in fieldwork have long taken for granted. Culture within these spaces no longer forms into systems, but rather becomes fluid, ephemeral, and contested. History can no longer be recuperated into teleological narratives that "once happened" and now can be told again and again in their inscribed versions. History, too, forms in a temporal space, contested because fragments of the past remain in the everyday of the present.

For the ethnomusicological fieldworker the boundaries between the past and present become themselves the "field," a space allowing one to experience and represent musical practices that are not simply inscriptions of the historical past or aural events of the immediate present. Although I examine one specific case of such a space, that of the Jewish musical past of Burgenland, I argue in this chapter that it is not unique, but rather representative of a wide range of ethnomusicological pasts. That there is no Jewish music to hear in Burgenland in the 1990s results from the devastation of the Holocaust, which in turn specifies the historical conditions of the Jewish musical past in this boundary region between Eastern and Central Europe. Still, it would not be correct to assume that there was a singular Jewish musical past in Burgenland and that this past, as a whole, simply ended with the Holocaust. The Jewish presence in Burgenland was historically in constant transition. Jews adapted to changing legal restrictions and responded with other culture brokers to fulfill the political agendas of both Habsburg and Esterházy rulers in the area.[5] It was the malleability of Burgenland's Jewish communities that suited them to the contested nature of the historical and geographical spaces in which they lived. Fieldwork in the ethnomusicological past attempts to reckon with that malleability, not to bound "Jewish culture" or to determine bounded repertories of "Jewish music."

The ethnomusicological past always possesses complex meanings and requires different forms of ethnographic representation. At one level, the events of history do calibrate the ethnomusicological past, as, for example, the events of the conflict between empires—Habsburg and Ottoman—provided the initial reasons for transplanting diverse settlements of ethnic and religious Others to Burgenland, and then the events of the Holocaust provided the grounds for eliminating the Jewish and Roma presence from Burgenland. At another level, the ethnomusicological past, like the present studied by ethnomusicologists, comprises ritual practices, which use musical performance to reproduce selfness or to confirm the meanings of community and polity. History is constructed through the actions of musical and ritual specialists. At still another level, the ethnomusicological past exists as a web of seamless everyday musical practices, each one producing myriad moments of history. The musical practices at these different levels may or may not be connected, but within the ethnomusicological past they form through *bricolage* into complex musical meanings. They interact with each other because, as processes formed out of performance, they occur within the boundary spaces between past and present.

The ethnomusicological past is not one past, but many. In this chapter I reflect on how ethnomusicologists might explore those many pasts. Throughout the chapter I employ several excursuses drawn from my own fieldwork, and I interleave these with more theoretical sections, in which I think through the ways in which different ethnomusicological pasts might be constructed. Together, these excursuses and methodological fragments do not constitute a method. I do not, myself, believe that they could, and perhaps this is an important caveat to keep in mind: Fieldwork, although it requires us to draw extensively from theory, is not a theoretical end in itself. It requires that we be prepared at all times for the unexpected and for the fluidity of experience. Fieldwork is at its theoretical best when it has the potential to respond to this fluidity and the experiences at the boundaries between cultures. I should like to argue in this chapter that ethnomusicological fieldwork may also be at its best when it brings us closer to the fluidity and experiences on the boundaries between the past and present.

Music in Burgenland's Jewish Pasts

Excursus: Remembering the Other.   "We always got along well with the Jews." "They were our neighbors, and we never had any problems." "When they made music, we were there; when we had a dance, they were there." "They were taken away so quickly, we had no idea." Burgenlanders today have, by and large, not forgotten their former Jewish neighbors and the Jewish culture of Burgenland. Their memory of Burgenland's Jewish past takes place through remembering and recollection. It is a memory, like many memories, that consists of fragments, pieced together to help the fieldworker complete his or her narrative.

One of the most disturbing aspects of my initial interviews in Burgenland was that I encountered consultants whose memory of the Jewish past was exclusively positive. Although I always attempted to retain my objectivity and not to intrude in an interview with questions that might unnerve, I found it difficult to believe what I was hearing. I responded with mistrust, with a feeling that I should later need to reinterpret the tales of a slightly tarnished, but golden past. I had no idea how literally I might report this mistrust in a future ethnography. Even now, I am not sure how an ethnographer interprets information from the field that deliberately avoids the truth; were the ethnographer in the position of knowing the truth better than others, fieldwork would either be unnecessary or would turn into a form of indictment.

The Burgenlanders were not telling me lies; they were not taking advantage of the trust we had established through my residence in the area; nor were their tales about a good-neighborliness distorted half-truths. Their memory of the Jewish past was positive; it was also confused by the disjuncture and destruction that they had reformulated to fit the memory they had constructed. Their memory of the Jewish past had always formed from a pastiche of understanding and misunderstanding. The collective memory I began piecing together also contained considerable gaps, those boundaries with the past that made it difficult for me to distinguish understanding from misunderstanding. This, too, is a quality of the fragmentary nature of memory.

Boundaries were very significant in the Burgenlanders' accounts of the Jewish past. I came to realize this when I gradually began to gather accounts of Jewish burial practices and the rituals accompanying these. Older Burgenlanders still remembered the public aspects of Jewish funerals, processions they had witnessed and laments they had heard. Death and the ritual practices that mark it have not disappeared from the remembering of the Jewish past; the narrativizing of death, in fact, serves as a discursive connective between past and present, for Burgenland Jews used literature in various forms to remember the dead whose lives formed

Burgenland's past (see, e.g., Wachstein 1926; Reiss 1995). Death figures into the remembering of the past in various ways. At the deepest level, there is the recognition that death in the Holocaust eventually greeted most of the Jews who were transported from Burgenland. At a surface level, there was the death of a single individual, a small girl in Burgenland, which terminated the blatant attempts to erase Jewish culture in Burgenland during the 1940s.[6] The death of the Jewish past also presses on the memory on an everyday level, through the insistent presence of Jewish cemeteries, which are everywhere to be found in Burgenland. Non-Jews did not pass beyond the boundaries of cemeteries; they did not take part in or observe the ritual that occurred when the community turned to its own religious practices. Just as death had arrested the attention of the Burgenlanders, it allowed them to recall music making and the musical practices that they imagined to take place beyond the boundaries:[7] the singing and prayer of the cortège; the singing emanating from beyond the cemetery's walls; the community's care for the bereaved family in the week and year after the death.

The fragments of Burgenland's remembered Jewish past are not all the same, and it was this realization that led to a further recognition that the tales I was hearing were not dishonest, nor were they attempts to cover up the atrocities of the past. Instead, the fragments of the Jewish past arose from different types of remembering. One set of memories resulted from the encounters between Jews and non-Jews, from a true sense of neighborliness that was necessitated by the large population of Jews in a multicultural society. Another set of memories resulted from the awareness of otherness, the inability to weave difference into the fabric of a single memory. These two sets of memories, I came to understand, were at odds with each other; in effect, they drove each other to even greater extremes with the passage of time. One set of memories increasingly focused on a shared past; the other set became ever more confused by the otherness of a culture whose fragments were never understandable. The differences and otherness of the Jewish past entered the narratives of the ethnographic present; though they remained untold, these narratives constantly shaped how both present and past were remembered.[8]

Crossing the Border Between Present and Past. Shifting boundaries have ceaselessly mapped out Burgenland's historical past. The province's cultural geography is less a product of what was or what is, than a constant process of realigning borderlines to separate one political entity from another. The peoples of Burgenland have themselves seldom been that political entity, but rather have physically constituted the boundaries that serve as the shifting cartographic traces of the past (see the essays in Baumgartner, Müllner, and Münz 1989). It was, moreover, an aggressive settlement policy that first peopled Burgenland with difference and otherness. In the seventeenth century, when the Ottoman Empire's threat to Central Europe seemed greater than ever,[9] the Habsburg Monarchy mustered diverse settlement groups from the empire and placed them on the open, fertile plains of Burgenland. The defensive role played by the province is evident even in its name, literally "the land of the fortresses." In particular, Saxons from northeastern Germany and Croats were given land to attract them to Burgenland.

The opening up of the border region similarly attracted Jews and Romas, but for somewhat different reasons. Jews settled in large numbers at the end of the seventeenth century largely because they had been driven out of the Hungarian provincial capital, Ödenburg (today, Sopron), in the wake of the failure of the second Turkish siege of Vienna in 1683 (Ernst 1987:233–37). Romas found Burgenland to be an opportunity to map their own culture of diversity and mobility onto the region's historical diversity, discovering a remarkable fit.[10] With the gradual and final exit of the Ottomans from Europe in the eighteenth century, Burgenland had become a collective of otherness. That otherness would shape its history until the present (see *Burgenland* 1993).

The political and national boundaries of Burgenland's history necessarily affected the boundaries of the many local landscapes in the past, not least among them those of the Jewish community. Once Jews had settled in significant numbers in this boundary region, there remained the problem of how and where to locate their communities. Initially, that is after the expulsion from Ödenburg/Sopron, the Hungarian aristocratic families, Esterházy and Batthyány, provided economic and political protection for the Jewish settlements, and for this reason most of these settlements are directly adjacent to the palace or fortress of the various Esterházy or Batthyány family members, most of which were located in small or medium-sized towns. Accordingly, the Jewish quarter lay directly across from the center of power and culture, locating Jewish cultural and religious institutions as close to that center as possible.[11] Although the local boundaries produced by these historical interrelations deliberately demarcated the landscape, the boundaries existed only to be traversed; their separation of Jewish and non-Jewish communities was figurative, but as such they made the complex multiculturalism of that landscape normative.

The shifting boundaries of Burgenland's historical landscape are not unique in Europe, and for Jewish regions of Europe they were relatively characteristic (Applebaum 1994; Wischenbart 1992). Indeed, "Jewish Europe" has never been characterized by fixed boundaries. The location of culture of Jewish communities in Europe has always occupied a region beyond the boundaries (Gruber 1992), where the lives of individuals and communities are less the product of regionalism or nationalism, but rather of in-betweenness (Bhabha 1994:1–9). We know the names of the regions beyond the boundaries, whose populations have historically been multicultural, but it is practically impossible to locate these regions on the maps of modernity. Burgenland, Galicia, Pannonia, Alsace, the Bukovina (see Applebaum 1994). These are just a few of the regions that are beyond the nation and outside of nationalistic histories (see, e.g., Deutsch and Pietsch [1990] and Noll [1991a], for studies of the ways music has articulated such histories). Otherness has different meanings within such regions, for it is not an otherness stamped on minorities by national-ist-driven racism. Instead, it is a mutual otherness, an otherness produced by get-ting along with others rather than by stereotyping and excluding them. It was the form of otherness expressed by Burgenlanders in the 1990s as they described their Jewish neighbors more than fifty years ago.

Burgenland represents the many different ethnographic conditions that con-nect the present to the past. The musical practices and repertories of the province are no less a conjunction of diverse ethnicities and genres (Dreo, Burian, and Gmasz 1988; *Burgenland* 1993). As a site of Jewish history Burgenland is a place to investigate Jewish music in rural Europe, a region to compare with Galicia or Alsace (Baselgia 1993; Bohlman 1993; Dohrn 1991; Stauben 1986[1860]). Burgenland is multiethnic and multicultural, hence giving a specific context to Jewish music in both the pre-sent and the past. It is a border region, defined not so much by a defined identity as by the processes of change that mean that identity must always be negotiated (see Baumgartner, Müllner, and Münz [1989]; for a depiction of a musician engaged in the negotiation of Burgenlander identity see Reiterits 1988). There was never a single Jewish identity in Burgenland; Jewish culture could never be neatly circumscribed. The issue then is not "finding Jewish identity" but finding the conditions that negated Jewish identity (Baumgartner 1988; Gold 1970; Klampfer 1966; Spitzer 1995). These do not lie in the simple assumption that modern residents interpret the Jew-ish past as a history belonging to another culture.

The tales from the field, instead, narrate an entangled past, and the voices of the present reflect their own entanglement in that past (Van Maanen 1988). As an eth-nomusicologist, then, I am motivated not by some presumed power to disentangle the present from the past. To imagine Burgenland's past as a world split between Jews and others might render the region comparable to what we call ethnic cultures throughout the world, but it would violate the historical dynamic that results from the constantly shifting boundaries between Burgenland's past and present.

The Past's Fieldworks

Excursus: Fieldwork and My Past.   Since dissertation research in Israel, begun in 1980, I have devoted much of my research to the study of Jewish music. Although the various projects I have undertaken examine different aspects of Jew-ish music, the music of European Jews, particularly Ashkenazic Jews in Central and East-Central Europe,[12] has provided the primary repertories at which I have looked. My methodologies have largely been historical, with my point of departure being the experience in the field. To study the musical life of the German-Jewish community of Israel, I engaged in fieldwork in Israel and Germany in the 1980s in order to understand processes of immigration in the 1930s (see Bohlman 1989a). To understand how new forms of Jewish broadsides mediated and represented the transformation of European Jewish community at the turn of the last century, I explored the urban spaces that facilitated this transformation as the turn of the next century approached (Bohlman 1989b). I placed myself in the spaces where Jewish communities had been, where Jewish music had been heard. What I encountered through fieldwork, however, consisted at best of the traces of what was, or might have been.

My engagement with the past has persistently been personal, and yet it has been personal in ways difficult for many of my consultants to comprehend. My engagement with the ethnomusicological past of Central Europe and Germany has not been an engagement with *my* past, nor with a past my family or ancestors would claim. I am not Jewish, and I have no reason to believe that my ancestors from rural Pomerania, Ireland, or Wisconsin might have been Jewish. I am also neither German nor German-American. I speak Hebrew and German, though both as languages I learned later in life and use with no special connections to ethnic or religious identity. The question then arises, is this relevant? Anthropologists and ethnomusicologists have long entered the field to study not their past but someone else's. The question about my own past is, in fact, very relevant because it is a question inevitably asked of me while I am in the field. Those with whom I consult in the field want to know who I am, where I come from, and how my identity relates to theirs. For various reasons, my answers to these questions are important to them, and I do not hesitate to explain to them that I am not Jewish, and it is not my ethnomusicological past I am trying to discover.

By responding to questions about my own relation to the past I am studying, I specify and alter the context for the fieldwork itself. At the most basic level, a new context develops, depending on whether the questioner is Jewish or non-Jewish. My response, then, is not simply a declaration of objectivity. Rarely does this contextualization of the fieldwork stop with the some sort of aphorism about ethnographers being engaged with someone else's culture anyway. Why, then, should I be interested in this particular past, which is not my past? Many motivations lie behind this line of questioning. For some Jewish questioners, the motivation is a sort of amazement at encountering an anomaly, a non-Jew studying Jewish culture. For some non-Jewish questioners, the motivation is to determine just how far they might go before I begin to lay the burden of European anti-Semitism on them. Am I going to blame them for what I might discover about the past?

The conversation about the nature of my past continues, gradually passing through a transformation itself: It establishes a new discourse between myself, my consultants, and those not present to enter into our conversation. For my consultants, my responses become important because they suggest that I do not come to the field with a set of claims I want to prove or for which I am hoping to unearth new evidence. We establish the past as an ethnographic domain that I can only understand through the newly contextualized discourse of the present. Within this discourse, it may well be that I become the exotic Other, for I come entirely from the outside to learn from those connected to their own pasts in one way or another.

I do not deny that my response about my own identity and my relation to the past I am investigating changes the ethnographic present; it alters the path along which the fieldwork will go. I also do not deny that my particular identity—a non-Jew from North America studying the Jewish past in another part of the world—may unleash some confusion that is never completely resolved. All these issues of identity, nevertheless, foreground the problem of studying the past; indeed, they focus fieldwork on how the identity of the past itself is thrown into contrast by how the discourse of the ethnographic present unravels the identities of both fieldworker and consultants. It becomes increasingly important to know why we want to understand this ethnomusicological past, and knowing why may, in the best of circumstances, draw us slightly closer to the past lived by others we can no longer know.

Ethnomusicology's Pasts

The various ways of remembering the past produce many different histories. The plural in the preceding section heading represents this, if even also its ambiguity. In entering the past from the present, ethnomusicology must reckon with a wide range of differences, but it must also welcome that range to some degree. Fieldwork, particularly if we do not force it to become a set of methods, opens up modalities of interpretation that allow ethnomusicology to recognize these differences. In the present section I embark on discursive excursions into some of the modalities that might effectively contribute to ethnomusicology's engagement with the present and past. I mean this range to be inclusive, not exclusive, and I thereby make no claim to pinning down methods or privileging one modality over another. Ethnomusicological fieldwork is personal—it must be, or it would be pointless—and the following modalities for turning fieldwork toward the past are also largely personal. They, too, must be.

These different modalities further allow us to recognize that each individual narrates the past not only as she remembers it through her own experiences, but in very selective ways. In the field, the past is conveyed to us through personal narratives and decisions about what to remember. This is evident in the ethnographic historiography that currently narrates the past of the Eastern Europe that was, in the West, synonymous with the world behind the Iron Curtain, the world of communism (Applebaum 1994; Ignatieff 1994). The resurgent Eastern European nationalisms of the 1990s, for example, selectively reflect the different types of past (for a history of the ways in which Western Europe imagined Eastern Europe, see Wolff [1994]). For nations secure in their national image emphasis falls on the struggle against communism as the underlying historical motivation for the past half-century. In the case of Poland this emphasis requires filtering out any other histories that might undermine the nationalistic image linking past and present, notably but not solely the nation's historical complicity with anti-Semitism (Hoffman 1993:34–35). The Balkan states, whose nationalism increasingly fends off national names and labels, have seemingly bottomless wells from which to draw different and competing histories. With all these nationalisms there exists the problem that "unwanted pasts" may infect the narrative of a "wanted present" (see Ignatieff 1994). In the fieldwork on which the excursions in this essay are based, the Holocaust stands—or rather its shadow lurks—as the archetypal unwanted past.

Ethnomusicological fieldwork, because of its concern with the narrative and performative agency of music, provides diverse ways of encountering these many pasts. In the following modalities I sketch these diverse ways, though without claiming to represent "the past." Different modalities render the voices of the past audible in different ways. Although each contains potential problems of audibility and therefore can only incompletely represent the past, they become ways of formulating fieldwork questions and of encountering many different pasts.

The Past as Other.   The easiest premise for encountering the past is to say it's different from the present. Those who lived in the past are the Others. It's an easy premise, but it's a dangerous premise, and for that reason I begin with a modality of approaching the past's otherness. For ethnomusicology othering the past some-times has the additional seductive quality of suggesting that one is addressing difference. The past contains the culture of the Other, and ethnomusicologists can therefore go about the business of contrasting it with the present. If the musical culture of the past is that of otherness, it becomes superfluous, even self-defeating, to connect it with the present and self. The music of the past was contained by the past; it stopped sounding, and to recuperate it for the present is only to museumize it and to pretend we can hear it. These are acts of exoticizing, of course, and to some extent such acts have increasingly been the subject of criticism within and without the social sciences (see, e.g., Fabian 1983). I wish to argue here that fieldwork in the ethnomusicological past must not be immune from such criticism.

The first musical scholar to approach the otherness of the past was not an ethnomusicologist, but an historical musicologist. In his *Music in Renaissance Magic* (1993) Gary Tomlinson employs a dialogical hermeneutics to draw himself closer to the world of Marsilio Ficino, who created songs intended to transform magic into efficacious results. Tomlinson approaches Ficino's world, but ultimately denies the ability to cross over into it, to know it as a self would know its own world. On one hand, the dialogical hermeneutics draws both Tomlinson and Ficino into a discursive space, but it seems only possible to confront each other in that space. The construction and very existence of this discursive space, nonetheless, depends on retaining otherness, in Tomlinson's study Ficino's otherness. Without otherness the space ceases to exist. To approach the musical past, Tomlinson depends on a discourse independent of fieldwork. Would fieldwork allow him or any other historical musicologist to go beyond the discursive space? That, in itself, is a purely theoretical question, and it is theory, ultimately, that Tomlinson claims. Ethnomusicological fieldwork, I have claimed, is not a theoretical end. The ethnomusicological fieldworker must not cling to otherness in order to approach it.[13]

The otherness of the ethnomusicological past may allow us at times to slip dangerously close to fetishization. It might seem convenient to enforce the space between present and past by observing that, of course, the musical practices of the past were different. But what if such a claim were itself foreign to those in the past? What if, as in the case of many Jewish liturgical practices, the sameness of the past was precisely a music that ascribed identity? The spaces between present and past are far more variegated than the discursive spaces constructed through theory. It is not otherness, pure and simple, that lurks on the other side of the space. Through fieldwork, however, it becomes possible to encounter this space and decide just how, if at all, it is negotiable, and to judge just how the other side relates to selfness.

The Past as "Self." The otherness of the past as an experience in which one did not participate is often inseparable from the selfness of the past as an experience to which one draws closer through its narration (cf. Ricoeur 1992:140–68). The past's selfness is a constructed experience, and yet the location of the "self" in the past is one of the most powerful motivations for doing fieldwork in the past. In analytical philosophy the hermeneutics of the self is not primarily concerned with discovering oneself, but rather with the conditions of sameness and, by extension, of identity. Were we to turn to this hermeneutics of self in the fieldwork experience, we should enter on a different process of constructing identity, both the identity of the past itself and the identity of those who inhabited the past.

The use of fieldwork to interrogate the past as self is problematic on several levels. For many who search in the past for filiopietistic reasons, in other words to glorify their forebears, the selfness of the past is ipso facto a means of glorifying the present. Indeed, one is made blind to the otherness of self. Only the visibly present characteristics of the past are thrown into relief. Much ethnic folk-music research suffers from this dilemma of selfness. The constructs of the present (e.g., hyphenated folk musics such as Italian-American, African-American, or Irish-American) should have existed in the past because they do, presumably, in the present. A more hermeneutic consideration of self, however, would insist on problematizing the identity of self. Whose self is it that the fieldworker seeks to discover? His or her own, or someone else's? Must we assume that the identity of the past bears a relation to the identity of the present? Whose past does the self narrate when telling tales from the past?

The selfness and the otherness of the past are not unrelated, and it may well be their relatedness that makes it possible for fieldwork to examine identity. The question posed by hyphenated ethnic musics might therefore become not what the history of Italian-American folk song is, but to what extent have certain folk musics been identifiable as Italian-American as opposed to Catholic-American, Calabrian-American, or Neapolitan popular song. The otherness and sameness of these identities coexist, and the past takes shape from the tension implicit in this coexistence. Fieldwork in the ethnomusicological past ideally reads beyond the simple presence of selfness and otherness to perceive how music brings competing identities into the tension of history.

The Past as Musical Object.   Throughout the history of folk-song scholarship, it is the musical object that has most completely represented the past. A folk song comes into existence in the past, assuming authority over the past through claims made for its age and timelessness. For this reason, the folk song serves political ends, not least among them the incontrovertible evidence that the national existed even before the nation, indeed *was* the nation waiting for the moment when it would be allowed to be born. Music's timelessness is returned to time through oral tradition, which, reproduced through tune families or patterns of variance, connects the past to the present. It is the musical object, nonetheless, that enters the present from the past. Recuperating that object through fieldwork makes it possible to obtain a piece of the past.

For much folk-song scholarship, it is the objectification of music that ultimately valorizes and essentializes the past. This valorization is nowhere more evident than in the study of narrative genres. The German ballad embodies *Geschichte* and *Geschichte*, that is, "story" and "history." One notion of *Geschichte* is the past; the other connects it to the present. The objective nature of music surviving from the past, however, also erases parts of the past. If the folk song survives until the present, it has also overcome the power the past may have exerted on it. The past of the song, therefore, turns into a vast temporal space of otherness, where change has not happened, or at least has not impinged on the identity of the musical object. Still, the musical object does encode a version of the past. Experiencing it in the present provides a mode of decoding, if indeed one mode among many.

The Past as Everyday and Mentalité.   Ethnomusicological fieldwork may seem ahistorical when it aims to capture the synchronic musical events of the everyday. The fieldworker going to a music culture other than her own describes a setting that simply is. It exists outside of history, and its musical events enter the ethnography as if the past and future of their existence have no particular bearing on the present. Synchronic interpretations contrast with diachronic, in which change either does or does not take place, but nonetheless possesses a dynamic of its own, distinct from that of the everyday (cf. de Certeau 1984).

The study of music in the everyday, however, also provides an historical framework for ethnomusicology, for it situates music in contexts that are independent of the extraordinary events of history, allowing for a different form of narrative imagination, the study of a *mentalité*. As the French historiographical school known as the *annalistes* discovered, the records allowing for a reconstruction of the everyday in the past assume very different forms, but they are nonetheless abundant. Observations concerning ritual performance or musical practices transmitted by oral tradition allow us gradually to understand who made music and where it was made. What distinguishes the everyday is how specific events stand out against the fabric of community life, thereby creating a subaltern historical dynamic.

The everyday musical life of rural European Jewish communities emerges from the records in its synagogues and in the discussions about the nature of ritual.

A rather more frightening everyday has been recorded in the anti-Semitic reports of ritual murder (see Hsia 1988) or the several dance forms that incorporate the typically Jewish, usually known simply as *Judentänze*. Such records reveal that the everyday required contestation and resistance for survival. From an ethnographic standpoint, however, such struggle in the everyday remains as prevalent at the end of the twentieth century as it was at earlier moments in the history of Jewish Europe. Observations the ethnomusicologist might make today concerning the struggle to maintain ritual observances in Hungary, notoriously anti-Semitic throughout much of the Cold War era, evoke the everyday contexts in which ritual observance in Burgenland might have taken place in the eighteenth century at the periphery of the court in Eisenstadt or after the shift of international borders in 1921. The musical practices of ritual provided the glue of an everyday whose history resulted from responding to the threat against it.

The Past as Oral Tradition. The fabric that makes the everyday legible is oral tradition. It is a quality of the culture of the past and the present, hence it serves in the methodologies of folklore and ethnomusicology by connecting past and present. Through the experience of oral tradition in the field, the ethnographer tries to create a text for reading culture by moving backward through time. By interpreting the music of the present as linked to something previous through processes of either stability or change, it becomes possible to read backward through the past to a moment, perhaps, when only oral tradition existed. In this way, oral tradition may even render the past timeless.

As a theoretical framework oral tradition may connect the present to the past in different ways. Frequently, in the popular imagination, it is oral tradition that allows a community or culture to believe that some core of musical practices from the past—some essence of the past—remains intact in the present. Nineteenth- and early twentieth-century European concepts of Jewish music, for example, held that the liturgical practices of the contemporary synagogue, if truly Jewish, had been transmitted orally from the time before the destruction of the Temple in Jerusalem. So persuasive was this belief that it provided a means of explaining away the surface traits different regional styles shared with the musics of neighboring or surrounding cultures. The surface, inscribed by modern notational practices, was not what counted, but rather the unbroken transmission from cantor to cantor, from daily service to daily service (see Idelsohn 1932:vi).

In the second half of the twentieth century, ethnographic theory has tended instead to privilege the processes of change that necessarily result from oral tradition. It follows that musical texts of the present are not those of the past, but metonymically they represent the past. Certain types of change, therefore, are predictable, say the substitution of references in folk-song texts that are more meaningful to contemporary singers; other kinds of change predictably do not happen, say when stereotypes of the characters in narrative folk song remain intact even when the surrounding field of meanings changes. The construction of otherness in

European genres such as the *Schnaderhüpfl* or in dance genres given names such as *Judentanz* ("Jewish dance") lead scholars to believe these are unchanging symbols of social criticism. Such constructions of otherness are often not meaningful in modern practice—images of Scottishness are not frequently reported by those dancing the *Schottisch*—and that is precisely the evidence that makes oral tradition a seductive means of approaching the past, for it functions without conscious maintenance of the past. Its power to connect present to past lies in its invisibility.

Past as Archaeology and Epistemic Knowledge. It is in the historiographic concepts of Michel Foucault that we most completely encounter the notion of understanding the past by encountering the ways in which its inhabitants constructed their self-knowledge (Foucault 1972). This epistemic knowledge is suggestive for the ethnomusicological fieldworker, not least because it resides in one of the premises with which fieldworkers struggle with objectivity in the present. The episteme in the archaeology of the past, however, produces a history through "the conditions of possibility" (Foucault 1970:xxii), and therefore we encounter it in the "space of knowledge" representing a music culture or community. Musical practices not only take place in this space of knowledge, but their performative nature means that they transform that space into a field for expressing identity.

The archaeological approach to the ethnomusicological past is potentially very productive. Musical practices are frequently central to identity and the knowledge of self, especially when groups must together make the decisions necessary for coherent performance. Epistemic knowledge does not reside at the surface of musical style; rather, it inheres in the spaces of a shared knowledge that makes performance possible. The shared knowledge of identity occupies many different spaces: the sacred space of religious ritual, the rules guiding performance in oral tradition or the knowledge of body that informs how individuals use dance to express their social connectedness. The knowledge of self is necessary for the continuation of musical practices, and hence it becomes a type of historical knowledge that connects past to present. Through fieldwork, it follows, one can attempt to locate musical knowledge that conveys a sense of self in its relation to the past. Methodologically, we have moved from perceiving musical objects in the past to understanding how music has historically served as a means of knowing the past.

Past as Contested Space. It is the performative nature of music that necessitates the interpretation of music within the spaces of past and present. Entering the field immediately brings the ethnomusicologist into the space where music has been performed, and the nature of that space reflects the influences that performance exerts on the space that has once contained it. The interaction between performance and space is political in the sense that the conditions of performance have resulted from various hierarchies, various pressures on the public space of music to contain and define its public, its audience. The space of the musical past is not infrequently a contested space, and the impact of that contestation on the present may provide palpable evidence for the fieldworker to interpret the past.

Music conveys the contested nature of public space in various ways. The multilingual nature of a border region, for example, penetrates the texts of the song repertories that fill that region. This is evident in the historical traditions of Slovakia, particularly along the trade routes that follow the Carpathian Mountains north toward Poland, Ukraine, and Galicia (Wischenbart 1992). The songscape of this range is marked by the mixture of German, Slovak, Czech, Hungarian, and Yiddish texts, vying to penetrate the spaces each ethnic or religious group has sought out for itself. The contested musical spaces of culture may result from the denial of other spaces, in other words the performance of a space formed through music's presence in ritual. Pilgrimage practices, currently revived in the late twentieth century as an alternative cultural space, allow pilgrims in the Carpathians to perform a temporally ephemeral world whose boundaries remain only in the traces of musical texts. The past as a web of contested spaces offers a radically different history and historiography (see, e.g., Taussig 1987), and it is the historiographic potential that is most suggestive for the fieldworker studying the past.

By recognizing the contested nature of the past's spaces, the ethnomusicologist shifts her focus from musical product to process. The interpretation of public spaces in which women dance in South India, for example, has enabled ethnomusicologists to rethink the nature of Karnatak music history. The shift of emphasis by ethnomusicologists studying the Holocaust from repertories to the spaces in which Jews, Romas, and homosexuals attempted to survive, have revealed remarkably intensive music cultures, where musical performance became the very struggle to survive (see, especially, Flam 1992). To know the past through musical performance requires more than decoding whatever texts might survive. Before it is possible to hear the voices of those long silenced, it is necessary to embark on the journey of fieldwork to locate the spaces given meaning by those voices.

Past as Narrative Space. The contested spaces of the past are rarely absent from the narrative spaces inscribed by those whose writings connect past to present. In his recent focus on the conditions of imperialism and its modern decay, Edward Said has trenchantly shown that the stories told in the past cannot escape the political connections to the world around them (1993:62–80, and passim). As a literary theorist Said interprets narrative as literature, and he particularly concerns himself with the English novel, the genre that ascended in importance with the British Empire and narrated its spread, destruction, and dilemma of decay in modernity. I should like to suggest in this section that other forms of empire and colonialism produce other narrative genres whose narrative spaces may open up the interpretation of the ethnomusicological past. In particular, I believe that the narrative capacity of music shapes quite different genres in which the spaces of the past are palpable.

The fieldwork I have done in Burgenland has benefited from an awareness of quite different narrative genres chronicling the complex history of European Jewry. There is even a musical novel, whose title character is a young Jewish pianist in Eisenstadt, Franz Werfel's *Cella oder die Überwinder* (1982[1955]). I have never been able to escape the impulse to read this novel as a parable for the Jewish musical past. Though raised in the musical city of Haydn, Cella's family struggled to provide the talented young pianist sufficient opportunity to nurture her talent. As the *Anschluß* with Nazi Germany approached in the late 1930s, it became increasingly apparent that Cella would have to leave Austria, as would her narrator father, who largely took charge of the girl's music education. Werfel failed to finish the novel before his death, although its fragments narrate several attempts to leave Austria after being driven out of Burgenland by fascist Austrian functionaries. The final chapters follow the father to the Swiss border, which he was able to cross, but beyond which he narrated no more. The narrative spaces are so troubling precisely because the destruction of Burgenland and the silencing of its music are so clearly represented by the novel.

Werfel was not the only Jewish novelist to narrativize the spaces of Jewish Europe, spaces with only fluid boundaries; nor was he the only Jewish novelist to weave music as a narrative device into his novels. These techniques permeate the novels of Joseph Roth, to take one notable example, whose characters in novels such as *Die Flucht ohne Ende* (1978[1927]) and *Das falsche Gewicht* (1977[1937]) move across the Jewish landscapes of Galicia and other regions that no longer exist. Marking these landscapes are the narratives of musicians and musical performances, taverns where Jews and Romas sing together, and small cities in Germany where Jewish conductors worship the Romantic ideals of Wagner. These narrative spaces remain confused and contested; Joseph Roth died in Paris in 1939, never fulling knowing the fate of the narrative spaces he had created.

Musical genres, too, evoke narrative spaces, which become means of hearing the voices of the ethnomusicological past. In Central Europe the ballad is the most obvious example of the creation of musical spaces that narrativize the past. The ballad, "Die schöne Jüdin" ("The Beautiful Jewish Girl," DVldr. 158), is one such narrative of a young woman forced to cross beyond the boundaries of the Jewish community, to confront the other because "she was ready to dance" ("zum Tanz war sie bereit"; for versions of "Die schöne Jüdin" see Dittmar 1992). The metaphors of space and community are unequivocal in this ballad; the resolution of the encounter with Christian Europe, nonetheless, remains equivocal in its options: suicide, conversion, departure from Jewish tradition. The narrative spaces of ballads, novels, or other genres are not real in the literal sense, but it is because they evoke images of the social spaces of the Jewish past that they open up potential connections to that past. Embedded in their narratives is a knowledge of self and community, a knowledge embodied by those who inhabited the spaces of the past. Today, sung by non-Jews, "Die schöne Jüdin," survives in the narrative spaces of Burgenland.

The Past as Performance.   Music lends meaning to the spaces of the past through performance, a physical meaning expressed by the physicality of performance. In the various approaches to the ethnomusicological past that I have sketched in this section, performance has been a fundamental, though not always emphasized, component of fieldwork itself. In this sense, I mean "fieldwork itself" as a means of encountering the past that is different from history as a practice of writing and writing about the past. Fieldwork is physical encounter; its historical capacity goes beyond the text to perceive meaning in the body.

To investigate the past as performance the ethnographer recognizes a mutually dependent relationship between the spaces in which musical performance took place and the physical, bodily acts that transformed those spaces. In the examples from my own fieldwork that punctuate this chapter the connection between space and body has been essential. My fieldwork in Burgenland has largely explored the spaces of music making: synagogues formerly filled with song and prayer, communities with complex mixtures of public spaces, shifting boundaries in border regions. No one can relocate the individuals who once performed within these spaces, but the memories of the past and the imagination of the everyday, informed by the musical texts and objects that were performed in the spaces, gradually bring the past into focus.

The interpretation of the past through performance relies on the premise that musicians perform in order actively to transform their bodies and the spaces they occupy. Historical ethnographers, particularly, have theorized that this active concern with the narrative potential of the body ultimately makes it an agent for the performance of history (Comaroff 1987; Comaroff and Comaroff 1992:215–33). When praying and singing in the synagogue, for example, worshipers clothe themselves differently according to the gender roles, hierarchical roles within ritual, and performative roles within the articulation of sacred texts and the remembrance of history. The interdependence of space, music, and ritual on the body is profound.

Musical performance in public spaces, too, acts aggressively to transform those spaces so as to act on history and consciousness.[14] Public performance of music, whether that of eighteenth-century ballad hawkers or twentieth-century rappers, is one of the most powerful means of arresting attention. By necessity, the fieldworker enters into these spaces in the present in order to have her attention arrested by the transformations that performers work on the spaces as historically shifting fields. Each performance, each moment shaped by musical practice, draws the fieldworker into a complex of meanings embodied by the physical spaces linking present to past.

Entering the Field of the Past

Berger's world no longer existed. The farther we went, the more we searched in vain for this vanished world.

Gerhard Roth, *Eine Reise in das Innere von Wien* (1991:57)

Excursus: Locating the Past, Finding Its Spaces.   The synagogue of Kobersdorf, one of the smallest of the Seven Holy Cities of Burgenland, stood empty in 1990 when I first entered it. Directly across the open space of the wide street surrounding the small, but newly refurbished castle/fortress of the former Esterházy residents of Kobersdorf, the synagogue was plainly visible to the tourists who came to Kobersdorf during the summer to see the outdoor theater productions in the courtyard of the castle. The summer productions were a new idea, welcomed and eagerly supported by local boosterism, to bring added revenue and a bit of recognition to this small town of several thousand, only a dozen kilometers from the newly permeable Hungarian border. Most of those attending the summer productions did not know that an abandoned synagogue stood in Kobersdorf. Although it fronted the broad street, the façade of the synagogue had received no care or repair since it was spared from destruction by local superstition (see note 6). There was no entrance from the street, traditionally no entrance because it was at this end that the *bima*, the pulpit and location of the Torah scrolls, stood; facing these, worshipers were turned toward the east, Jerusalem, but more immediately toward the Esterházy castle and the Hungarian border.

With Manfred Fuchs, the Mayor of Kobersdorf, but by profession a music teacher and choral director, I fought my way through the tangle of weeds and brush that guarded the synagogue's front door at the back of the building. Fuchs had brought the keys, but, to his surprise, there was no need to use them; the door was unlocked. Inside, the sanctuary was silent; not even roosting pigeons were about to disturb the silence. I had entered a space outside of time, at least outside of the fifty-two years since the building had last been occupied. The synagogue's silence remembered those fifty-two years, a period during which, I learned later, no one knew what to do with the synagogue.

Questions of ownership had not been answered; the Jewish *Kultusgemeinde* in Vienna, the official administrative body for the Austrian Jewish community, simply did not know what to do with the building, or with the other spaces of Kobersdorf's Jewish community left silent by the Holocaust. Manfred Fuchs had developed a concept for the synagogue, which would turn it into a concert space, for use, especially, in the performance of Jewish music. We were witnessing at that moment just how good the acoustics were, though the space was entirely devoid of furniture and human occupants, who might otherwise inflect and distort the acoustically live surfaces of plaster and wood. As a concert hall, and not least in conjunction with the summer theater festival, the synagogue would serve as a means of remembering the past. The interest was there, and probably also the local investment from the mineral-water bottling company just outside of town, but too many questions lingered. The town had been told that the space was still sacred, and to use it as a concert hall would mean desacralizing the space. Only the Austrian Jewish community could do this, but communications from Vienna indicated that it was not exactly clear how one did such things. At the very least, a rabbinical official from Israel would have to come to Kobersdorf, and it was not entirely clear whether the synagogue should be stripped of its sacredness anyway. The synagogue stood, its space silent, not yielding its memories of the sounds that once filled it. It remained a space inhabited by the past.

The Jewish musical past in Kobersdorf resided in many of the town's spaces, and it was my growing sense of these spaces, which I explored through summer fieldwork in 1990 and 1991, that gradually allowed me to perceive something of the Jewish music that once filled them. The Jewish spaces of Kobersdorf formed during the eighteenth century and assumed more specific shape during the nineteenth century, when the town's Jewish population grew to almost 50 percent of the total. Kobersdorf was also one of the Burgenland villages that had a large population of Protestants, about half of all Christians living there, and the village was divided lengthwise on the two sides of the main street into Protestant and Catholic sectors. The Hungarian castle was the major political and cultural space of the town. There was one other political parsing of the space, namely the border between Hungary and Austria (Hungarian and Austrian parts of the Habsburg Empire), just outside of town until 1921, when the village and its environs were absorbed into Austria.

The diverse cultural, political, and religious spaces created remarkably complex musical spaces. That religious institutions embodied spaces in which different sacred musical practices were maintained goes without saying. What must be said, however, is that these spaces crossed and intersected with one another. Those with whom I spoke in the early 1990s remembered musical practices that took place in the village spaces and, particularly, in the movement between the spaces. The *Schulklopfer* (lit.: "school ringer," with "school" used in Yiddish as "synagogue" and in German as school) walked the streets of Kobersdorf, calling Jewish residents to prayer and mustering the children for religious instruction.

Secular musical practices were also mobile and dependent on the fluid nature of Kobersdorf's spaces. On the same street that separated the synagogue from the castle and only a few buildings south of the synagogue was a building standing at the intersection of the road to the former border crossing and the main street flanked by Protestant and Catholic sectors. The building, in many ways, epitomized the spatial confluence of Burgenland's history. The building had been the Jewish tavern, a secular space necessary for the maintenance of Jewish identity in a multicultural society. As a Jewish tavern, it provided kosher meals, overnight accommodations for travelers moving between the different parts of the empire, and a space for public music making.

Contemporary residents remembered all these functions, particularly because they had participated in them. It was in the tavern that they participated in the everyday Jewish musical life of Kobersdorf. They participated not as Jews, but as Kobersdorfers and Burgenlanders. The musical life embodied by this space, moreover, was not just Jewish, but Kobersdorfer and Burgenlander. Different dance bands played there, and indeed active exchange of musical repertory and style was facilitated by the public nature of the tavern's intersection with the village's fluid spaces. The celebrations following Jewish weddings, obviously, took place in this space, but Jewish musicians did not play at these; Roma bands from the area did. There was no irony in this, for Jewish bands played at Roma weddings. Jewish musicians also played at Christian celebrations and with Christian and Roma musicians. The most important and publicly visible ensemble in the village, moreover, was the Kobersdorfer Salonorchester, an ensemble that toured widely throughout western Hungary and eastern Austria. The Salonorchester was the pride of Kobersdorf, and its members were mostly Jewish, all Jewish in the memories of contemporary residents. As a musical ensemble the Salonorchester extended the public spaces of Kobersdorf to the many places it played. The mix of musicians and the complex cultural conditions of music making in the village were reconfigured at each performance.

The Jewish tavern, however, was silent in the early 1990s. It had been a private home for many years. Roma musicians were infrequent performers in the village. Local wind ensembles and choral groups performed in public, but their repertories were regional and national. The spaces in which Jews had made music, however, were still there, and it was these spaces that gradually provided me with a means of making the past legible and audible. The cemetery, virtually untouched, remained a space to enter; its entrance house, with materials used in caring for the bodies of the deceased left where they were, provided me with a space through which I could symbolically enter the past. The silence I first heard in the synagogue was everywhere in the village, but everywhere it was different. I entered the spaces of the Jewish past, and gradually the ways in which music filled them became evident to me. When they joined me in these spaces of the Jewish past, the Kobersdorfers remembered them again, and they returned to them—to dances, to weddings, to concerts of the Salonorchester—at least in their imaginations. Gradually, the boundaries between the spaces of the present and the past blurred, and fieldwork was bringing me into contact with the ethnomusicological past in vivid, unexpected ways. Occupying the spaces that had once been filled with Jewish music, the modern residents of Kobersdorf and I were drawn closer to a Jewish musical past that had been silent for half a century.

The New Europe and the People without Ethnomusicological Pasts

If the people without a past are happier or unhappier than we is something I first need to find out. Surely, knowledge of the past could also be a burden. I only fail to conceive, however, that there could be a people that lives only for one day and one day alone without being conscious of the names of their ancestors.

Herbert Rosendorfer, *Briefe in die chinesische Vergangenheit* (1983:27)

This chapter is not a call to ethnomusicologists to become more historical. Much is made these days about rapprochement between ethnomusicology and historical musicology, and it is customary to argue that ethnomusicologists should at base be as historical as the historians. Historical musicology, however, does not employ fieldwork, and its view of the past often reflects this all too painfully. It reflects this because of the human neglect that its methods sometimes uncritically accept. To state it bluntly by rallying the examples most common in this chapter, there is no presence of Jews and Jewish musicians in the music history constructed by historical musicologists for Europe, which is their fundamental historical domain. The contested spaces of empire and border region do not make it into music histories; the musical practices of the everyday did not happen.

I want to conclude this chapter by focusing on Europe, in fact on the New Europe, which is, I want to suggest, an extraordinarily important domain for carrying out fieldwork in the past. Europe poses a special problem because of its historicization of itself, its obsession with a certain type of historical understanding of its identity. The modern trope of this identity is the nation, and that trope influences many modern forms of musical identity: folk song, national songs, religious sectarianism, to name a few obvious cases. Much of the concern for identity in the New Europe derives from a long tradition of privileging sameness and scorning otherness. In particular, it is the tradition of privileging sameness that has made ethnomusicological fieldwork extremely difficult. Much folk-song fieldwork, for example, has been devoted to shoring up old boundaries (e.g., in northern Italian Südtirol, where German, not Italian, songs are customarily collected).

Fieldwork has traditionally not addressed the fluid nature of boundaries, nor has it looked beyond cultural boundaries to the music cultures of those who are not contained by them. Europe, as an historical and cultural domain of musical practices, has been a place where fieldwork has been difficult because of the assumption of sameness, the assumption that there has been *a* history of Western art music, if not of Western music in general. The extensive sameness that we encounter in this overwhelming historiographic concern with self has encumbered the use of fieldwork to study Europe.

Modern musical scholars, however, remain encumbered at their own risk. The rise of the New Europe—the reconfiguration of culture and historical memory following the fall of communist state systems in Eastern Europe—has again foregrounded the tendency of nationalisms and ethnic groups to engage in selective processes of memory (Applebaum 1994; Ignatieff 1994). The past, at the present moment, is an increasingly competitive arena, in which one group's memory must validate its claims on land and history through destruction or erasure of another group's memory. New musical repertories and new musical practices have emerged, which nevertheless achieve validity through their putative connections to the past. Music again becomes a performative medium for making the contested spaces of past and present public. Musicians perform the histories of Europe on street corners throughout Europe, intensifying the narrative space that the past will occupy (Bohlman 1994).

The setting for fieldwork is there, on the street, in the public sphere that mixes old and new musical voices. There are additional European voices that will not be heard in the New Europe, especially the historical victims. The silence of Jewish communities in Burgenland is but one example. Romas, Sintis, and other groups of Gypsies are another case of racism that refuses to become invisible. More recently, Turkish residents of Germany have become another, though the historical connections to Europe's buttressing of itself against Muslims has not entirely been forgotten in the long history of Europe. Outside the course of Western art music's past, there exist and have long existed forms of identity embodied by the spaces of the cabaret or the social spheres in which women, gays and lesbians, or workers have made the music that voiced their own histories. History's victims have come to represent new boundaries of Europe (e.g., the Sami in the north) and within Europe (e.g., the reemergence of pilgrimage routes, performed by the estimated one hundred million Europeans who make pilgrimages each year). The spaces of the imperial past have neither disappeared nor become less serious in their contestation of Europe's present, witness Sarajevo's framing of the twentieth century (cf. Marcus 1993).

The historical problems of the European past, strikingly, have again emerged in the problematic struggles of the New Europe. The disjuncture between past and present—the disjuncture that fieldwork necessarily confronts—has become more precarious and more compelling as a social space the ethnomusicologist must investigate. This disjuncture may efface and blur the boundaries between past and present, intensifying the immediacy of engaging in fieldwork in the ethnomusicological past and present. As Eva Hoffman observed in the epigraph that opens this chapter, no place, however idyllic, is innocent of history. It is that absence of innocence that urges the ethnographer to look for new forms of history and to struggle to understand the reasons for the disjuncture between past and present. These are the troubling realities that characterize fieldwork. These are the conditions that connect musical practices in the present to those in the past, conditions ethnomusicology can address because it must.

Notes

1. During my fieldwork in Burgenland I benefited enormously from the counsel from and experiences I shared with Gabriele Burian, Walter Burian, Manfred Fuchs, Franziska Pietsch, and Rudolf Pietsch. I should like to express my gratitude for that counsel and experience, as well as to the National Endowment for the Humanities (Summer Stipends) and the Alexander von Humboldt Foundation for their financial support of fieldwork in Burgenland during 1990 and 1991.

2. Burgenland still has a higher percentage of Hungarians, Croats, Romas, and Protestants than any other province in Austria. Croatian, for example, is an official language in many grade schools in middle and southern Burgenland, and Hungarian provides a special track for some high schools (*Gymnasien*) that emphasize modern languages. The historical presence of Romas is still evident in the many settlements that surround villages in Burgen-

land, whereas the presence of Protestants is announced by the extensive use of stone in church architecture, for example in the building of steeples. Ethnic diversity in Burgenland is official and fully present in the public sphere (Baumgartner, Müllner, and Münz 1989). For recorded examples of the diverse musical traditions of Burgenland see the first volume of *Tondokumente zur Volksmusik in Österreich* (*Burgenland* 1993).

3. The ballad, "Die schöne Jüdin" ("The Beautiful Jewish Girl"), remains in oral tradition. A recording of a version from Deutschkreuz is included on *Burgenland* (1993), which, though sung by non-Jews, survives in one of the Seven Holy Cities.

4. Johannes Fabian interpellates the many ways in which anthropology must remove cultures from time in order to construct the images of the Other that appear in ethnographies. By removing the Other from temporal frameworks that the anthropologist would represent as his or her own, it follows, the Other becomes understandable, framed as an object that can be pondered and studied; see Fabian 1983. Isolating images of the Other through ethnomusicological fieldwork remains the primary focus of the essays in *Deutsche Gesellschaft für Musik des Orients* 1981.

5. Burgenland was a region in which the Austrian and Hungarian parts of the Habsburg Monarchy, in effect, overlapped. Ruled primarily by the Hungarian throne, that is by the Esterházy family, Burgenland's courts served as a political and cultural transition to the Austrian seat of the empire in Vienna. We witness this clearly in the biography of Joseph Haydn, who spent most of his life as a court composer in the service of the Esterházy family in Burgenland.

6. The story of this death is recalled as follows. In order to demonstrate the power of the National Socialist regime in Vienna, a decision was made in the early 1940s to demolish all the synagogues of the Seven Holy Cities in a single day, one after the other, with crowds of residents gathered to witness the disappearance of the last visible traces of Jewish culture. School children were marched to the sites of demolition, and when the sixth of the seven synagogues was blown up, a brick or stone struck a girl in the head, killing her immediately. The Burgenlanders saw this as a sign that the acts of demolition were wrong, if not the implementation of evil, and the seventh synagogue, which still stands in Kobersdorf, was spared.

7. Jewish cemeteries were never inside the walls of a European city, and therefore quite literally occupied a space beyond the boundaries. In one of the Seven Holy Cities, Kobersdorf, the Jewish cemetery was even on the other side of the international boundary with Hungary, and local residents remember how many mourners would stop at that border rather than accompanying the corpse beyond the Hungarian borderpost.

8. John Van Maanen (1988) compares the different forms the tales encountered and produced by fieldworkers assume, subsuming these under three large categories: realist tales, confessional tales, and impressionist tales. Issues of right and wrong, truth and falsehood, and understanding and misunderstanding shape all three tale types, thereby enriching and complicating modern ethnography.

9. The Ottoman occupation of Buda began in 1541, ending only in 1686, and during this period Burgenland, as the western part of the Pannonian basin of Hungary, became the final bulwark against an invasion of Vienna.

10. The earliest Roma settlements of Austria, those in Burgenland, first appeared in the sixteenth century and included Romas largely from the areas of present-day Hungary and Croatia. The history of Roma settlement in the area has historically been of such significance

that Romas who descend from the early settlements are simply called *burgenländische Roma,* which distinguishes them from all other Roma, Sinti, and Lovara groups in Austria.

11. In Eisenstadt, summer home of the Esterházy court, as well as to the musical career of Franz Joseph Haydn, this is strikingly evident, for the Jewish community is much closer to the palace than the Christian sections of this small city, now the provincial capital of Burgenland (Klampfer 1966).

12. The vernacular of Jewish communities in these areas has been German, rather than Yiddish, since roughly the beginning of the nineteenth century.

13. For a more ethnographic approach to the Other in the past and the past as Other, see Michael M.J. Fischer's study of the historical contestation of Polish identity (1993).

14. Klaus Theweleit takes the body's presence as an historically situated vessel for performance as a metaphor for radically disjunct cross references that at once intensify historical consciousness and confuse it by transforming it into a field of restless signification. Musical performance transforms Theweleit's notion of the body into an unceasing proliferation of historical meaning (1988).

Selecting Partners

Questions of Personal Choice and Problems of History in Fieldwork and Its Interpretation

An enormous ethnographic literature exists from Eastern Europe consisting of literally thousands of monographs and articles in the multiple languages of the area, with fieldwork and its interpretation beginning in the early nineteenth century. In my definition of fieldwork, I include gathering, reading, and interpreting historic and contemporary ethnographic literature produced by others working in the same region where I am conducting fieldwork. My intent in this chapter is to examine the implications of incorporating into my fieldwork process selected materials from this vast body of historic and continuing ethnographic literature of several Eastern European countries. When researching areas where there is a substantial ethnographic literature, I believe it is appropriate and necessary for contemporary fieldworkers to listen to the voices of living and deceased ethnographers along with the voices of local performers and other community members of the region being studied.

Fieldwork is an individual experience that takes place in time (at or through a specific time), and fieldwork often results in an ethnographic record outside of time (an interpretation of the fieldwork experience made available to others anytime through a written text). I can relate my fieldwork experiences by means of a written text, and I can know something of the fieldwork experiences of others through their texts. In both cases, the written text is an interpretation by the author (derived in part from fieldwork experience) and an interpretation by the reader (derived in part from the author's text). Discussion of fieldwork from the perspective of either writer or reader is difficult without somehow examining the meanings of "cultural authority" and "cultural interpretation." Important here is not only the researcher's background, training, and relationship with those whose cultural norms are under study, but also the ideas fieldworkers gain from earlier ethnography in their areas—the texts that provide one of the bases for a comparison of interpretations of culture.

Much of the ethnographic literature in Eastern Europe is produced by field-workers who work in their native country. A truism in ethnography is that one working in his or her native land brings a unique and valuable perspective to field-work and its interpretation, yet such a fieldworker is also open to a wide variety of experiences. Some ethnomusicologists, myself included, rely heavily on interpretations of culture made by scholars or commentators from that culture. This is especially logical in parts of the world where local fieldworkers have created a large number of written texts, an ethnographic literature. Although it is important to use the views of native researchers, there is no self-evident methodology to light the way, nor is this usage the only option for the foreign fieldworker who approaches an ethnographic literature written by local fieldworkers. Why should one expect agreement in interpretation among any group of native researchers? An indiscriminate and uncritical use of native ethnographic literature—that is, regarding it as producing inviolate results—creates the impression of a "culture member formula" that probably does a disservice to both native and nonnative researchers. According to a "culture member formula," fieldwork and its interpretation by any except culture members is discredited because it is nonnative, not based on the lifetime experience of a culture member. The problem is that several different culture members, several lifetimes of experience, can produce quite different interpretations of "their" culture. In such a case, how does the nonnative interpret the conflicting views of several native ethnographers, and how do native fieldworkers explain their diversity of interpretation to nonnative colleagues? At its worst, the "culture member formula" is a search for an ultimate answer, a final fieldwork choice in the form of special partners who are above critical consideration, an attempt to find people whose backgrounds ostensibly make them suitable candidates for producing a magic formula that everyone else can plug into with impunity.

This is not the selection of partners I discuss here. I do not regard anyone's interpretation of culture as inviolate, final, or best, and that includes any single native ethnographer. It includes my own work as well. Diversity of opinion is characteristic of the ethnographic literature from Eastern Europe, as it is of ethnography from other parts of the world. How that diversity is measured or qualified is a crucial part of the interpretive process of the reader. More important, it is a necessary part of a fieldworker's interpretation. In this chapter, I make a distinction between living ethnographers (those with whom it is possible to interact) and dead ethnographers (those to whom one can only react), and between the work of native and nonnative fieldworkers. However, I believe such distinctions can be overemphasized; they easily lead to placing the fieldwork of others into negative categories such as "theirs" as opposed to "ours," and in extreme cases into the "culture member formula." I regard those colleagues whose fieldwork I incorporate into my own work as partners. This includes colleagues both of the present and the past. Our partnership is primarily characterized by the trust and respect inherent in using another's fieldwork interpretations, not by immediate interaction between two people. Our contact point is not a social context, but the written text. When I incorporate their texts into my work, I not only read a document, I take on at least part of their fieldwork and interpretation as my own, albeit usually in modified form. I do not believe I do this naively or without a critical examination of problems. Trust and respect are most valuable when after critical examination they can be said to be appropriate.

In the chapter's initial section, "Fieldwork and Personal Choice," I consider the implications for my work of choosing from among a diversity of opinion, resulting in a selection of research 'partners' among this cacophony of metaphorical and real voices. In the second section, "Fieldwork and the Past," I discuss some of the issues raised in diachronic, ethnographic methodologies, primarily those that I and others practice in Eastern Europe. In the section, "Fieldwork and Interpretation," I describe limitations of methodologies practiced by many ethnomusicologists when applied to diachronic settings, with examples from the musical past and present of Ukraine. Finally, in "Fieldwork and Culture History in Ukraine" I examine some of the implications of combining chosen materials and data collected and interpreted by past ethnographers with what I and my contemporaries collect and interpret today.

Fieldwork and Personal Choice

As a social activity, fieldwork is a selection of a series of working relationships, each with its particular and special obligations and responsibilities. These relationships can be with a wide range of people: local performers, informed or uninformed listeners, native scholars, foreign scholars with the same area or subject specialization, academic colleagues, librarians and archivists, and virtually anyone with a knowledge or experience of a topic under consideration. Who we choose and why we choose them can be among the most important questions we face, influencing the outcome of nearly all professional activities. The selection process can be strange, haphazard, and drawn out, with dead ends and false starts. It does not always follow neat and simple rules, and it contains a degree of useful chaos. The process is not necessarily part of a dialectical method of analysis that weighs alternative interpretations against each other. Perhaps it is ideally not a two-way effort at all, but a true cacophony of voices. We need not necessarily answer these voices to learn from them. Our selection of working relationships need not be any more limited than we want it to be, and can be inclusive of literally all those whom we choose, living or dead, on virtually any level of interaction. In pursuing fieldwork processes, we take part in what Michael Oakeshott calls "a conversation," in which "the diverse idioms of utterance which make up current human intercourse have some meeting-place" and in which "they may differ without disagreeing" (1991[1959]:489).

Long and sometimes bitter years of foreign control and repressive political administration make issues of cultural authority and interpretation sensitive in many parts of the world. I work in an area with such a history, Eastern Europe. I have occasionally heard music researchers and other ethnographers stating that an outsider cannot possibly understand all the complexities of the region, a frequently voiced complaint directed at all fieldworkers not native to an area (cf. Nettl 1983:259). This point is probably well taken, although it is also useful to remember that native scholars in Eastern Europe, as in other parts of the world, do not agree among themselves on their interpretations. There is not, nor has there ever been, a single interpretive voice. Everyone, native and foreign researcher, is involved in an ongoing process of selecting those with whom it is most useful or most comfortable to work; no one person or school is representative of, or has a monopoly on native interpretation. The diversity of the fieldwork experience is not only an unalterable given, it can be seen as a positive feature, one of the major factors in the development of all disciplines that rely on fieldwork for primary source material, including ethnomusicology.

One aspect of the discussion on cultural authority has questioned any person's ability to make proper use of this material, to translate its subtleties into a text.[1] In fact, the very concept of "culture" as a whole unit is frequently questioned. Individuals of a given group of people are never in uniform lockstep. Most social anthropologists agree that a complex of cultural elements can differ greatly among individuals of a group (e.g., Rosaldo 1993[1989]). The nature and outlines of "a culture" are partly a theoretical construct of the researcher. An authoritative interpretation of "a culture" that is inclusive of all the views of each member of an entire population is not possible. This includes "a music culture." If one assumes that social- or culture-based research must always lead to hard and fast or unvarying rules, or to fixed boundaries of the normative as opposed to the uncommon, then admitting to such a tangle of complexity is indeed a problem. But if one places this research and the concomitant problems of interpretation in the context of the humanities, it gains a different intensity and begins to get interesting. A conversation is joined that is probably as old as the human being. The conversation is about none other than the nature of reality.

Due to this complexity, if fieldwork is to be undertaken, unique choices must be made by the ethnographer. As fieldwork experiences vary so greatly, the selection of the voices to be considered most valuable or useful is difficult. Does each choice reflect a cultural bias of the fieldworker? How can the fieldworker sort out differences in interpretation that normally and inevitably arise with the passing of successive generations of researchers?

This leads to a basic question: Is fieldwork conducted in the past as useful as that conducted today? I do not have in mind here controversies surrounding questions of authenticity and veracity in research, rather I am asking if fieldwork conducted forty, eighty, or one hundred and twenty years ago can be regarded equally with present-day fieldwork. Or, is present-day fieldwork more useful than that of the past? Will our fieldwork be regarded as uninformed or even deranged in fifty years? Then does the passing of time preclude usefulness or applicability in the literature of the social sciences or the humanities?

There are good reasons to ask these questions. With academic fashion changing every few years, an enormous number of secondary sources are more or less out of circulation, no longer touched by students, almost as if these studies were never written. Much of the energy of a large number of researchers, including many ethnomusicologists, seems to be taken up in following and adapting to academic fashions—"current intellectual trends"—even to the point where a search for the new is uncomfortably similar to a pursuit of the trendy. This and similar pursuits George List diplomatically refers to as the wish to be *au courant* (1979:4). William Roseberry more pointedly calls it "the politics of academic consumption," suggesting that successful or "correct" academic writing requires that one discover then follow current academic fashions, utilizing the most up-to-date sources, theories, methodologies, and buzzwords (1991a:126); as if one were a consumer walking through a market seeking products that promise to make a person "better" ("slimmer, healthier, faster, cleaner, or more productive"). Viewed in this context, the "marketplace of ideas" seems to be a consumer's market. I am not suggesting that the passing parade of academic fashions ought to be disregarded, although a healthy skepticism seems in order. Among other things, academic fashions help broaden the focus with a wide variety of possible research modes and methods as well as theories, especially if viewed from the perspective of a historiographer. Of course, all interpretations are not equally accepted by all academics, nor should they be. By necessity, certain interpretations are preferred as more interesting, more useful, or more authentic—or regrettably as more fashionable and up-to-date. We select those partners, living and dead, with whom we wish to work. And how could it be otherwise?

In making the selection of partners, how do we judge or evaluate the research of others, especially when it is conducted in parts of the world we have never been to, or that of the past? This is a central problem in the discussion of cultural authority and interpretation. On what do we base the broad trust explicit in our acceptance of another ethnographer's interpretation, either from a different part of the world or of a different time? Does such a set of criteria even exist? Is the inclusion or exclusion of other voices in our work based on decisions no more involved than notions of what constitutes current academic fashion? This is a crucial question in considering fieldwork conducted in the distant past. If the past is another place, another country we can never visit, as described by David Lowenthal (1985) and others, how do we evaluate its fieldwork? As academic interests shift through time, as is normal, is all past research to be regarded as less than useful, even quaint? If not, then who chooses what is to be regarded as informative long after authors are gone? What are the complexities in the relationships between living fieldworkers and those from the past?

Fieldwork and the Past

The thousands of sources that make up the ethnographic literature from Eastern Europe pose several problems with regard to questions of cultural authority. Some of these parallel problems from other parts of the world. The literature can be classified in various ways, for example based on region, population group, time period, language, or other factors. Considering for now a language classification, each of the constituent parts of this literature can be regarded as part of the national or native literatures that exist virtually everywhere in the world; that is, ethnographic studies undertaken and written by scholars native to a particular area of the world: Hungarian language literature about Hungarian music, Japanese language literature about Japanese music, and so on. On the other hand, a part of the literature from Eastern Europe consists of studies in which ethnographers of one cultural heritage conduct fieldwork among a people of a different cultural heritage, but both groups live within the political boundaries of one state. Such fieldworkers often interpret their findings in languages different from those of the people under study; this is also usual for foreign fieldworkers. This fieldwork scenario is common to several areas of the world; for example, Swedes and other Scandinavians conducting fieldwork among Saami; Japanese among Ainu; Americans, Canadians, and Mexicans among Native Americans; Spanish-speaking researchers from Chile and Peru among Andean peoples; urban-born Brazilians and others among Amazonian peoples; Chinese among Tibetans; Russians in all parts of Central Asia and Eastern Siberia; Russian fieldworkers in Ukrainian villages; Ukrainian fieldworkers in Russian or Belarussian villages; Poles among Belarussians, Ukrainians, and others; Hungarians among Slovaks and Romanians; and numerous combinations of collectors and distinct groups of villagers in India and Indonesia, various states in Africa and Southeast Asia, and elsewhere. If written out in its worldwide totality, this list would be quite lengthy.

In the history of fieldwork in Eastern Europe, while fieldworkers of one national group often conducted research among villagers of another group, especially in the pre-World War I Austro-Hungarian and Russian Empires, most fieldwork was conducted within what ethnographers considered their national, as opposed to imperial, boundaries. The data gathered from peasant populations the ethnographers thought of as "theirs": Ukrainian researchers among Ukrainian villagers, Serbian researchers among Serbian villagers, and so on.[2] One way to regard these fieldworkers is as native ethnographers in their own country. Another way to view them is as elites distinct from the peasant populations among whom they worked. The mostly urban-born and/or highly educated ethnographers were culturally different from, and carried a specific type of national consciousness not shared by, the peasant populations they studied. This situation evokes a social relationship similar to Robert Redfield's "great and little traditions," with native ethnographers part of the "great tradition," even as they took part in the study of the "little traditions," largely products of peasant populations (1962). In a more general way, this social dichotomy still applies today to demographic considerations in many regions of the world. Generalizing still further, a characteristic dichotomy in ethnography for most fieldworkers, both native and foreign, is the level of their wealth and education as well as degree of mobility as measured against that of the people among whom they work.

Even in cases of "native ethnography," then, there is not always a clear picture deserving of unequivocal or unambiguous self-righteousness. To paraphrase Judith Becker, ethical ambiguity in ethnography is no one's separate and definitive domain, either in the present or the past (1991:396). Now as then, when one sits down to write or travels virtually anywhere in the world to a fieldwork site— whether in native or foreign lands—the ambiguity is already well established as part of personal and professional life. Over time or through personal effort ethical ambiguity can be altered, but it probably cannot be eliminated.

Much of the earliest ethnographic literature from Eastern Europe is largely philological in nature and difficult to utilize today. It was formulated through period-specific strainers that compromise much of the data. Among these strainers was the search for national origins and signs of evolution. In North America a similar search was underway at that time, the quest for the origins or at least the evolution of "primitive man." One or the other, the national or the primitive, was the typical topic of ethnographic and folklore studies in most parts of the world until the early twentieth century or even later. More specific to fieldwork in Europe (Eastern and Western) from the early nineteenth century was the use of urban poetic standards in transcribing texts collected in the field.[3] One rarely heard the actual voices of the villagers under study until the second half of the nineteenth century, and transcriptions of village musical performances were not common until then.[4] In the 1860s and 1870s, ethnographers began to spend greater amounts of time in the field recording and describing the village voice. Chubyns'kyi in Ukraine and Kolberg in Poland are but two of several examples.[5] By the 1890s, dozens of ethnographic journals were published in Eastern Europe, and by the early 1900s there were many more.[6] At any given moment there were probably dozens, sometimes hundreds of ethnographers conducting fieldwork in Eastern Europe, covering thousands of villages. The publications included articles, monographs, encyclopedias, and bibliographies, and continued for decades. The result was an enormous ethnographic literature with thousands of articles and books detailing aspects of village life, including music. Taken as a whole, I think it is no exaggeration to call this the most detailed and comprehensive early literature on peasant society and culture in the world.

Obviously this literature has to be approached critically. Enormous changes have taken place in Eastern Europe over the last hundred years. The villagers and the fieldworkers of the 1930s were already different from those of the 1890s, and those of the 1990s are different than those of the 1930s. If this literature is to be utilized (and not everyone agrees that it should), care must be taken to understand the differences in outlook and standards in the material from various time periods. I incorporate from this literature diachronic components when conducting current fieldwork. My approach is to select aspects of rural culture described in the ethnographic literature, examine them as they exist and change through time, and compare them to one another and to current practice (e.g., Noll 1991a). This is more or less similar to approaches of several colleagues from Eastern Europe (e.g., Czekanowska 1972; Iashchenko 1962). The results can be seen as a culture history (cf. Merriam 1964:277–302; Merriam 1967), or cultural history, or as part of a more general historical ethnomusicology. Regardless of how it is named, much of my fieldwork is part of a larger ethnographic effort conducted over a period of about a hundred and fifty years by hundreds of fieldworkers whose research was in the same regions, in the same villages, and occasionally with the same families as those I work with now. This ethnographic effort includes colleagues actively engaged in fieldwork today. I am interested in a dovetailing of the present and the past. I will even go so far as to state that there is some doubt in my mind if "culture" and "history" can be meaningfully separated as independent ideas.

Historical ethnomusicology, especially that type I think of as part of the culture history of peasants, is probably not a topic or methodology all ethnomusicologists are interested in, although the diachronic methods that I and others use in Eastern Europe have parallels among scholars researching the music of other parts of the world, especially in terms of area studies. The list of such scholarship is long and those included show great variety in method.[7] In addition to these, there is a wide variety of diachronic approaches among ethnomusicologists interested in broad or comparative problems concerning historical ethnomusicology, such as Stephen Blum (1975), Blum et al. (1991), Alan Merriam (1967), Bonnie Wade and Ann Pescatello (1977). There are various diachronic methodologies and/or interpretations proposed by several anthropologists that are useful for ethnomusicologists, among others William Roseberry (1991a), Marshall Sahlins (1985), Eric Wolf (1982), and earlier, Franz Boas (1936). Among European social anthropologists there is an important series of publications devoted to diachronic considerations; for example, Kristen Hastrup (1992) and David Lowenthal (1985). In addition, there are interesting comments by historians on the use of diachronic interpretations by anthropologists (e.g., Fernand Braudel 1980a[1958]; M. I. Finley 1987[1975]:102–19). I have in mind here not a diachronic approach such as "acculturation" (cf. Nettl 1992:381–86), but the use of an ethnographic text from the past as a source. In spite of all this activity, some ethnomusicologists in North America and Western Europe are reluctant to engage the historical ethnographic literature from any region of the world, especially that from Eastern Europe. This reluctance is present even among some Americans and West Europeans who conduct research on music in Eastern Europe. Some virtually ignore the historical literature and concentrate largely on synchronic methods and approaches. Their claim is that little or nothing can be done with the ethnography of the past. They believe it should be rejected virtually out of hand because the aims, methods, and ideologies of ethnographers of the past differ from those of our time. According to this view, problems stemming from differences in cultural perceptions of reality and ideological background between "them" and "us," or between "then" and "now," are so great as to prevent an honest appraisal of this literature today, or that the data are tainted because of these differences.

This view has widely accepted merit. The social sciences, including ethnomusicology, are ideally in a state of constant renewal, testing assumptions and seeking to explain anew, or to examine different aspects of their subjects. No book, no study is written forever, and it would be foolish to believe otherwise. This said, however, it seems to me that some elements of the primary source materials gathered in fieldwork are not the use-and-discard stock of academic fashion. They are not merely products of the imagination, although they are partly that. Ideologically based generalizations and ethical ambiguities are present in all ethnography, both present and past. After all, people write ethnography. There are numerous difficulties in abstracting data from an ideological background, but this applies no less to data collected by the living than to that of the deceased (data new and old). In spite of difficulties, ethnographers routinely incorporate data and ideas selected from the fieldwork of others in their own work. The point here is that all types of field data are not regarded as identical by most researchers. Selection takes place as a matter of course.

Problems of cultural authority and the interpretation of fieldwork from the past are not entirely different from problems of contemporary fieldwork. Contemporary ethnographers routinely find common ground in their work and ideas, even when they have different backgrounds, hold different views, and use different methodologies. In the same sense, today we can probably find common ground with many of the ethnographers of the past. In other words, it is neither realistic nor desirable that contemporary colleagues agree on all points of methodology or ideology, and the same can apply to relationships with ethnographers from the past. Differences in perception exist between contemporary and historic ethnographers, but these differences do not have to be a hindrance; they do not preclude an attempt to learn from others, and I can think of no reason why they automatically exclude the use of ethnographic materials gathered in the past. The function of the interpretive process in both synchronic and diachronic settings is complex, tied to the identities and perspectives of reality carried by an individual and a social group.

Although the living can communicate with one another, no interaction is possible with the deceased authors of historical ethnographic literature. One can only react to their work. They are silent partners, and in order to learn from them it is necessary to approach their work with care, critically appraising each aspect of the literature. When possible, it is useful (if not necessary) to know what their aims were as well as their methods of conducting fieldwork. This obviously helps evaluate the degree of possible interest each individual work retains for current ethnographers, but it is not a simple matter. Because of the wide range of aims and needs, ideologies and research strategies of ethnographers both in the past (here the writers) and today (the readers), I hesitate to suggest any specific instruction regarding the use of this material. Individual needs of the present and the quality of individual work in the past make generalizations difficult. The most that can be said, I think, is that with caution and an intimate knowledge of the history and languages of the area, researchers today can sort through that which they regard as not usable and choose that which they feel can be learned from the literature.

If this is not true, and if utilizing ethnographic texts of the past is beyond the pale for scholars of the present, then all fieldwork-derived texts written in our lifetimes must, in their turn, be excluded from consideration by future scholars. Or are we arrogant enough to believe that we hold special keys to knowledge that no one before us has managed to grasp, a knowledge that makes current fieldwork and our texts ontologically different from those of the past and therefore automatically deserving of special treatment in the future? Periodic exclusion of sets of past ethnographic texts would mean that fieldwork-derived information is to be considered time dated, like a box of cornflakes. Here only fieldwork undertaken by a current generation would be valid for interpretation (read consumption) by that generation of researchers (read shoppers), with each future generation only interpreting the data it collects for itself. The result would be that only the synchronic is valid stuff for the contemporary. This is one aspect of "the promise of the new and different" (Tyler 1986:124), a principle feature of the scientism of the nineteenth and twentieth centuries. Prominent here is the allegorical search for the proper key, the needed technology or metalanguage, which supposedly allows the world to swing into clear view for the first time. All can see who are holders of the key or who are novitiates to the mysteries of the technology. Human beings are seen as limited by neither biology nor temperament, but only by faulty technology; improve the technology, methodology, or science and you automatically improve the human being. Although aspects of this ideology are embraced by most social scientists, it is far removed from, even antithetical to, the cultural relativism that is ostensibly shared by many of them, including most ethnomusicologists. Conflicting views are held on this topic (compare Becker and McDaniel 1991; Bozeman 1984; Braudel 1980a[1958]; Christensen 1991; Nettl 1985; see also Clifford 1986a:109–10; Tyler 1986:134–35).

If we accept that we profit from the experiences of past ethnographers, the next critical questions are, what do we learn from an historical ethnographic literature and what are we to do with it? On the most basic level, the texts left behind by past ethnographers in Eastern Europe can be treated as a record of the ideologies and concerns of the researchers themselves as well as their time, although I see no reason to consider these texts any more or less referential or tied to their time than any other set of texts, and they are much more. Critically qualified, they are a record of the people under study, just as they were intended to be. Today (for us), they can be seen as a primary source about the past. Many decades before the term was used by Clifford Geertz (1973b) and others, "thick description ethnography" was normal practice for large numbers of fieldworkers in Eastern Europe. Regardless of the allegorical meanings and referential features and functions of these texts, they offer data that can be used in a number of ways. This is especially true when multiple references to the same elements or topics of a culture present quantifiable information that can be treated in ways similar to methods used by social historians who utilize records of births, deaths, and employment. The record is data that can be (and invariably is) interpreted in different ways by different scholars, an ethnography of cultural products and resources that can be examined much as an anthropologist treats cultural phenomena. The ethnographic literature of the past has both a historical and an ethnographic function.

The literature is "fragmentary," as Stephen Tyler (1986:131) suggests of postmodern ethnography; that is, it is not always organized around familiar categories such as kinship, social structure, or religion. It covers a wide range of material and expressive culture, but is particularly rich as a record of ritual customs of the village. Concerning music, records describe a wide range of discrete activities and elements. Among those that interest me are types of instrumental ensembles, the dominant types of ensemble repertory, the roles of different types of musicians in the village and their place in the village social hierarchy, the economic concerns of instrumental musicians and the role of music making as one part of their family income, differences in repertory between women and men and between people of different age groups, gender-based differences in the degree and kind of control of the social calendar, the social organization inherent in the realization of certain genres, the specificity of performance contexts for various genres, the regionalization of certain music practices, types of religious elements in music practice, the interrelationship of the music of different ethnic groups, and the challenges and problems in using notated transcriptions for analysis. In the historical literature, I am able to observe how these activities and elements change through time in a demonstrable way.

Fieldwork and Interpretation

Interpretation of fieldwork is necessary if the ethnographer is to write a text. The interpretation itself is a series of choices made by the ethnographer that provides the means for a future reader to understand what is often a staggeringly complex and sometimes confusing mass of detail—chaos by any other name. In other words, reduction is unavoidable. A written text is (among other things) an explicit reduction of experience. How the reduction takes place is crucial to the interpretive process of both writers and readers. In many if not most cases, writers choose to use an interpretive model already known to their readers. In ethnomusicology this often means using a model that is applicable to many situations and parts of the world, with broad comparative possibilities. This provides an immediate basis for establishing an interpretation that is at least in part common to writers and readers alike, which among ethnomusicologists means among people researching music from literally anywhere in the world.

Such commonality has both benefits and problems. Concerning the latter, I believe it is important to acknowledge the limits of those interpretative "models" used widely in ethnomusicology that divide the human sociocultural world into binary oppositions, such as "tradition and change," "Western (or Westernized) and non-Western," "insider and outsider," "emic and etic ethnography," "subculture and superculture," "stratified and nonstratified," "private and public," "proletarian and bourgeois," "subjective and objective ethnography," "primitive and modern," "cultural survivals and cultural changes," "big country and little country," "cooked and raw," and even "capitalism and socialism." Whatever uses they might have, such binary models are limiting in nature and tied to specific parameters. They are also negative in that they force a narrow interpretation prescribed by the very terms used in the analysis. Although one can discuss such limits as part of the normal function of language; as a necessary result of an interpretation, semiotic codes, or theory; or as a kind of shorthand that provides a broad comparative basis for discussion, neither this "normality" nor this need for discussion changes the fact that binary oppositions cannot reflect the complexities of the social and musical world of most people. One reason such models exist is to reduce complexity into a simple idea easily accessible to readers, which means for ethnomusicologists a model applicable to multiple contexts in several parts of the world. This methodology often uses small amounts of data to formulate sweeping general theories.

Perhaps the most compelling reason for their wide use in the social sciences (and in the academic world in general) is that they offer a convenient way to construct paradigms of social theory, a convenience that is part of the ever-present dialectical method of analysis common in ethnomusicology (Nettl 1991:273). It seems to be ingrained in scientific inquiry, or stated another way, an integral aspect of the ideology of scientism. Even the question of whether or not such a method of analysis is successful or possible is itself couched in binary terms; as William Roseberry suggests, such theoretical binary oppositions, or antinomies, point to "irresolvable conflicts between mutually exclusive sets of assumptions—between, for example, those who take a science of society as their goal and seek precise explanations of social processes and those who deny that such an explanatory science is possible and seek instead interpretive understanding of social life" (1991b:30).

As I see it, the main problem with these models is their overly reductive and limiting characteristics which are evident when considered in a diachronic analysis.

I illustrate this problem with an example from the musical past and present of Ukraine. Most readers are probably familiar with staged musical ensembles from Eastern Europe, those that came into existence in the years when the countries of the region were ruled by organized elites professing an allegiance to Marxism-Leninism. Here large numbers of performers render arranged versions of a supposedly "national" or "folk" music, usually performed by government-financed folklore ensembles staffed by professionals. The differences can be enormous between the music of this sanctioned, officially patronized music and the actual music practices of rural society. The most widely viewed and listened to type of ensemble of what is called *bandura* music in Ukraine fits this profile: large ensembles dating from the 1920s with professionally trained musicians singing in bel canto a repertory consisting largely of generic folk songs, composed ditties in popular style, and arrangements from the European classical repertory, but not utilizing the genres or styles of music of villages (Iashchenko 1970).

The music of these *bandura* ensembles is presented by its administrators and practitioners as if it were based on, or a continuation of, older village music practices of the blind peasant minstrels of Ukraine, the *kobzari* and *lirnyky*, and thus a long-standing Ukrainian music practice. As in many other parts of the world, this popular and officially sanctioned representation of cultural history has a complex history. The instruments, repertory, and performance practices of these giant folklore *bandura* ensembles have virtually nothing in common with village music practice. One of the instruments of the blind peasant minstrels, a plucked lute known to villagers as *kobza*, was small, handmade, and of village design, with no two exactly alike.[8] The performer, always male and virtually always blind, earned cash by performing in public places, often next to churches and monasteries, as well as in small town market squares and in village streets walking from house to house. A pupil studied privately for a few months or years with a blind village minstrel, accompanying him on his travels. He had to turn over to his teacher whatever earnings he produced during the learning period in payment for his lessons. A minstrel usually performed only solo (not in ensemble), or at most sang in duet.[9] His repertory consisted mostly of *psal'my* (a religious genre with textual themes derived largely from the Bible) and *dumy* (heroic epics based on Cossack myths and historical events), with a smattering of dance tunes and satirical songs.[10] Two blind mistrels, here hurdy-gurdy players, are shown in the photograph on the next page.

The music of most minstrels was characterized by recitative, tempo rubato, and a thin head voice, with many performers hovering in the upper tenor register, as clearly demonstrated in transcriptions in Mykola Lysenko (1978[1874]), Filaret Kolessa (1969[1910/1913]), Volodymyr Kharkiv (1930), and from wax cylinder recordings from Kolessa's and Kharkiv's fieldwork. This music practice was unmistakably different from the widely distributed fare of the large ensembles, which features an instrument that is mass produced (*bandura*), a repertory that is wholly secular, a bel canto vocal style based on popular idioms of the twentieth century, a

Two blind minstrels (lirnyky) *and their boy guide, ca. 1900. Photograph from the Center for the Study of Oral History and Culture (Kyïv).*

musical context of the concert stage, ensembles of either or both men and women, and formal music education derived mostly from notation, often taking place in a music school or conservatory.

In spite of these and other differences, the staged *bandura* ensemble is widely accepted as a product of the Ukrainian rural past and is proudly used as a musical symbol of a national heritage. The solo performances in the older style, on the other hand, are little known today to the majority of people. What are the results of an application of the most common binary "model" in ethnomusicology, the one that presupposes "a traditional and a modern" (or its counterpart "traditional and Westernized")? The urban staged ensemble is widely accepted as quintessentially Ukrainian, whereas the older village style is not; that which is newer and urban based is regarded as "traditional" and of rural heritage. Is this right or wrong? When asking "whose cultural reality is under question," it seems that the concept of "tradition" is not an absolute, but derives from one's view and experience. The idea of "tradition" derives largely from either interpretation or the institutionalization of an idea (cf. Hobsbawm and Ranger 1983). The binary model of "traditional and modern" in Ukraine, as in many other cases, brings more confusion than clarity. It is part of an institutionalized system of valuation. As such it is limited as either description or analysis, and seems to me to be frequently used in poor judgment by ethnomusicologists. Values are a necessity in an interpretation of fieldwork. The question is, which values or whose values do we choose and why? (cf. Seeger 1965:2).

A more recent approach labels the older style as part of an "ethnographic present," here a past music practice that continues in the present as part of a self-conscious and deliberate program (cf. Clifford 1986a:111–13). Yet the blind minstrels did not survive. They have no present. Most of the blind minstrels were gone from village musical life by the 1950s, probably eliminated through radical and deliberate repression by state authorities (mostly in the 1920s and 1930s) and through a gradual change in village culture over a period of several decades. A small number of minstrels survived into the 1970s and 1980s. Today there are about fifteen sighted performers using some of the blind minstrels' performance practices and styles. In the northwestern regions of Volyn' and Polissia, blind harmonia players continue performing some elements of the music of the blind minstrels (Noll 1993b).

Here a specific set of concerns reflect political and social currents of several decades. Examining this music through the ethnographic literature of the nineteenth and twentieth centuries is not a search for origins that are largely unknown. Furthermore, it is not "salvage ethnography" (cf. Marcus and Fisher 1986:165–66). There are people living in Ukraine today who are neither performers nor administrators but who remember and recognize the performance practices of the older style. They understand the differences between it—a native music practice—and the staged *bandura* ensembles invented in the twentieth century. These are primarily elderly villagers and a few urban intellectuals. A few of them remember or understand how and why the differences just described were created and institutionalized in the Stalinist period, then maintained over a long period of time, and who carried out these actions.[11] In other words, the differences in music aesthetic, performance practice, and expectation described earlier are not merely part of a generational differentiation in perception; they are not some event or object; they did not just happen. They are not described or analyzed within the confines of reductive abstractions such as "tradition" or "change." I would argue that they are better described within the context of many social institutions that were developed by specific people under specific circumstances for specific reasons.

There are significant questions of cultural authority and culture control here that need to be examined. Whose cultural reality is to be considered? Whose lives are to be addressed? Which social group, which set of musical standards, which kind of social and economic organization is to be studied and from whose perspective? If "a music culture" is to be studied, whose will it be, given that views of participants differ? If perspectives change through time, which time period is to be addressed, or how can the change through time be described? Obviously not everyone in Ukraine shares the same experiences or interpretations of the music of the blind peasant minstrels. Layers of meaning derived from the music vary greatly among culture participants. From the perspectives of state and party administra-

tors involved in repressing blind peasant musicians there is one set of interpretations, from the perspectives of repressed village musicians quite another, from the
surviving family members yet another, from the viewpoints of village musicians
who were not repressed there is another, and from the perspectives of elderly non-
musician villagers yet another. Former villagers who moved to the city during the
Stalinist period often have yet another set of interpretations. From the experiences
of contemporary village youth—a group with virtually no personal experience of
this aspect of Ukrainian culture history—is another set. Furthermore, perspectives
of the 1990s will likely lead to different interpretations of these questions than the
perspectives of the 1930s. Who is doing the examining and what perspectives do
these people bring to the ethnographic context? Finally, to what extent is it possible
to compare these sets of interpretations with musical practices and contexts in
other parts of the world?

Are the music practices of thousands of people spread over several generations
best described within the self-limiting framework of a binary opposition, or perhaps
simply as part of an "ethnographic present"? When is it useful to reduce a complex
reality to a simple equation? What does this reduction tell us? How does it shape our
possible interpretations of the social or musical world? Whose social structure,
whose history, whose music aesthetic are we concerned with? If the social world is a
complex of multiple structures and histories, how do our efforts to understand this
world reduce its meaning, complexity, and significance in crucial ways, perhaps hidden behind a mask of social science jargon? Fieldwork includes the consideration of
multiple realities of many different kinds of people as well as institutions, all of
which exist in the present and through time, continually changing. The past is
describable as a complex of processes developing over years, decades, centuries, and
as a series of specific moments in time. The present is describable as multiple structures and cultural conventions as well as personal visions and individual experiences. How does one conduct research that reflects the complexity of human organization, experience, and thought, both on the level of groups and that of
individuals, in both the past and present? What are the consequences for interpretation (writer's and reader's) when the ethnographic text, an explicit reduction of
experience, is engaged?

Fieldwork and Culture History in Ukraine

Fieldwork is a problem-producing activity. It does not necessarily lead to answers.
Numerous interpretations are usually possible from given fieldwork experiences.
The reduction of a complex reality to a simple theoretical equation is one of the
seemingly necessary (and perhaps endless) consequences of ethnographic interpretation. There are no secret formulas for finding a balance between unique ethnographic detail and wide theoretical comparison. Focusing attention on the one
detracts from the other (cf. Geertz 1973b). For example, the concept of "colonial-

ism" is an abstraction, a theoretical equation used for comparative purposes. The concept is so widely applied, however, that it is fraught with shallow stereotypes. It refers to such a variety of political and social experiences worldwide, that on the whole I prefer to leave it to publicists. Much the same applies to "hegemony," a prominent buzzword in current academic fashion, the multiple meanings of which I believe make it nonspecific and overgeneralized for distinct ethnographic or historical contexts. Since all social, not to mention political, contact intrinsically engenders some degree of hegemony, when examining specific situations the concept is reductive to an almost hopelessly extreme degree. Both concepts reduce unique detail to neutral clogs in what are proposed as overarching theoretical systems. For my purposes these systems are not useful because they too radically reduce the particular to undifferentiated fodder for a theory.

On the other hand, ethnographic details need to be rationalized as abstractions derived from fieldwork material for comparative purposes if fieldwork is to have more than a personal meaning. My approach in Ukraine is to research selected aspects from the history of music there, but without trying to construct a systemic or theoretical framework for all music practices of all people and all times in the region. I eschew all social evolutionary schemes, unilinear or otherwise, as too radically reductive (and perhaps unsound). I am especially interested in those elements of music practice from the Stalinist period, when most of the culture controls mentioned earlier were put into place, and specifically in providing a detailed account of the effects of the administrative controls developed for the blind peasant minstrels and their music. I use written sources (published and unpublished), sound-recorded material, and oral histories. The latter I collect from various participants of the time period in question, including administrators, villagers who are not musicians, village musicians and their families, and ethnographers. Finally, I attempt to show the influence of institutions and ideas from the past on current music practice. I am trying to incorporate material collected today with that collected in the past, a dovetailing of synchronically and diachronically derived texts.[12]

The great changes in music practice in Eastern Europe that occurred between approximately 1920 and 1950, but especially at the time of collectivization, can be seen in the context of significant changes in social organization. These changes cannot be described or analyzed simply by reducing them to the concepts of "colonialism," "hegemony," "tradition and modernity," or by applying similar reductive formulas. One generalization that pertains to music in most of the East European socialist world is that village community centers—"houses of culture" and "clubs" fostering a statist view and practice of music—were built throughout the region (Kondufor 1989; White 1990). These community centers were part of a series of great webs or networks of regional, national, Soviet-wide, and even East European-wide institutions intended to change and control area norms of expressive culture, and in this they were largely successful (Lapidus 1978; Noll 1994a; and Solomon 1978).

In Soviet lands of the 1920s and 1930s, large ensembles became the mainstay of official (supported or prescribed by government agencies) musical life and all that was associated with state or party, even in the villages, where the "houses of culture" and the "clubs" were the means to both distribute and administer the statist program. Much that did not fit into this program was repressed. Urban administrators assumed enormous power over rural expressive culture (Fitzpatrick 1992:115–48). Using the network of community centers as their vehicle, they replaced some of the music contexts of civil society with newly created holidays and places for performance. They tried to replace some religious observances with state holidays that included music. They created new secular village gatherings that were devoted to distributing party ideology.[13] State administrators took over the functions of providing the contexts for many of the musical performances in the village. These performances were usually on stages in the community centers, for audiences often compelled by authorities to attend in order to hear political speeches. The administrators brought performance content into line with official ideology by censoring texts and "recommending," that is, forbidding any but certain types of performance practices, particularly by favoring melodies based on popular Soviet (instead of regional) styles of the day, with texts praising Stalin, Lenin, the party, the Red Army, and so forth. These administrators published repertory lists that prescribed acceptable repertory, largely arrangements of selected generic folk songs, music by Soviet composers, and revolutionary songs (for lists concerning the music of the bandurists, see Khotkevych 1930b and *Repertuar* 1934). The state's economic patronage of musical performance was often provided by people with little or no relation to village music practice. This patronage was extended to a handful of selected blind minstrels, those who took on the prescriptions mandated by the state, while all peasant minstrels had their music practices proscribed. For the most part, state patronage was provided to sighted (usually urban) professionals and amateur *bandura* enthusiasts. Virtually all musicians receiving government economic patronage used a sanitized repertory either invented by or acceptable to party authority, performing most often in ensembles sanctioned by the state.

This was a radical departure from village performance practice, much of which was characterized by specific genres that were rendered only in specific performance contexts by specific people, each context having its own unique repertory and performance practices (e.g., weddings, spring rituals, summer rituals, Christmas caroling, and *dosvitky* or "evening gatherings" of unmarried girls) (Noll 1994b). The change took place abruptly, put into place mostly over the span of a decade. In other words, this is not a topic that adapts easily to the concept of "acculturation." It was an administrative course largely devised and carried out by urban dwellers who developed as quickly as possible institutions and networks to promote specific kinds of cultural contacts between urban and rural populations (Noll 1994a). Nowhere was the change as radical as that imposed on the blind peasant minstrels and their music. Blind minstrels and itinerant peasant musicians of all kinds in Ukraine and Belarus, southwestern Russia, and elsewhere were forbidden to travel from village to village, as had been their custom, effectively ending their way of life, including the economic basis of their music practice.

I have found and conducted interviews with numerous surviving members of the families of repressed minstrels. In several cases, they were the same families researched in the 1920s by Volodymyr Kharkiv (1929), Borys Luhovs'kyi (1926, 1993), and Oleksandyr Malynka (1929), or even earlier by M. Speranskii (1904). By combining the oral histories that I collect from family members with material ethnographers collected in the past directly from the minstrels, I am able to construct a history from approximately the turn of the century to the 1990s. Part of this is an attempt to understand how, why, and by whom the repression of this music and these musicians took place, as well as the continuing impact of this repression today. According to those I have interviewed, the methods of proscribing the music of the blind minstrels most often included threats of arrest. Some minstrels were beaten, others apparently arrested and imprisoned. Some starved to death in the purposely engineered famine of 1932–1933, their blindness probably contributing to their losses. Others may have been shot, and many laid down their instruments out of fear or confusion and ceased to perform. Still others survived, and stopped performing only in the 1950s or so when the state began to provide subsidies for the blind and the handicapped as well as pensions for the elderly in villages.[14]

The process of developing socialist cultural norms can be interpreted in various ways. What are the implications of any such interpretation for an understanding of both current and past practice as well as in a discussion of cultural authority? My interpretation is that the past administrators of party and state were occupied with the development of a "parallel culture"; that is, socialist cultural norms that paralleled, and were intended to largely replace, the cultural norms of civil society (Noll 1991b and 1993a). This parallel culture is still in place. In the end, it did not totally replace the expressive culture of civil society, although its institutions provide the economic, aesthetic, and contextual basis for most of the officially sponsored music practices throughout Eastern Europe in the socialist period, and to some extent still today.

How do native scholars interpret this process? Here there are problems and no simple answer. As noted, the construction of socialist norms in expressive culture, including many of those still in place today, took place largely in the Stalinist period. This period was not a vacuum in which no ethnographic research was carried out. However, most of the research of the time was conducted in line with specific administrative policies of party and state. Public dissent from these policies put the researcher at great risk. Thus, a fieldworker was directed to travel to specific villages and collect songs and sayings about Lenin, the party, Stalin, the army, and Soviet luminaries. The material was collected largely from village party activists, policemen, army recruits and veterans, komsomol participants, brigade leaders on

Klyment Kvitka. Photograph from the Center for the Study of Oral History and Culture (Kyïv).

collective farms, and the like—not exactly a representative sampling.[15] The village voice, by its absence in this literature, seems today all the louder and more significant, and can be regarded as one measure of a cultural authority that is not at all synonymous with political authority.

A significant number of the researchers were physically repressed. Some were shot, others perished in the Gulag prison system, and still others were imprisoned but survived. Andryi Khvylia, executed in 1937, was a folklorist who at one time was the editor of a prominent Stalinist folklore journal in Ukraine (Khvylia 1937; Tabachnyk and Pohrebniak 1989). Nina Zahlada, executed in 1938, was an ethnographer who conducted research on material culture (Borysenko 1992). Hnat Khotkevych, shot in 1938, was a novelist, playwright, bandurist, and music researcher. His monograph on musical instruments in Ukraine is still often cited in Ukrainian language publications (Khotkevych 1930a). Kateryna Hrushevs'ka was perhaps the greatest authority of her generation on the blind minstrels of Ukraine (e.g., Hrushevs'ka 1927). She lost her job in the early 1930s, was sentenced to prison in 1937, and died in a labor camp in 1943. Borys Luhovs'kyi conducted extensive fieldwork among street musicians of Chernihiv in the 1920s (Luhovs'kyi 1926 and 1993). He hung himself in 1937 while in prison awaiting a political trial. Sofiia Tereshchenko was an active fieldworker who collected material on, among other things, village wedding rituals (e.g., Kryms'kyi 1928). Arrested in 1930 , she died in 1947, two years after her release from labor camp (Vlasiuk and Lykhach 1994). Kost'

Koperzhyns'kyi published a series of articles on winter village rituals, providing probably the most detailed descriptions of these music contexts in the historical literature (Koperzhyns'kyi 1929). He spent several years in a prison camp, then was exiled for life to Leningrad. Klyment Kvitka is the Ukrainian ethnomusicologist perhaps best known internationally. He was arrested in the early 1930s and spent an unknown amount of time in a prison camp in central Asia. He survived the ordeal, but was exiled for life to Moscow, specifically not allowed to return and conduct research in Ukraine (Ivanenko 1970). He lived nearly twenty years in exile, although he never again published anything of significance (see figure on facing page).[16]

Still other fieldworkers conformed to state and party demands, enabling them to continue fieldwork but only along closely monitored channels. In 1929 and 1930 many Ukrainian researchers, particularly those working in the Academy of Sciences, were either arrested or threatened with arrest as the Stalinist political machine went into full gear.[17] Before these arrests began, the ethnomusicologist Volodymyr Kharkiv was active as a fieldworker and was an associate of Kvitka's in the Music Bureau of the Ethnographic Commission, Ukrainian Academy of Sciences in Kyïv. His work was extraordinary for its time. Unpublished manuscripts derived from Kharkiv's fieldwork in the late 1920s are among the most detailed, extensive, and informative primary sources on the blind minstrels from that period, including dozens of music transcriptions made from wax cylinders recorded in the field (Kharkiv 1929, 1930). Then Kharkiv was arrested along with others. Upon his release, he became a different kind of researcher, one who conformed to the demands of party and state, collecting in fieldwork expeditions mostly material about Stalin, Lenin, the party, army, komsomol, collectivized agriculture, and so on, primarily from village representatives of party and state authority, but occasionally from other villagers (e.g., Kharkiv 1932, 1937). Kharkiv apparently regularly reported to political authorities on his activities in the field. He later moved to Moscow.

These are only a few examples from the history of Ukrainian ethnography from the Stalinist period. Today an interpretation of the fieldwork of that time must obviously be tempered by acknowledging the particular constraints under which these people worked, or could not work, or had to modify their working methods. Of equal importance is that these constraints were to have lasting consequences, still evident today. In Soviet Ukraine, no ethnographic journal of acceptable standards was published between 1931 and 1957, after which time many of those who might have helped continue or revive ethnographic research were either dead, in exile, in prison, or too scared to get involved. A generation of fieldworkers was virtually wiped out, and competent research emerged again only in the 1960s. Ethnography itself was apparently considered dangerous to the state, and was closely controlled and monitored right up to the collapse of the Soviet state in 1991. This control was Union-wide but especially heavy in parts of the Soviet Union outside of European Russia. Even in the early 1970s, ethnographers whose fieldwork and publications fell outside of allowed limits lost their jobs.[18] No department of ethnography/ethnology (what in North America would be called "cultural anthropology") was allowed at a university; rather, ethnography was treated as a minor aspect of Ukrainian history. A kind of subdepartment was finally established in Kyïv in 1991. A department of ethnomusicology has been slowly emerging at the Kyïv Conservatory since the late 1980s. Patterns that originated in the Stalinist period continued to develop over the decades, becoming part of the interpretive function of Soviet ethnography. Until recently, Ukrainian interpretations of the Stalinist period did not mention the repression of either musicians or musicologists. The topic was off limits entirely and could not be safely broached. This situation has changed, and articles are slowly appearing that describe those decades more fully (e.g., Khai 1989; Noll 1993a).

The main point in this description of the Stalinist period music culture is to illustrate both the problems and the usefulness in employing elements from the history of the state structure for the economic patronage and distribution of expressive culture and research in the area, as well as the difficulties one would face in conducting and interpreting fieldwork without this knowledge. It is important, I believe, to acknowledge these difficulties. Much of today's state-patronized music practice in Eastern Europe is part of, or derives from, a long-standing and restrictive state policy that might appear neutral from a synchronic perspective. However, when considered diachronically, including the massive repression of musicians and music researchers in the Stalinist period, this same system of institutions appears anything but neutral. The music practices and institutions developed by a repressive administrative authority in the Stalinist period ought not to be viewed as a normative function of the state. The enormous costs in human life and local culture that the development of those practices and institutions entailed ought to give pause to any fieldworker who comes into contact with them. Some of these institutions were common in parts of Eastern Europe until recently or are still present today. I am extremely skeptical of an ethnomusicology or an anthropology of aesthetics that uncritically treats the Stalinist period as if it were unrelated to the present, and these institutions as if they were just another mechanism for state support of expressive culture. Virtually all discussions on cultural authority are in general agreement that the ethnographer needs to place critical value at some point on that which is researched. This ought to include that which is brutally repressed. A respect for the inhabitants of the past is no less appropriate than for the living.

Of course, even the most detailed account of the history of village music and music scholarship will not answer all questions or solve all problems. A diachronic method has limitations, just as a synchronic method does. We cannot live someone else's history any more than we can live someone else's daily life. Our understanding of either the past or the present can never be complete or final, nor can we escape the allegory of our own interpretations. We can, however, use what knowledge of the past we have available, either as a study in its own right or as a supplement to current fieldwork. The latter is a necessity if we want to analyze those elements, structures, and ideas that exist through long periods of time, generations or even centuries, and continue to impact on the present. I know of no reason to believe that problems inherent to the interpretation of culture are better discussed by deliberately excluding relevant diachronic data. Nor do I know of any reason to assume that a diachronic component in either conducting or interpreting fieldwork is inherently any more or less allegorical than a synchronic one.

Conclusion

Fieldwork's complexities increase when it becomes desirable to link one's own fieldwork material with that of ethnographers from the past. I have no blueprint for how this should be done. I have few answers for the many questions I pose here. I certainly cannot provide a succinct definition or even a description of fieldwork that might apply to all situations, and I do not think that guidelines for using historical ethnographic literature are possible to formulate. For all of these issues there are many variables, including the needs and ideologies of fieldworkers as well as the social relationships with those they work most closely. Although fieldwork leads to a variety of such relationships, it seems that the primary yardstick the ethnographer has for measuring success, usefulness, authenticity, or interest level is the opinion of colleagues, a sometimes dubious but always frightening dependency that often resembles a search for the fashionable.

Much of my fieldwork in Eastern Europe is geared toward complementing that of the area's native ethnographers, both past and present. I do this not in order to conform to some native cultural interpretation. There is no single native interpretation. Current research does not reflect a lockstep "reimagining of the past" or process of "reinterpreting history" that applies to all scholars. Especially since the fall of the Soviet state, most discussions on the peculiar history of this part of the world are many-sided and are not well described by prevailing academic clichés. If for no other reason than out of due respect for colleagues, living and dead, who share or once shared the particular fieldwork domain in which I am currently involved, the unique voices of these ethnographers ought to be incorporated into discussions that reach the international academic community. A familiarity with and use of their materials opens me (or any foreign fieldworker) to data, methodologies, and interpretations that might otherwise go unnoticed or remain little known.

However, I have another reason for considering my research as one of many voices in a larger ethnographic study of the region, a reason that reflects my choices in fieldwork methods, emphases, and aims. In spite of whatever flaws they carry, either individually or collectively, the many fieldworkers of Eastern Europe have left a unique and valuable ethnographic legacy, one aspect of which is an opportunity for the application of diachronic methods to a wide assortment of problems that are usually approached without the benefit of an historical literature about the society and culture of peasants. Comparative interpretations that span periods of time might be no less important, valuable, or interesting than comparative interpretations that span territory.

Notes

1. The literature on cultural authority is extensive and found in publications of (among others) historians, anthropologists, folklorists, and ethnomusicologists, but the discussion is too broad to describe in detail here. One well-known view from an anthropologist is Clifford 1983. More recent comments on this discussion in anthropology include essays by Clifford, Tyler, and Marcus (all from Clifford 1986a). In ethnomusicology, Becker and McDaniel (1991) and Titon and Dornfeld (1992) provide a brief overview as well as a bibliographic survey on the subject in anthropology and ethnomusicology. For earlier and somewhat different comments from a historian, see Braudel 1980b [1960].

2. Sources examining questions of national consciousness in the development of the ethnographic literature in Eastern Europe include Hofer (1968, 1969) and Sugar (1969); compare to Hobsbawm and Ranger (1983).

3. One of many examples of altering village-derived materials to make them fit urban poetic standards of the time is Tsertelev (1827). There are numerous criticisms of this practice in the ethnographic literature from the late nineteenth and early twentieth centuries: e.g., Hrushevs'ka (1927:xvi–xvii, cii, and cviii).

4. Among the most detailed music transcriptions of the time are those of Mykola Lysenko (Lysenko 1978 [1874]; Chubyns'kyi 1877).

5. Pavlo Chubyns'kyi published a seven-volume series, his *Trudy*, between 1872 and 1879, based on his expeditions through villages in 1869–1870 (e.g., Chubyns'kyi 1874, 1877). Oskar Kolberg published dozens of regional monographs in the second half of the nineteenth century based on many village travels (e.g., Kolberg 1979[1867]).

6. Periodicals of uneven quality began to appear as early as the 1870s, but by the 1890s a full-blown professionalism was evident in ethnographic publications in most of Eastern Europe. Some of the most important Ukrainian ethnographic journals and their years of publication are: *Sbornik kharkovskogo istoriko-filologicheskogo obshchestva* ("Collections of the Historical Philological Society of Kharkiv," 1877–1922), *Kievskaia starina* ("Kievian Antiquity," 1882–1906), *Etnohrafichnyi zbirnyk* ("Ethnographic Anthology," 1895–1929), *Materiialy do ukraïns'koï etnol'ogiï* ("Materials on Ukrainian Ethnology"—the name varied through time— 1899–1929), and somewhat later *Etnohrafichnyi visnyk* ("Ethnographic Bulletin," 1925–1930) as well as *Pervisne hromadianstvo ta ioho perezhytky na Ukraïni* ("Primitive Society and Its Survivals in Ukraine"—1926–1929) and *Muzyka* ("Music," 1923–1928). Similar publications existed in large numbers at that time in virtually every region of Eastern Europe.

7. There are several such parallels. One is the treatment of early research on the music of Native American Indians (e.g., the writings of Francis Densmore, Walter Fewkes, Alice Fletcher, and others) by such scholars as George Herzog, Gertrude Kurath, and Bruno Nettl. A more recent example is Robert Witmer (1991). Historical research on East Asian music is one of the most prominent in historical ethnomusicology; for example the works of Laurence Picken and his students (cf. Widdess 1992). Much (but not all) of this research is qualitatively different

from that from Eastern Europe, as it is focused primarily on the classical music genres of elite populations as well as sources of music notation, as in the research on Japanese music in publications of Shigeo Kishibe, Robert Garfias, Eta Harich-Schneider, William Malm, and others. Of interest is that scholarship on the music of Japanese peasants was nearly non-existent until the 1930s (Embree 1943). Each country in East Asia has a unique history of research, but detailed studies of peasant music practices were rarely a part of that research until at least the 1920s and more commonly the 1940s, 1950s, or later (Wong 1991), from roughly fifty to a hundred years later than in Eastern Europe. Even today there is a paucity of research on music among peasants for some regions of East Asia, an astounding lacuna given the fact that the area contains the largest concentration of peasant populations in the world.

8. Blind peasant minstrels performing *lira* (hurdy-gurdy) and *kobza* (a plucked bowl lute) were common in villages up to the 1930s. *Lira* performers were known over a wide territory, including (using current borders) eastern and southern Poland, virtually all of Ukraine, most of Belarus, and southwestern regions of Russia, mostly those bordering both Belarus and Ukraine. *Kobza* was known principally in certain Left Bank regions of Ukraine, especially in the Chernihiv, Poltava, and Kharkiv regions. The *kobza* of Romania is a different plucked lute; that of the Polish highland region, Podhale, is a bagpipe. In the late nineteenth century the strings of the Ukrainian *kobza* normally numbered anywhere from eight to about thirty, and were tuned diatonically. The twentieth century *bandura* is also a plucked bowl lute, but is larger and mass produced in factories. It has about sixty strings and is usually tuned chromatically.

9. An extraordinarily large literature (little known outside of the region) exists concerning the *kobzari* and *lirnyky* of Ukraine and the *lirnyky* of Belarus, eastern Poland, and southern Russia as well as the men and women *startsi* and *starchykhy* ("wandering beggars") of Eastern Europe. Most of this literature comes from the nineteenth and early twentieth centuries. Several hundred sources can be listed. A few of these are: Bezsonov (1861–1864), Borzhkovskii (1889,) Demutskii (1903), Hnatiuk (1896), Horlenko (1884), Hrushevs'ka (1927), Kolessa (1969 [1910/1913]), Krist (1902), Kvitka (1928), Lysenko (1978 [1874]), Nazina (1989, e.g., pp. 203–5, no. 143, "Prytcha pra bludnaha syna"), Slastion (1902), Speranskii (1904), and Tykhanov (1899).

10. Much of the literature from the nineteenth and early twentieth centuries on *kobzari* and *lirnky*, and virtually all of the literature from after 1930 is flawed regarding repertory. The pre-Soviet scholars were primarily seeking *dumy*, often to the exclusion of everything else. In the Soviet period, most scholars simply ignored the religious aspects of the minstrels' repertory. As a consequence, the repertory of the blind minstrels is widely but mistakenly thought to have consisted primarily of secular genres, either the epic *dumy* or dance music. The most comprehensive treatment of repertory in the pre-Soviet period is Speranskii 1904. A comprehensive study on repertory from the Soviet period is the fieldwork of Borys Luhovs'kyi (1926, 1993), most of which was undertaken between 1924 and 1926.

11. In 1993–1994 ten Ukrainian researchers and I conducted fieldwork interviews with more than four hundred elderly villagers in five regions of Ukraine, in a project made possible with funding from IREX (International Research and Exchanges Board), Special Projects Grant. Researchers used a questionnaire devised by project participants that focused on expressive culture of the 1920s and 1930s. Longer oral histories were taken down from some of the villagers.

12. I conducted fieldwork in several regions of Eastern Europe, particularly in Poland (1980–1983 and 1989) and Ukraine (1989–1996), with shorter research trips to Moldova, Slovakia, Belarus, and Russia. Research in Poland was made possible by the Wenner Gren Foundation for Anthropological Research, the University of Warsaw, the Polish Academy of Sciences, and the University of Washington. Research in Ukraine has been made possible by several organizations, including IREX (International Research and Exchanges Board) in 1989–1990, with funds provided by the National Endowment for the Humanities, the United States Information Agency, and the Academy of Sciences (Soviet, Ukrainian, and Moldovan), and in 1993–1994 by an IREX Special Projects Grant. From 1993 to 1996 research was supported in part by a Fulbright Fellowship. Shorter trips between 1990 and 1992 were funded by the Smithsonian Institution (Office of Folklife Programs), the Harvard Ukrainian Studies Fund, the Harvard Ukrainian Research Institute, and the Ryl's'kyi Institute of Art, Folkloristics, and Ethnology of the Ukrainian Academy of Sciences *(Instytut Mystetstvoznavstva, Fol'klorystyky ta Etnolohiï im. Ryl's'koho)*. None of these organizations is responsible for the views expressed.

13. Much of the data I have about the music and music contexts of this period come from unpublished sources (manuscripts) held in archives as well as from interviews I conducted in Ukrainian villages among the elderly. The former includes Kharkiv (1929), *Materialy z istoriï* (1922, 1934?), *Lysty* (1926), and *Proiektyvnyi Plan* (1925). In addition, there are dozens of published sources from the period that inadvertently provide a vivid and eye-opening account of the phenomenal organizing prowess of the Soviet bureaucracy and its effects on the music of the village; a few of these are Anonymous (1938), Bilokopytov (1934), K-ii (1928), *Muzyku na front* (1931), Mykoliuk (1929), and Polotai (1940). See also Noll (1993b).

14. For a more detailed examination of the blind peasant minstrels and their repression during the Soviet period see Noll (1993b), which also provides bibliographic information with most sources in Ukrainian and Russian.

15. See, for example, Hrinchenko (1939), and Kharkiv (1937). For a brief description of this literature in English see Odarchenko (1962/1963:93–94).

16. Some of Kvitka's collected articles were published by Volodymyr Hoshovs'kyi in two volumes, in Russian, mostly translations from texts originally published in Ukrainian (Kvitka 1971/1973). Another two-volume set, edited by Andryi Ivanyts'kyi, consists mostly of texts not published in Kvitka's lifetime (Kvitka 1985/1986).

17. In these years of wholesale arrests, many were held for only a short time but were later arrested again, often with lethal consequences. See Kondufor (1992) which contains the biographies of many ethnographers and others involved in fieldwork who suffered this fate.

18. One of the most prominent ethnomusicologists of those repressed in Ukraine during the Brezhnev period was Leopold Iashchenko, whose book on multivoice singing in Ukraine (1962) is still the standard work on the subject. In the early 1970s he was fired from his job at the Ryl's'kyi Ethnographic Institute in Kyïv, and thereafter made a living through various jobs outside the academic world. He currently lives in Kyïv and directs a choir.

The Ethnomusicologist, Ethnographic Method, and the Transmission of Tradition

However else they may identify themselves and each other, fieldworker and subject are first and foremost human beings. It is this shared identity that makes fieldwork, with both its problems and its accomplishments, a meaningful mode of mutual learning.

Georges and Jones, *People Studying People* (1980:3)

Most ethnomusicological discussions of the transmission of tradition attempt to document and interpret the manner in which music is communicated over time within a particular setting, giving attention to both the interpersonal dynamics and communication technologies of these processes.[1] However, I will focus my inquiry neither on the native carriers of tradition nor on the materials these traditions convey. Rather, I propose to take a reflexive turn and to discuss the role of the ethnomusicologist who, while seeking to document the transmission process, becomes a part of it.[2]

I will approach this subject by drawing on instances from my own field experiences and those recounted by colleagues in the literature. I wish to move discussion beyond an appreciation of the impact of "relational knowledge" (Rosaldo 1993 [1989]:206–8)[3] on ethnographic interpretation and writing to explore more deeply a type of reciprocity and grounded action that is a surprisingly frequent outgrowth of the ethnomusicological research progress. I will suggest that an idiosyncratic theoretical stance and working methodology give rise to this outgrowth of ethnomusicological research and that it likely has its roots in the close but conflicted relationship of ethnomusicology with other disciplines.

It is necessary to sketch a brief disciplinary perspective, to which I will return again later in this essay. In terms of its intellectual history and the training of its researchers, ethnomusicology has been shaped by the often contradictory worlds of historical musicology and anthropology. For the historical musicologist, the transmission of tradition is such an implicit aspect of her activity that it has largely escaped critical scrutiny. Any card-carrying historical musicologist would readily acknowledge that she is implicated in the continuation of the tradition studied. From its inception in 1885 as one part of the larger field of musical scholarship within which comparative musicology was subsumed, historical musicology has had as an important adjunct to its scholarly mission the (re)discovery, interpretation, and perpetuation of musics of the Euro-American art music tradition. Indeed, the American Musicological Society each year presents the Noah Greenberg award "to stimulate active cooperation between scholars and performers by recognizing and fostering outstanding contributions to historically aware performance and to the study of historical performing practices" (*American Musicological Society Directory* 1993:7). The annual conferences of the society feature special recitals and concerts of compositions not otherwise widely heard and performed.[4] Thus, musical manuscripts surviving only in scattered archives have been unearthed, reconstructed, edited, and performed by historical musicologists as a matter of course. To quote Joseph Kerman's appraisal of musical scholarship in *Contemplating Music*, "any scholarly edition of music is an invitation to a performer, and musicologists have been known to press such invitations quite hard, lobbying, consulting, and masterminding . . . concerts when they are given a chance" (1985:185).

Indeed, the central polemic among historical musicologists vis-à-vis the act of performance and their own role in transmitting (and even reinventing) tradition seems to center largely around issues of authenticity versus creativity in the act of musical reconstruction and performance practice.[5] Musicologists do not generally question whether they *should* be active in the process of transmitting musical tradition; rather they simply debate *how* closely they should adhere to historical precedent and in what manner the questions arising from lacunae in their sources can or should be answered. Most ethnomusicologists have been trained as undergraduates in music departments operating under the system just described, the same venue in which the vast majority of ethnomusicology professors eventually find their institutional homes.

This long-standing interaction between scholarly documentation and the act of performance has had its influence on ethnomusicological theory, most notably in the notion of "bi-musicality" advanced by Mantle Hood. The founder of the first major ethnomusicology program at UCLA, Hood felt that "the training of ears, eyes, hands and voice and fluency gained in these skills assure a real comprehension of theoretical studies" (Hood 1960:55). Hood was secondarily concerned that training and performance in Western music constrained ethnomusicologists studying other traditions. Hood did not just write about the importance of becoming bi-musical (or multimusical) and gaining cross-cultural musical experience through performance. He established an ethnomusicology curriculum including native performers, who were brought to UCLA to instruct students in a range of musical traditions. Early Hood students went on to found other programs at Wesleyan, Michigan, Seattle, and elsewhere. Becoming bi-musical became an increasingly common norm among ethnomusicologists, who capitalized on their bi-musicality by carrying out truly participatory participant-observation in the field.

In contrast, raising the possibility of the involvement of the anthropologist in the transmission of tradition evokes a response quite opposite from that in historical musicology. Anthropologists have also generally not addressed this issue explicitly; only the most recent revision of the American Anthropological Association Principles of Professional Responsibility (1990) strengthens and personalizes the statement of responsibility to the "people whose lives and cultures anthropologists study," mentioning for the first time the possibility of both the "positive and negative consequences of [the anthropologists'] activities and the publications resulting from these activities" (Fluehr-Lobban 1991:274–275).[6] Indeed, although the record shows that anthropologically trained ethnomusicologists have also actively participated in musical performance in the field, they have done so most often to ensure reciprocity and/or to test their understanding of musical data they have gathered. To cite an example from an ethnomusicological study carried out by a scholar trained primarily in anthropology, Steven Feld allowed himself to be represented as a "song man" within his own culture to the Kaluli (for whom he played recordings of Charlie Parker) (Feld 1990(1982):11). Feld also composed and performed Kaluli songs for his research associates to test hypotheses about "constraints upon form" (p. 13).

Yet even anthropologically trained ethnomusicologists have been influenced by Hood's maxim. In a study advocating a "musical anthropology," Anthony Seeger moves somewhat beyond Feld in incorporating musical performance for heuristic purposes. Seeger dedicates his book *Why Suyá Sing* (1987b) "in memory of the songs we sang," and describes in some detail the folk music styles ranging from bluegrass to African songs that he and Judy Seeger taught to the Suyá. In some cases, Seeger acknowledges that he altered folksongs learned from his uncle, Pete Seeger, "to fit a pattern easily recognizable to the Suyá" (Seeger 1987b:20). In honoring a request by the Suyá that he collaborate in publishing a recording of their music (pp. 23–24),[7] Seeger's activities in fact come very close to the sort of ethnomusicological participation in the transmission of tradition I seek to examine here.

Thus, ethnomusicological activity in the transmission of tradition appears to draw on musicological commitments to the preservation of musical tradition wedded to anthropological concerns regarding reciprocity and social responsibility. Apart from the disciplinary implications and the insight they provide into the values of different fields of study, discussion of the role of the fieldworker in the transmission of tradition lays bare an aspect of the intensely human nature of fieldwork and raises at the same time slippery issues in the ethics of ethnographic research that have been little discussed.[8] Most discussions of ethics have tended to focus on interpersonal relations both during and after fieldwork, and only incidentally to address the impact on the musical tradition itself.

Ethnography and Transmission

My concern with this subject did not emerge initially on a theoretical level. Rather, an experience in the field several years ago pushed me toward a new set of considerations concerning the role of the ethnomusicologist. Let me describe in some detail the ethnographic event, and its broader context, that served to throw this consideration into relief.

For nearly a decade I have been doing fieldwork with Jews of Syrian descent who live in Brooklyn, New York. The project began as a team effort with my New York University graduate students and the Syrian community (detailed in Shelemay (1988)). I have continued research on my own since concluding the team project in 1986 and expanded its boundaries to incorporate multilocale fieldwork among Syrian Jews in Mexico and Israel.

Some background is needed to frame the following discussion. Some seventy years after their migration from Aleppo to the New World, a community of more than 30,000 Syrian Jews in the New York metropolitan area sustains a strong Judaeo-Arabic identity expressed, in part, through many aspects of musical performance. The central musical repertory is a corpus of paraliturgical hymns called *pizmonim* (sing. *pizmon*), which have newly composed Hebrew texts set to borrowed Arabic melodies. The *pizmon* tunes are adopted from popular songs in the Arabic musical tradition, whereas the Hebrew texts contain biblical and liturgical allusions, as well as veiled references to individual members of the community for whom the songs are composed and to whom they are dedicated. The multivocality of the songs and the memories sustained in separate channels of text and tune provide wonderful material for social and historical analysis, but that is not our subject here. The focus of the original research project on the *pizmonim* emerged directly from suggestions of knowledgeable Syrian community members who wanted to record as many of the 500 extant songs as possible. The initial team research project recorded performances of nearly two hundred *pizmonim*, and deposited copies of all in a community archive, which members of the research team also helped catalogue and organize.

The event that highlighted issues concerning transmission took place in the Syrian community on March 14, 1990, and was mounted to honor Meyer "Mickey" Kairey, a man then in his late sixties who for many years has been a mainstay in the Syrian community's religious life. One of Mickey Kairey's most notable activities has been the teaching of *pizmonim* to Syrian young people. Mickey Kairey played an important role as one of the chief research associates for the *pizmon* project and on many occasions shared his expertise.[9]

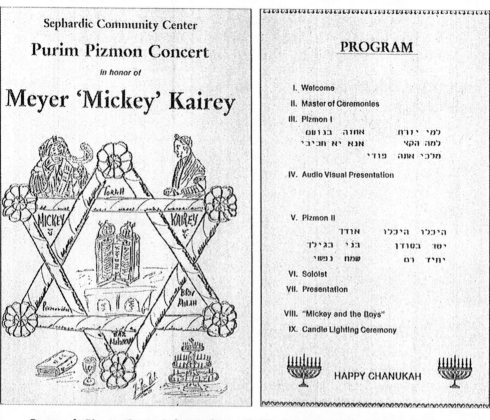

Program for Pizmon *Concert in honor of Meyer "Mickey" Kairey. March 14, 1990, Sephardic Community Center, Brooklyn, New York.*

The concert, attended by an overflow crowd of approximately 350 people, was held at the Sephardic Community Center in Brooklyn, the institutional center of the Syrian Jewish community. The program[10] included two different "sets" of *pizmonim* sung by a choir of young boys accompanied by an ensemble of Middle Eastern instruments; a third group of solo songs was performed by Isaac Cabasso, Mickey's uncle and himself a beloved lay cantor. The climax of the evening was the presentation of an oversized framed certificate to Mickey containing the signatures of some 1000 of his students trained between 1955 and 1990. See page 195 for an example of congratulations placed in a dedication book produced by families grateful for Mickey Kairey's role in transmitting *pizmonim*.

Midway through the program, there was an audiovisual presentation about Mickey's life and work. Slides traced Mickey's career, including pictures of his synagogue and of his *pizmon* teacher and mentor, Eliyahu Menaged. There were images of his family, photos from his years of military service during World War II, and innumerable references to his love of music of all kinds, including Stan Kenton and the Big Bands of the 1940s. Slides showing Mickey training young boys for their Bar Mitzvahs were accompanied by commentary and recordings made by students of these lessons. Suddenly, I heard on the recording my own voice asking Mickey a question about a *pizmon;* it had obviously been taken from the tape of a session we had held some five years earlier when Mickey taught *pizmonim* to me and my students. Although the concert overtly celebrated the role of the individual in the transmission of tradition, in this case Mickey Kairey's enormous contribution, I had not realized that I was a part of Mickey's experience just as he was part of mine. The ethnomusicologist had been folded into the experience of Mickey and his community, one very small link in the chain of transmission leading from their past to the future.[11]

If I had any doubts that the ethnomusicological presence had become a factor in the transmission of tradition, they were resolved quite coincidentally during an interview that took place shortly after the concert. The young Syrian cantor with whom I spoke discussed the revival of *pizmon* singing he believed to be present among young people in the Syrian community. He further suggested that a catalyst for the revival was events like the concert the prior evening, a performance genre that had emerged in the wake of the team project (personal communication, B. Zalta, 16 March 1991).

Clearly, the Syrian music project had left more of a trace than recordings of music and oral histories in an archive. Six years after its inception, it had been absorbed into the fabric of both community activity and individual memory. At this intersection of life and scholarship converge formal, institutional relationships, such as that established between the Sephardic Community Center and New York University in terms of copyright and royalty agreements for the record we coproduced (Shelemay and Weiss 1985) and a complex network of close individual friendships between me, several of my students, and some two dozen individuals within the Syrian-Jewish community.

Reviewing my journal, project correspondence, and other residue of our long association, I found other instances of my own activity that directly touched on the processes, personnel, and politics of transmission. Let me briefly set forth a few examples.

In June 1986, I was asked to write to the United States Immigration Service on behalf of a visiting cantor from Israel whom the largest Syrian synagogue in Brooklyn wished to retain on a permanent basis. Here I invoked my authority as a professor and used my knowledge of the tradition to aid the community in a matter of great importance to them. In fact, as an ethnomusicologist, I was actually quite concerned about this turn of events, since the distinctive Aleppo musical tradition sustained in Brooklyn was under pressure and undergoing a significant amount of

IN HONOR OF

OUR BELOVED PIZMONIM TEACHER

MEYER "MICKEY" KAIREY

The Graduating Class

of 1970

Magen David Yeshivah

שי"ר ושובה הל"ז ורחמו

DEAR MICKEY,

Just wanted to thank you for teaching us Ta'amim and Pizmonim, and for preparing us for our Bar-Mitzvahs. We sing the Pizmonim every Shabbat, and now our children are beginning to pick up the tunes.

You should be very proud that our great traditions are being carried out throughout the community due to your tireless efforts.

Sincerely,

Jack and Bert Hidary

Tributes from Dedication Booklet for Meyer "Mickey" Kairey distributed March 14, 1990, Sephardic Community Center.

change precisely because of the influx of talented Israeli-born cantors who carried different streams of Sephardic tradition. In my letter, I purposely omitted this information and consciously played a role directly affecting transmission in a direction about which I was personally ambivalent but that the community desired.

In 1987, I was asked by a leader of the community to give him information that would help defuse a growing concern among local rabbis that so many of the melodies used in Syrian *pizmonim* are of secular and/or even of Christian or Islamic origin. Specifically at issue was the *pizmon* "Mifalot Elohim," which borrows the melody of the well-known Christmas carol "Oh Tannenbaum." It is almost certain that rabbinical skepticism about the broader issue was provoked in part by the publication of our recording two years earlier and the subsequent high profile of our collaboration in what had become known as "the Syrian music project." In response to this request, I wrote a letter giving my associate information on several controversial, borrowed melodies, and provided a rationale that could be used in justifying the tradition:

I do not think the original sources of these melodies should be of any concern to you or the community. There is a longstanding tradition in Jewish music (both sacred and secular) of borrowing melodies from the surrounding society. This tradition is as widespread in Ashkenazic circles as in your own pizmon tradition, only the sources of the melodies differ because of the different geographical settings. Music is always part of the surrounding cultural milieu and I know of no tradition that is "pure" and does not borrow a variety of things with which it is in contact. The very nature of musical expression is that it is transmitted from person to person across geographic, social, and cultural boundaries. (Kay K. Shelemay, letter of June 9, 1987 to a member of the Syrian community)

In this case, then, I explained the transmission process in order to justify, and ultimately, to preserve it.

The publication of the record *Pizmon*, which included a selection of *pizmonim* taken from recordings made during the first year of our joint project, had other unanticipated outcomes as well.[12] The record was chosen by the American Folklife Center for its Selected List (American Folk Music and Folklore Recordings: A Selected List 1985), and it also won a prize from the national association of Jewish community centers. Both awards were a source of shared pride for everyone involved. However, the publication of the record, and the "first annual *pizmon* concert" around the same time in 1985, raised perceptions outside the community that the Syrian men who had come together for music sessions comprised a group.[13]

My interaction with these individuals outside formal recording and interview sessions increased as we began to get invitations from area cultural institutions and universities: Generally, the Syrian men were asked to perform and I was asked to give a lecture or long introduction that explained the music to be sung. The men with whom I worked were quite comfortable with this arrangement despite the obvious asymmetries; indeed, they had invited me to speak at the first *pizmon* concert and suggested to the sponsor that I participate when they received the first invitation to perform outside the community.

I now realize that this was only the beginning of my increasingly active role in the transmission process, one that paralleled the deepening friendships between myself and several individuals in the community. A pivotal event took place on November 15, 1987, when we were invited to perform a combined lecture/concert at a community center on the Lower East Side of Manhattan. As I led off the session with a talk explaining the Syrian musical tradition, the elderly audience comprised largely of Jewish immigrants of Eastern European descent got very restless. Every time I mentioned the connection of the Syrian-Jewish tradition to Arabic music and used the word "Arabic," members of the audience hissed.[14] After several such incidents, Moses Tawil, the nominal leader of the Syrian men who were to sing *pizmonim*, stood up from where he sat behind me on stage and joined me at the microphone: "We are businessmen and we don't have to be here," he said emphatically. "We are interested what Professor Kay has to say and want to hear it. Please be quiet."

I can't say that Tawil's admonition improved the audience's deportment—I still consider this talk the worst single public lecture experience I have ever had—but it was an enormously important moment of warmth and bonding between myself and the Syrian men present. From that moment forward, I received invitations to family events, Bar Mitzvahs, wedding anniversaries, and holiday celebrations. And the closer we became, the more I was called on to play a role in perpetuating the tradition.

Therefore, I would like to argue that as ethnomusicologists become engaged in research with living musical traditions and the people who carry them, they both intentionally and unwittingly become caught up in the processes and politics of transmission of tradition. Sometimes their interventions support continuity; at other times they engender change. I believe that these interactions are not conceptualized as formal, scholarly acts, but are carried out relatively unconsciously on a much more personal level as the study of tradition shifts almost imperceptibly to occupy a relational space situated between scholarship and life. As relationships "in the field" mature from the initial formality of scholar/informant (if indeed there is the luxury of ample time and access) to more collegial and personal ones, the fieldworker inevitably moves beyond the management of cultural capital into the negotiation of human relations in the field.

Transmission and Tradition

As I began to reconsider what in retrospect appears to be my surprisingly active role in the transmission processes within the Syrian community, I reviewed my other past fieldwork projects—multiple urban and rural research projects in Ethiopia, a combined archival/ethnographic experience at an American synagogue in Houston, a notably unsuccessful six month experience with a new music group in New York City—and looked for similar patterns. Indeed, they were there and I can only conclude that such patterns are much more prevalent than ethnomusicologists generally acknowledge. In what follows I would like to identify and briefly discuss three ways in which the fieldworker is most frequently implicated in the process of transmission: preserving tradition, memorializing tradition, and mediating tradition. No doubt there are more, and any one ethnographic experience might give rise to varying combinations of the three at one time. As part of the process of definition, I'll set forth some brief examples from my own experience and those gleaned from the ethnomusicological literature. Almost without exception, these situations inevitably arise at the point of intersection of life and scholarship—they begin at moments when the study of a tradition becomes part of the life of the tradition itself and relationships in the field deepen to a more interactional model.

Preserving Tradition

If any aspect of the ethnomusicologist's entry into the transmission process is generally acknowledged, it is the presumption that ethnomusicological activity works on one level to preserve. Although the ethic of preservation was long an unquestioned part of the ethnographic process, and older paradigms led earlier scholars to seek out and study certain traditions since they would otherwise "be lost," it seems clear that the very process of studying any musical tradition is tantamount to participating in an act of preservation.

Frequently the role of the ethnomusicologist as preserver of tradition is acknowledged or even desired by people within the tradition itself. To take but one example from the literature, Barbara Smith recounts how she learned bon-dance drumming among Japanese immigrants in Hawaii, became a member of a club, and "beat the drum" at bon dances one summer (1987:211). A few days after the second bon dance at which she performed, she was told that a member of the community had commented: "Now it is safe for us to die, because if Professor Smith is drumming there will always be someone to drum for our souls" (p. 211). Smith goes on to relate that her drumming encouraged some young people to learn to play and that there has not been a shortage of drummers since!

There are most certainly instances where the ostensible "informant" charges the "ethnomusicologist" with the responsibility of transmitting tradition. A graphic example occurred in my own work in northern Ethiopia among the Beta Israel (Falasha). One day, an elderly Beta Israel priest looked at me solemnly and said: "In twenty-five years, only you will know our prayers" (Shelemay 1989:xviii). He was both acknowledging a reality of the transmission process within his own community and making me aware of my responsibility to preserve his tradition.

It strikes me that preservation is therefore not just an outgrowth of now dated scholarly paradigms, but at least in some circumstances, both an acknowledgment of the realities of a musical change and part of an implicit contract between the ethnomusicologist and the tradition's native carriers. This contract may be particularly crucial in the case of "insider" research, when the scholar shares wholly or in part the identity she studies.

The bon-dance drumming example cited earlier also highlights a type of preservation I have not personally experienced,[15] but that is most common in the field at large. Although all ethnomusicologists transmit speeched knowledge and recorded music, many further transmit musical tradition through re-creating the act of performance itself. In this manner, the performative nature of the ethnomusicologist's unit of study lends itself to replication, both before and after the ethnographic research period. Many ethnomusicologists today teach the music they learned in the field. Although one may question this activity as an act of appropriation, I believe that it is not generally regarded as such by the native carriers of the tradition or by the ethnomusicologist. Rather, it can be viewed as part of the very human process of passing on a world of expression that is inordinately private. How can one read John Miller Chernoff's description of his acquisition of Ghanaian drumming techniques (Chernoff 1979) and not acknowledge that he, like his teacher, sustains this music as "a bodily memory?" (Connerton 1989).[16] Theories such as Mantle Hood's "bi-musicality" allow for much more than an entry into musical learning; they implicitly move the ethnomusicologist toward the preservation, replication, and active transmission of tradition.[17]

Memorializing Tradition

Although we tend to conceptualize transmission in terms that are communal and social, in fact the workings of the process are intensely personal and idiosyncratic, the source of the tradition being a teacher (the informant, or more appropriately, the research associate), the receiver a student (the ethnomusicologist). The tendency of ethnomusicology to extrapolate from the individual to the group combined with longtime anthropological traditions supporting anonymity for subjects of research, has resulted in fewer traces of memorializing in our literature. But there are examples. Bruno Nettl has written an ode to his favorite teachers (1984) in which he discusses and memorializes the men who once would have been called his informants.[18] Likewise, the autobiography of Frank Mitchell, *Navajo Blessingway Singer*, was in part "a realization of Frank's wish that a book on his life would live after him" as well as a sense of "family unity" growing out of his long years of collaboration with the editors (Mitchell 1978:5). Frisbie and McAllester acknowledge that their relationship with Frank Mitchell was an intensely human one that progressed from an initial development of rapport, through work on various projects, to a lifelong friendship with mutual obligations and responsibilities (p. 5). That this book is dedicated to the memory of Frank Mitchell is not coincidental.

Mediating Tradition

Navajo Blessingway Singer also leads us into a third mode of transmission—mediation. In addition to memorializing Frank Mitchell, Frisbie and McAllester mediate between him and the wider world: "Frank, of course, is the author of *Navajo Blessingway Singer*. Our job has been to collect the data, edit the narration and, with the assistance of able interpreters, put it into English" (Mitchell 1978:8). In one sense, every time a scholar quotes or paraphrases an interview or conversation, he mediates tradition. Some researchers have in fact referred to themselves as mediators. Alan Lomax doesn't consider himself a "reviver so much as a stander-in-between," perceiving an important part of his responsibility to "find the best folk singers . . . and get them heard everywhere" (cited in Sheehy 1992:329). Beth Lomax Hawes put it even more strongly in comments made at a 1981 Folk Arts Panel meeting: "That's right, we're meddlers!" (Titon 1992:316).

Mediation takes many forms and may not be restricted to an intermediary zone between the community and outsiders. In addition to "mediating" for my Syrian research associates, giving talks to introduce their performances to audiences unfamiliar with the *pizmon* repertory, I also was asked to assume this role within the community. At a gathering of the extended Tawil clan and several hundred other Syrian families in a Catskill mountain resort one Passover in the late 1980s, Moses Tawil arranged for me to give a public lecture on the Syrian-Jewish musical tradition; the majority of the audience at my talk were Syrian Jews. Mediation can therefore entail not just translating for those outside of the tradition, but also participating in raising awareness of the tradition within the community itself.[19]

I suggest then, that many (if not all) ethnomusicologists preserve, memorialize, and mediate traditions on a fairly regular basis, in large part because of what I would term the "bracketed performativeness" of the materials they study. Both in the field and afterward, this is emphatically not a theoretical issue. One learns music by doing and remembers by repeating, whether through live performance or sound recordings. Ethnomusicological data in the musical domain are replicable in a way in which other types of ethnographic data are emphatically not. I would propose, therefore, that the involvement of the ethnomusicologist in the transmission of tradition is an old and deep aspect of the ethnomusicological research process, emerging in large part from the nature of its data.

From a disciplinary perspective, here we encounter head-on the ethnomusicologist's bifurcated identity, which draws at once on musicological commitments to performance and anthropological tenets of noninterference. The tension between these approaches has surfaced intermittently in the literature, moving one past leader of the field to write that the ethnomusicologist "does not seek the aesthetic experience for himself as a primary goal (though this may be a personal by-product of his studies), but rather he seeks to perceive the meaning of the aesthetic experience of others from the standpoint of understanding human behavior" (Merriam 1964:25). Only in more recent ethnomusicological writing are there explicit acknowledgments of the shared involvement that emerges in the field. In the words of one ethnographer:

> There is no substitute in ethnomusicological fieldwork for intimacy born of shared musical experiences. Learning to sing, dance, play in the field is good fun and good method. Being an appreciative audience is an especially important form of musical exchange. Savour the joy of being a student again; establishing a close relationship with a master musician is a common and successful approach in ethnomusicology (Myers 1992:31).

But if "play" in the field is to be based on good methods, then ethnomusicologists require guidelines for a situation rife with ethical and practical problems. Moving to a more prescriptive mode, it would seem that ethnomusicologists and others who become implicated in the transmission process could well consider the following points:

- If we are bound explicitly or implicitly to preserve what people have taught us, we must document it carefully and deposit it faithfully in archives.
- Our work should be timely, to permit both dialogue with the living and meaningful memorial of the dead.
- We should honor confidence and protect it when necessary, but be equally ready to acknowledge and celebrate individual expertise and artistry when they are freely and openly given.
- We should share the fruits of our labors, whether by repatriating tapes, providing materials for use within the community and/or by individuals within it, or through sharing financial rewards such as royalties.
- If fieldwork is to be a truly humanistic pursuit, we must erase what has been termed "the mistaken dichotomy," the false divide thought to separate academic research from public sector work. We must accept responsibility not just for the impact of our entry into the field, but for our abiding relationship to it and our teachers long after we have "left" (i.e., discontinued research).
- If we are to be truly coeval in time with the men and women who are our teachers (Fabian 1983), we must engage in collaborative processes. Collaboration in turn helps to reduce power assymetries and assures greater congruency between ethnographic goals and the sensitivities of individuals and communities.
- We must acknowledge more openly that in many situations, the entering scholar may at times be perceived to be an authority and to possess a degree of power that will inevitably be invoked in the pursuit of real life. We are obligated to use our knowledge and power, should they be conceived as such, in the best interests of the people with whom we work.
- Occasionally, we will encounter situations in which our goals are not those of the community or in which we are entrusted with materials that we are explicitly charged with keeping secret. In these rare instances, our best course is silence or withdrawal. We need to preserve a place in the oral tradition of pedagogy where we can discuss the unsuccessful and the discarded.

Ultimately, the acknowledgment of fieldwork as a problem in human relations offers a pathway through the thicket of issues surrounding the ethnographic process and the potentially intrusive role of the fieldworker. This seems to be congruent with a trend in both ethnomusicology and anthropology to develop a practice-informed theory (Titon 1992).

Most of us are well aware that we do not study a disembodied concept called "culture" or a place called the "field," but rather encounter a stream of individuals to whom we are subsequently linked in new ways. Given the increasing interest in what Arjun Appadurai has called "deterritorialization," I would suggest that human relations may be the most promising residue of a field once conceptualized as local, stable, and bounded (Appadurai 1991:192). We can begin by teaching and practicing an ethnography that acknowledges a reality of sharing and interaction, one predicated on negotiated relationships.

Notes

1. In one sense, the "transmission of tradition" is a tautology, since the etymology of the word, from the Latin *traditum*, refers to anything that is transmitted or handed down from the past to the present (Shils 1981:12). By "musical transmission" I refer to any communication of musical materials from one person to another, whether in oral, aural, or written forms, without regard to the time depth of the materials transmitted. For the sake of discussion here, I will focus primarily on the role of live musical performance in this process, and secondarily on musical materials mediated and conveyed by technologies such as the LP, cassette, or compact disc.

2. This chapter, written during a 1992–1993 fellowship year funded by the National Endowment for the Humanities, is an expansion of an article published under the title "The Ethnomusicologist and the Transmission of Tradition," *The Journal of Musicology* 14(1):35–51, 1996. The initial version of this paper, titled "Intersections of Life and Scholarship: Human Relations in the Field," was delivered at Brown University in 1992. I thank Gregory Barz and Timothy Cooley for both the invitation to Brown and their subsequent comments on the resulting chapter.

3. Rosaldo has suggested that "relational knowledge," which constitutes a shared expressive form on the "borderland" between ethnographer and "subject," "should be regarded not as analytically empty transitional zones but as sites of creative cultural production that require investigation" (Rosaldo 1993[1989]:208).

4. Even such prosaic forums as business meetings can celebrate the reentry of a composition into the repertory. The 1993 annual meeting of the AMS featured the first performance of a recently edited and published chamber work by Ruth Crawford [Seeger] (Tick 1993). Editor Judith Tick describes herself as a type of musicological midwife in the rebirth of this composition, which she was thrilled "to send out into the world" (Tick, personal communication).

5. For a rare and explicit critique of the search for authenticity in musicologically inspired performance, see Richard Taruskin (1982). Taruskin comes close to acknowledging the role of the musicologist in the transmission of tradition, in his comments on a story credited to Dmitri Shostakovich: "What's a musicologist? I'll tell you. Our cook, Pasha, prepared the scrambled eggs for us and we are eating them. Now imagine a person who did not cook the eggs and does not eat them, but talks about them—that is a musicologist. Well, we're eating them now, and even cook up a few on occasions, as when we do a little discreet composing to make a fragmentary piece performable . . ." (Taruskin 1982:349). That discourse about authenticity in editions intended for performance is still a very lively issue can be seen in Frederick Neumann's article, "Improper Appoggiaturas in the Neue Mozart Ausgabe" (1992).

6. Ethical guidelines or codes of ethics adopted by various American anthropological societies since 1949 are printed together for the first time in Fluehr-Lobban 1991:237–69.

7. *A Arte Vocal dos Suyá* (1982) jointly published by Seeger and the "Suyá community."

8. Mark Slobin has pointed out that ethical issues were not discussed at all in the eth-

nomusicological literature until the 1970s, and that ethical awareness in the field remains in an "embryonic state" (Slobin 1992a:331). Slobin's discussion, however, does not move beyond "the bounds of problems raised by the earlier modes of inquiry" (p. 332).

9. I also worked closely with and interviewed his brother, Hyman Kaire (the two brothers spell their name differently), and late sister, Sophie Cohen.

10. The cover of the program booklet contains symbols of Mickey Kairey's active musical role in liturgical and life cycle events. Alert readers will note that the table of contents contains the inscription "Happy Chanukah" at the bottom. The concert, originally planned to coincide with the Chanukah holiday in December was postponed to the March Purim observance due to a family emergency.

11. The individual who had prepared the commentary accompanying the slide show later told me that she had originally included my own singing of a *pizmon* on the tape, just like those of the young boys Mickey trained, but later deleted the excerpt in fear that it would offend more traditional members of the community who adhered to religious prohibitions concerning the hearing of a woman's voice.

12. This in contrast to its planning and execution, which were quite straightforward and largely without complications. All the performers signed consent forms, and the royalties (of which in the end there were none!) were to be divided between the Sephardic Archive and New York University. Assignment of royalties to the performers was not an issue; they were for the most part affluent musical amateurs for whom the receipt of money would have been highly unacceptable.

13. This is a surprisingly common phenomenon, the development of what has been termed new "performance frames" growing out of the impact of ethnomusicological fieldwork. See Sheehy (1992:332). Also, see Dyen (1982), for a detailed case study of this phenomenon in the sacred harp tradition.

14. The Arabic musical tradition is generally unfamiliar to Jews outside of the Middle East and, for some, including members of that particular audience, evidently carries negative associations stemming from the ongoing Arab-Israeli conflict. This contrasts markedly with the great pride in and nuanced understanding that many Syrian Jews have of Arabic music.

15. Largely because I've been a woman studying esoteric male musical traditions, whether in Ethiopia or Brooklyn, my own opportunities for performance in the field have necessarily been limited.

16. See Chernoff's account (1979:104) of studying drumming with Alhaji Ibrahim Abdulai, who remarked that "teaching with the hand is more than teaching with the mouth."

17. Long before the notion of bi-musicality spurred performance by ethnomusicologists and sparked revival, fieldworkers had actively intervened in the transmission of tradition. A notable example is that of John Lomax, whose studies of cowboy songs and frontier ballads (1910) "aimed to feed back song lore into the stream of oral tradition" (cited by Sheehy 1992:326).

18. I would note that the most striking examples of preserving, memorializing, and mediating tradition have been recounted initially in the oral tradition of the field, i.e., in lectures only later published. This is true of Nettl (1984) and Smith (1987), both of which were first presented as Charles Seeger Lectures at annual meetings of the Society for Ethnomusicology.

19. Repeated mediation of these different types also led to one of the most interesting acts of exchange in my academic career. In April 1991, Moses Tawil was invited to speak at

the meeting of the Coalition for the Advancement of Jewish Education. He telephoned to ask if he could borrow a copy of my Passover Catskill lecture along with the accompanying tape of musical examples to use for his talk; he reassured me that he would credit me at the beginning of the presentation. I sent him the materials he requested; he reported that the talk went well.

Chasing Shadows in the Field

An Epilogue

[One] who approaches the world with faded similes and borrowed metaphors is a
jaded epigon or dilettante. . . . No matter how acute an insight may be, nor how
faithful a reproduction, nor how impressive a portrayal; though it may even arouse
our admiration for its author's gift of observation, it is still far from being a poetic
vision. The perfect statement of a fact, the fashioned material itself, evokes no meaning. It is only the *vision* of a fact which unveils its meaning and lets us divine it.

Franz Werfel, *Between Heaven and Earth* (1944):39–40

Experiencing and Representing Shadows

The goal of the year-long colloquium series sponsored by the graduate program in
ethnomusicology at Brown University from which the majority of these essays
emerged was to shift the focus of recent writing, research, and teaching in the discipline of ethnomusicology away from issues of representation toward matters of
experience. The essays in *Shadows in the Field* suggest that a major paradigm shift
in ethnomusicological thought has occurred, embracing a "new fieldwork," as
Titon suggests, that focuses more on the "doing" and "knowing" of fieldwork than
on the representing of fieldwork. Each author in this volume identifies a need to
enter into a dialogue with historical colleagues—both in and out of the field—but
they all nevertheless respond to a call to acknowledge their individual being-ness in
contemporary fieldwork. Ultimately, what ethnomusicologists do in the field is not
totally separable from what they do out of the field, yet much of the focus in ethnomusicological writing and teaching until now has centered around analyses and
ethnographic representations of musical cultures instead of on the rather personal
world of the understanding, experience, knowing, and doing of fieldwork.

The contributors to this volume present themselves as doers of fieldwork, con-
curring that it now dominates the paradigm of contemporary ethnomusicology, yet,

for each author, the issues concerning what to "do" with experiences after leaving the field are perhaps not as easily distinguished from what to "do" in the field as they once were. This has led each author to question the boundaries he or she constructs around the place called "the field." Experiences reflect changes in language, and language reflects changes in experiences—just as knowing and interpretation are interdependent. As the substance, politics, methods, and theories of ethnomusicological field research have been recast, so have the expectations and responsibilities.

Field research is now a prescribed liminal state for ethnomusicologists, an anticipated, supported, and funded *rite de passage*. Field research, as Titon suggests in this volume, has become the primary act constituting contemporary ethnomusicology in the academy—defining both academic positions and publications. Rice concurs, proposing in his chapter that field research has become *sine qua non* for ethnomusicologists. Contemporary ethnomusicology can no longer deny the shadows they cast in the field, as ethnomusicologists advance distinct ways of experiencing, listening, performing, reading, writing, and shifting the discipline, as Titon proposes, toward an ontology focused more specifically on "being-in-the-world-musically."

As ethnomusicology, anthropology, and other social sciences confront one crisis of representation after another—jargon to some, provocative insight to others—the responsibilities for representing and interpreting musical performance are now shared by both author *and* reader. The border crossings between fieldworker and field-reader are permanently blurred. No longer the "harmless drudge," ethnomusicologists openly engage questions concerning cultural authority, representation, power, and agency (Nettl 1983:1). It is little wonder that the contemporary ethnomusicologist agonizes when putting pen to paper, doubts the validity of research agenda, questions all forms of authority and representation, and chases shadows in the field.

It is ironic, therefore, that in this volume we turn toward the act of ethnographic writing to give voice to our reflections on the changing philosophies of field research and to re-experience issues and concerns "of the field." If there was an adequate or acceptable way of "music-ing" or performing our ethnography within this volume I am sure that many authors included here would embrace it. Yet, the very act of giving language to field research might be a way of integrating the experiences both "in" and "out" of the field, either while still in the field or relying on research from fieldwork of quite some time ago (see Barz in this volume).

Chasing Shadows

What do we see when we acknowledge the shadows we cast in the field? What do we hear, smell, and taste? In their forward and backward glances, the authors in this volume explore the distinct roles they act out while performing and reconstructing field research. Will field research continue as an integral part of ethnomusicological theory or of its method? Or will distinct theories emerge that will dominate future ethnomusicological discourse? If so, where does field research of "the past" fit into these theories? What new directions is ethnomusicological field research taking?[1] What good can come of it all? Such questions are unique to the new fieldwork and have not yet been addressed in a significant way in any of the standard guides to ethnomusicological or anthropological field research theory and method. As they interact with contemporary and historical field research models, contemporary ethnomusicologists define individual ways of interacting, often improvising and inventing new methods and theories in the field.

A degree of separation between experience and representation has been a traditional feature of ethnographic field research in the social sciences. This assertion persists in many contemporary studies despite the recent "crisis of representation." The two quotations that follow demonstrate an historical and contemporary reassertion of the bifurcation of field research from ethnography, of experience from representation no longer embraced in the new fieldwork. The first selection below is from the field guide, *Notes and Queries on Anthropology*, first published in 1874:

> [The investigator] *must assume the attitude of a learner,* not of a teacher. . . . The music of every people, whether vocal or instrumental, has its own characteristics, and can be estimated rightly only on the *evidence* supplied by *accurate* records. *General impressions*—even those of a trained European musician—*are of little value unless the sounds and phrases which they describe can be reproduced.* Music may be recorded either in writing, or by means of the phonograph or other recording instrument. (Frake 1964[1874]:33 and 315, emphasis added)

This dictum indicates that one of the main objectives of the field researcher of musical performance is to document by means of "accurate records" before any observation can be of "value." The second quotation, similar in spirit to *Notes and Queries*, appears in the recently issued field manual compiled by the Society for Ethnomusicology (Post et al. 1994), in which the notion of documentation or writing as separable from ethnography or representation is reaffirmed:

> Respect your informants' beliefs and traditions. You may object to attitudes or behaviors on a personal level, but in your role as researcher, do not pass judgement. . . . Ethnomusicologists are part of a process whereby musical traditions all over the world are recorded, documented, studied, written about, and made accessible to new audiences. . . . Effective documentation can make data valuable not only for the researcher returning from the field with a large body of information to organize, analyze, and interpret, but also for future generations of scholars. (Post et al. 1994:54, 5–6)

The Society for Ethnomusicology manual reiterates the prominent position of documentation in ethnomusicological field research; the manual asserts that field research relationships, human relationship are perhaps not authentic interactions in and of themselves. Along this line of thinking, "informants" give, and the "researchers" take—how could it really be otherwise given this posture? There is little room in this dialogue for the exchange of ideas, information, or traditions in the field; true mutuality is neither a primary goal nor is it encouraged. Both manuals present field research as it has been traditionally conceptualized—a means to an end with ethnography as the goal. Both manuals accept experience's legitimacy only as data; being musical-in-the-world becomes reduced to recorded, "accurate" documents, documents that can be studied in the laboratory.

The authors in *Shadows in the Field* address issues of documentation, but not as a field guide or manual for the next generation of field researchers; the essays offer few prescriptive recommendations concerning what to do while engaged in field research. Specifically avoided are questions one should ask in the field, specific methods to employ, definitions of what music is and what it is not, and identification of what musical facts are and are not. Rather, the authors engage in a forum, openly questioning the position of field researcher in the new fieldwork.

Shadows in the Field poses tough questions concerning who we are as field researchers in relation to the people with whom we work, live, study, and grow in the field. All the authors approach their experiences in the field as a way to confront questions concerning who they are as field researchers and what they signify to the people they work with (and to themselves). In addition, each author attempts to reach beyond traditional academic discourse to redefine the way we read, ultimately suggesting changes in representation that involve an acceptance of multiple truths, multiple epistemologies that would lead to a "creative diversification" of ethnographic writing that James Fernandez has called for (1993:180). Ethnography in this sense becomes an integral part of the translation of experience, an extension of the field performance, and ultimately a form of performative writing. For most field researchers the period of "translation" is frustrating, where nothing, including the self, is as it seems, and many are now beginning to realize that field research itself is just such a period of "translation."

Shadows in the Field does not present a complete story; the authors intentionally leave doors open, ideas unfinished, and research still in process. It is an important time for these essays to emerge—an experimental moment in contemporary ethnomusicology—as researchers and informants, scholars and friends, stand close enough to each other that the outlines of their shadows merge, blurring the definition of Self and Other in field research. The negotiation of individual and communal experience, the processes of forming relationships, the representation of musical ethnography—contemporary ethnomusicology is challenged in many unique ways, most importantly to listen, feel, question, understand, and represent in ways true to one's own experiences. *Shadows in the Field* contributes its voices to an ongoing conversation in which we allow, as Werfel suggests in the quotation opening this epilogue, the "visioning" of a musical fact to bring us closer to understanding and knowing what it means for ourselves and others to "be-in-the-world-musically."

We stand now at a critical moment in the field of ethnomusicology. The new fieldwork has become a reality for many field researchers, for both experienced and younger scholars, as we continue to listen and learn from those we engage with in field research. The new fieldwork resists musical sound as "text" (subjects of interpretation), and weaves experience and representation into the same fabric. Each of the ethnomusicologists in this volume issues a call for the integration of field research experience with the representation or communication of that experience. Each author acknowledges and approaches an understanding of the agency of the individual field researcher both in and out of the field, chasing whatever is hidden behind the shadows he or she casts in the field. It is to be hoped that the discipline of ethnomusicology will be encouraged to take these ideas, thoughts, and methodologies into classrooms, seminars, conversations with colleagues at home and in field research situations, and explore them in ethnographic writing.

Notes

1. This very question of the direction of field research in ethnomusicology is beginning to be taken up by, of all people, students in the discipline. A forum titled, "Fieldwork in Contemporary Ethnomusicology," was sponsored by the Student Concerns Committee of the Society for Ethnomusicology at their 1995 annual meeting in Los Angeles. Students are at the forefront of experimental change in the discipline of ethnomusicology, particularly in the focus on experience in the new fieldwork.

References

Abbreviations

IMFE   Instytut Mystetstvoznavstvo, Fol'klorystyky ta Ethnolohiï im. M.T. Ryl's'koho, Akademiia Nauk Ukraïny ("Ryl's'kyi Institute of Art, Folkloristics, and Ethnology, Ukrainian Academy of Sciences").

Abrahams, Roger D. 1970. "A Performance-Centered Approach to Gossip." *Man* 5:290–301.
American Folk Music and Folklore Recordings: A Selected List. 1995. Washington, DC: American Folklife Center, Library of Congress.
American Musicological Society Directory. 1993. Philadelphia: American Musicological Society.
Amiot, Jean Joseph Marie. 1779. *Mémoire sur la musique des chinois, tant anciens et modernes.* Paris: Nyon.
Anonymous. 1938. "Stalins'ka konstytutsiia i vybory do Verkhovnoï Rady URSR v narodnii tvorchosti." *Ukraïns'kyi fol'klor* 4:114–35.
Appadurai, Arjun. 1991. "Global Ethnoscapes: Notes and Queries for a Transnational Anthropology." In *Recapturing Anthropology: Working in the Present,* edited by Richard G. Fox. Santa Fe, NM: School of American Research Press.
Applebaum, Anne. 1994. *Between East and West: Across the Borderlands of Europe.* New York: Pantheon.
Asad, Talal, ed. 1973. *Anthropology and the Colonial Encounter.* London: Ithaca Press.
Atkinson, Paul. 1990. *The Ethnographic Imagination: Textual Constructions of Reality.* New York: Routledge.
Babiracki, Carol M. 1991. "Musical and Cultural Interaction in Tribal India: The *Karam* Repertory of the Muṇḍas of Choṭānāgpur." Ph.D. diss., University of Illinois at Urbana-Champaign. Ann Arbor: University Microfilms International.
Bahuchet, Serge. 1985. *Les Pygmés Aka et la Forêt Centrafricaine.* Paris: Selaf.
Bartók, Béla. 1976. *Béla Bartók: Essays.* Edited by Benjamin Suchoff. New York: St. Martin's Press.
Baselgia, Guido. 1993. *Galizien.* Frankfurt am Main: Jüdischer Verlag.

Bauman, Richard. 1975. "Verbal Art as Performance." *American Anthropologist* 77:290–311.

Baumgartner, Gerhard. 1988. *Geschichte der jüdischen Gemeinde zu Schlaining*. Stadtschlaining: Österreichisches Institut für Friedensforschung und Friedenserziehung.

Baumgartner, Gerhard, Eva Müllner, and Rainer Münz, eds. 1989. *Identität und Lebenswelt: Ethnische, religiöse und kulturelle Vielfalt im Burgenland*. Eisenstadt: Prugg.

Beaudry, Nicole. 1988. "Singing, Laughing and Playing: Three Examples from the Inuit, Dene and Yupik Traditions." *Canadian Journal of Native Studies* 8(2):275–90.

————. 1992. "The Language of Dreams: Songs of the Dene Indians (Canada)." *The World of Music* 34(2):72–90.

Becker, Judith, and Lorna McDaniel. 1991. "A Brief Note on Turtles, Claptrap, and Ethnomusicology," and "A Page on Turtle Relations." *Ethnomusicology* 35(3):393–98.

Béhague, Gerard, ed. 1984. *Performance Practice: Ethnomusicological Perspectives*. Westport, CT: Greenwood Press.

Bell, Diane, Pat Caplan, and Wazir Jahan Karim, eds. 1993. *Gendered Fields: Women, Men and Ethnography*. London: Routledge.

Berliner, Paul. 1993[1978]. *The Soul of Mbira: Music and Traditions of the Shona People of Zimbabwe*. 2nd ed. Chicago: University of Chicago Press.

Bezsonov, P. 1861–1864. *Kaleki perekhozhie. Sbornik stikhov i izsledovanie*. Moskva (six volumes).

Bhabha, Homi K. 1994. *The Location of Culture*. New York: Routledge.

Bilokopytov, O. O. 1934. "Vykryty i roztroshchyty do kintsia natsionalizm na muzychnomu fronti USRR." *Radians'ka muzyka* 1:18–44.

Blum, Stephen. 1975. "Towards a Social History of Musicological Technique." *Ethnomusicology* 19(2):207–31.

Blum, Stephen, Philip V. Bohlman, and Daniel M. Neuman, eds. 1991. *Ethnomusicology and Modern Music History*. Urbana: University of Illinois Press

Boas, Franz. 1936. "History and Science in Anthropology, a Reply." *American Anthropologist* 38:137–51.

Bohlman, Philip V. 1988a. "Missionaries, Magical Muses, and Magnificent Menageries: Image and Imagination in the Early History of Ethnomusicology." *The World of Music* 30(3):5–27.

————. 1988b. *The Study of Folk Music in the Modern World*. Bloomington: Indiana University Press.

————. 1988c. "Traditional Music and Cultural Identity: Persistent Paradigm in the History of Ethnomusicology." *Yearbook for Traditional Music* 20:26–42.

————. 1989a. *"The Land Where Two Streams Flow": Music in the German-Jewish Community of Israel*. Urbana: University of Illinois Press.

————. 1989b. "Die Volksmusik und die Verstädterung der deutsch-jüdischen Gemeinde in den Jahrzehnten vor dem Zweiten Weltkrieg." *Jahrbuch für Volksliedforschung* 34:25–40.

————. 1991. "Representation and Cultural Critique in the History of Ethnomusicology." In *Comparative Musicology and Anthropology of Music: Essays on the History of Ethnomusicology*, edited by Bruno Nettl and Philip V. Bohlman. Chicago: University of Chicago Press.

————. 1993. "Musical Life in the Central European Jewish Village." In *Modern Jews and Their Musical Agendas*, edited by Ezra Mendelsohn. Issue of *Studies in Contemporary Jewry* 9. New York: Oxford University Press.

_____. 1994. "Music, History, and the Foreign in the New Europe." *Modernism/Modernity* 1(1):121–52.

Borland, Katherine. 1991. "'That's Not What I Said': Interpretive Conflict in Oral Narrative Research." In *Women's Words: The Feminist Practice of Oral History*, edited by Sherna Berger Gluck and Daphne Patai. New York: Routledge.

Borysenko, Valentyna. 1992. "Etnohrafichna ekspedytsiia na Polissia 1934 roku." *Rodovid* 3:30–36.

Borzhkovskii, Valerian. 1889. "Lirniki." *Kievskaia starina* 9:661–704.

Bourdieu, Pierre. 1977. *Outline of a Theory of Practice*. Cambridge, UK: Cambridge University Press.

_____. 1991. *Language and Symbolic Power*. Cambridge, MA: Harvard University Press.

Bowen, Eleanor S. (Laura Bohannan). 1964. *Return to Laughter*. Garden City, NY: Doubleday.

Bozeman, Adda. 1984. "The International Order in a Multicultural World." In *The Expansion of International Society*, edited by Hedley Bull and Adam Watson. Oxford: Clarendon Press.

Brady, Ivan, ed. 1991. *Anthropological Poetics*. Lanham, MD: Rowman and Littlefield.

Braudel, Fernand. 1980a [1958]. "History and the Social Sciences: The Longue Durée." In *On History*, translated by Sarah Matthews. Chicago: University of Chicago Press.

_____. 1980b [1960]. "Unity and Diversity in the Human Sciences." In *On History*, translated by Sarah Matthews. Chicago: University of Chicago Press.

Briggs, Jean. 1970. *Never in Anger: Portrait of an Eskimo Family*. Cambridge, MA: Harvard University Press.

Bruner, Edward M. 1986. "Ethnography as Narrative." In *The Anthropology of Experience*, edited by Victor W. Turner and Edward M. Bruner. Urbana: University of Illinois Press.

Buelow, George J. 1980. "Kircher, Athanasius." In *The New Grove Dictionary of Music and Musicians*, edited by Stanley Sadie. London: Macmillan.

Burgenland. 1993. Vol. 1: *Tondukemente zur Volksmusik in Österreich*. Accompanying booklet edited by Sepp Gmasz, Gerlinde Haid, and Rudolf Pietsch. Vienna: Institut für Volksmusikforschung.

Cantwell, Robert. 1984. *Bluegrass Breakdown: The Making of the Old Southern Sound*. Urbana: University of Illinois Press.

Carnap, Rudolph. 1966. *An Introduction to the Philosophy of Science*. Edited by Martin Gardner. New York: Harper Torchbooks.

Caws, Mary Ann. 1986. "The Conception of Engendering, The Erotics of Editing." In *The Poetics of Gender*, edited by N. K. Miller. New York: Columbia University Press.

Cesara, Manda. 1982. *Reflections of a Woman Anthropologist: No Hiding Place*. London and New York: Academic Press.

Chenoweth, Vida, and Darlene Bee. 1971. "Comparative-Generative Models of a New Guinea Melodic Structure." *American Anthropologist* 73:773–82.

Chernoff, John Miller. 1979. *African Rhythm and African Sensibility: Aesthetics and Social Action in African Musical Idioms*. Chicago: University of Chicago Press.

Christensen, Dieter. 1991. "Erich M. von Hornbostel, Carl Stumpf, and the Institutionalization of Comparative Musicology." In *Comparative Musicology and Anthropology of Music: Essays on the History of Ethnomusicology*, edited by Bruno Nettl and Philip V. Bohlman. Chicago: University of Chicago Press.

Chubyns'kyi, Pavlo. 1874. *Trudy etnografichesko-statisticheskoi ekspeditsii v zapadno-russkii krai.* Tom 5. S. Peterburg: Gosudarstvennoe Russkoe Geograficheskoe Obshchestvo.

_____. 1877. *Trudy etnografichesko-statisticheskoi ekspeditsii v zapadno-russkii krai.* Tom 4. S. Peterburg: Gosudarstvennoe Russkoe Geograficheskoe Obshchestvo [includes 138 melodies transcribed by Mykola Lysenko].

Cixous, Hélène. 1991. *"Coming to Writing" and Other Essays,* edited by Deborah Jenson, translated by Sarah Cornell et al. Cambridge, MA: Harvard University Press.

Clifford, James. 1983. "On Ethnographic Authority." *Representations* 1(2):118–46.

_____. 1986a. "On Ethnographic Allegory." In *Writing Culture: The Poetics and Politics of Ethnography,* edited by James Clifford and George E. Marcus. Berkeley: University of California Press.

_____. 1986b. "Introduction: Partial Truths." In *Writing Culture: The Poetics and Politics of Ethnography,* edited by James Clifford and George E. Marcus. Berkeley: University of California Press.

_____. 1988a. *The Predicament of Culture: Twentieth-Century Ethnography, Literature, and Art.* Cambridge, MA: Harvard University Press.

_____. 1988b. "On Ethnographic Authority." In *The Predicament of Culture: Twentieth-Century Ethnography,* edited by James Clifford. Cambridge, MA: Harvard University Press.

_____. 1990. "Notes on (Field)notes." In *Fieldnotes: The Making of Anthropology,* edited by Roger Sanjek. Ithaca: Cornell University Press.

Clifford, James, and George E. Marcus, eds. 1986. *Writing Culture: The Poetics and Politics of Ethnography.* Berkeley: University of California Press.

Code, Lorraine. 1991. *What Can She Know? Feminist Theory and the Construction of Knowledge.* Ithaca: Cornell University Press.

Comaroff, Jean. 1987. *Body of Power, Spirit of Resistance: The Culture and History of a South African People.* Chicago: University of Chicago Press.

Comaroff, John, and Jean Comaroff. 1992. *Ethnography and the Historical Imagination.* Boulder, CO: Westview. *(Studies in Ethnographic Imagination.)*

Connerton, Paul. 1989. *How Societies Remember.* Cambridge, UK: Cambridge University Press.

Coover, Robert. 1993. "Hyperfiction: Novels for the Computer." *New York Times Book Review,* August 29, pp. 3, 8–12.

Cowan, Jane K. 1990. *Dance and the Body Politic in Northern Greece.* Princeton, NJ: Princeton University Press.

Cruikshank, Julie. 1988. "Telling about Culture: Changing Traditions in Subarctic Anthropology." *The Northern Review* I (summer):27–39.

Czekanowska, Anna. 1972. *Ludowe melodie wąskiego zakresu w krajach słowiańskich* (Przegląd dokumentacji źródłowych próba klasyfikacji metodą taksonomii wrocławskiej). Kraków: Polskie Wydawnictwo Muzyczne.

Dallmayr, Fred R., and Thomas A. McCarthy. 1977. *Understanding and Social Inquiry.* Notre Dame: Notre Dame University Press.

de Certeau, Michel. 1984. *The Practice of Everyday Life,* translated by Steven Rendall. Berkeley: University of California Press.

Demutskii, P. 1903. *Lira i ii motivy.* Kyïv: Leona Idzikovskago.

Deutsch, Walter, and Rudolf Pietsch, eds. 1990. *Dörfliche Tanzmusik im westpannonischen Raum*. Vienna: A. Schendl. (*Schriften zur Volksmusik* 15)

Deutsche Gesellschaft für Musik des Orients. 1981. *Musikologische Feldforschung—Aufgaben, Erfahrungen, Techniken.* [Musicological Field Research: Conditions, Experiences, Techniques.] Hamburg: Karl Dieter Wagner.

Dilthey, Wilhelm. 1989. *Introduction to the Human Sciences.* Edited by Rudolf A. Makkreel and Frithjof Rodi. Princeton, NJ: Princeton University Press.

Dittmar, Jürgen. 1992. *Deutsche Balladen mit ihren Melodien* 9. Freiburg im Breisgau: Deutsches Volksliedarchiv.

Dohrn, Verena. 1991. *Reise nach Galizien: Grenzlandschaften des alten Europa.* Frankfurt am Main: S. Fischer.

Dreo, Harald, Walter Burian, and Sepp Gmasz, eds. 1988. *Ein burgenländisches Volksliederbuch.* Eisenstadt: Verlag Nentwich-Lattner.

Drewal, Margaret Thompson. 1992. *Yoruba Ritual: Performers, Play, Agency.* Bloomington: Indiana University Press.

Dumont, Jean-Paul. 1978. *The Headman and I.* Austin: University of Texas Press.

Dyen, Doris. 1982. "New Directions in Sacred Harp Singing." In *Folk Music and Modern Sound,* edited by William Ferris and Mary L. Hart. Jackson: University Press of Mississippi.

Ellingson, Ter. 1992a. "Transcription." In *Ethnomusicology: An Introduction,* edited by Helen Myers. New York: W. W. Norton.

———. 1992b. "Notation." In *Ethnomusicology: An Introduction,* edited by Helen Myers. New York: W. W. Norton.

Ellis, A. J. 1885. "On the Musical Scales of Various Nations." *Journal of the Royal Society of Arts* 33:485–527.

Embree, John. 1943. *Japanese Peasant Songs. Memoirs of the American Folklore Society.* Vol. 38. Philadelphia: The American Folklore Society.

Emerson, Robert M., Rachel I. Fretz, and Linda L. Shaw. 1995. *Writing Ethnographic Fieldnotes.* Chicago: University of Chicago Press.

England, Nicholas M., Robert Garfias, Mieczyslaw Kolinski, George List, and Williard Rhodes. 1964. "Symposium on Transcription and Analysis: A Hukwe Song with Musical Bow." *Ethnomusicology* 8(3):223–77.

Ernst, August. 1987. *Geschichte des Burgenlandes.* Vienna: Verlag für Geschichte und Politik. (*Geschichte der österreichischen Bundesländer*)

Fabian, Johannes. 1983. *Time and the Other: How Anthropology Makes Its Object.* New York: Columbia University Press.

———. 1990. *Power and Performance: Ethnographic Explorations through Proverbial Wisdom and Theater in Shaba, Zaire.* Madison: University of Wisconsin Press.

Feld, Steven. 1990[1982]. *Sound and Sentiment: Birds, Weeping, Poetics, and Song in Kaluli Expression.* 2d ed. Philadelphia: University of Pennsylvania Press.

Fernandez, James W. 1993. "A Guide to the Perplexed Ethnographer in an Age of Sound Bites." *American Ethnologist* 20(1):179–84.

Finke, Laurie A. 1992. *Feminist Theory, Women's Writing.* Ithaca: Cornell University Press.

Finley, M. I. 1987[1975]. *The Use and Abuse of History.* New York: Penguin Books.

Fischer, Michael M.J. 1993. "Working through the Other: The Jewish, Spanish, Turkish, Iranian, Ukrainian, Lithuanian, and German Unconscious of Polish Culture; or, One Hand Clapping: Dialogue, Silences, and the Mourning of Polish Romanticism." In *Perilous States: Conversations on Culture, Politics, and Nation,* edited by George E. Marcus. Chicago: University of Chicago Press.

Fitzpatrick, Sheila. 1992. *The Cultural Front. Power and Culture in Revolutionary Russia.* Ithaca: Cornell University Press.

Flam, Gila. 1992. *Singing for Survival: Songs of the Lodz Ghetto, 1940–45.* Urbana: University of Illinois Press.

Fluehr-Lobban, Carolyn. 1991. *Ethics and the Profession of Anthropology: Dialogue for a New Era.* Philadelphia: University of Pennsylvania Press.

Foucault, Michel. 1970. *The Order of Things: An Archaeology of the Human Sciences.* New York: Pantheon Books.

———. 1972. *The Archaeology of Knowledge and the Discourse on Language,* translated by Alan Sheridan. New York: Harper & Row.

Frake, Charles. 1964[1874]. "Notes and Queries in Ethnography." *American Anthropologist* (special publication) 66(3, pt. 2):132–45.

Gadamer, Hans-Georg. 1992[1975]. *Truth and Method.* 2nd rev. ed. New York: Crossroad.

Geertz, Clifford. 1973a. *The Interpretation of Cultures.* New York: Basic Books.

———. 1973b. "Thick Description: Toward an Interpretive Theory of Culture." In *The Interpretation of Cultures.* New York: Basic Books.

———. 1983. *Local Knowledge.* New York: Basic Books.

———. 1988. *Works and Lives: The Anthropologist as Author.* Stanford: Stanford University Press.

Georges, R. A., and M. O. Jones. 1980. *People Studying People: The Human Element in Fieldwork.* Berkeley: University of California Press.

Gluck, Sherna Berger, and Daphne Patai. 1991. *Women's Words: The Feminist Practice of Oral History.* New York: Routledge.

Goffman, Erving. 1959. *The Presentation of Self in Everyday Life.* Garden City, NY: Doubleday.

Gold, Hugo. 1970. *Gedenkbuch der untergegangenen Judengemeinden des Burgenlandes.* Tel Aviv: Olamenu.

Golde, Peggy, ed. 1986[1970]. *Women in the Field. Anthropological Experiences.* 2nd ed. Berkeley: University of California Press.

Goldstein, Kenneth. 1964. *A Guide for Field Workers in Folklore.* Hatboro, PA: Folklore Associates, Inc.

Gourlay, K. A. 1978. "Towards a Reassessment of the Ethnomusicologist's Role in Research." *Ethnomusicology* 22(1):1–35.

———. 1982. "Towards a Humanizing Ethnomusicology." *Ethnomusicology* 26(3):411–20.

Gravel, Pierre Bettez, and Robert B. Marks Ridinger. 1988. *Anthropological Fieldwork: An Annotated Bibliography.* New York: Garland Publishing, Inc.

Gruber, Ruth Ellen. 1992. *Jewish Heritage Travel Guide: A Guide to Central and Eastern Europe.* New York: John Wiley & Sons.

Guilbault, Jocylene. 1993. *Zouk: World Music in the West Indies.* Chicago: University of Chicago Press.

Hale, Sondra. 1991. "Feminist Method, Process, and Self-Criticism: Interviewing Sudanese Women." In *Women's Words: The Feminist Practice of Oral History,* edited by Sherna Berger Gluck and Daphne Patai. New York: Routledge.

Harrison, Frank, ed. 1973. *Time, Place and Music: An Anthology of Ethnomusicological Observation c. 1550 to c. 1800*. Amsterdam: Frits Knuf.

Hastrup, Kirsten, ed. 1992. *Other Histories*. London and New York: Routledge.

Heidegger, Martin. 1978. *Being and Time*, translated by John Macquarrie and Edward Robinson. Oxford: Blackwell.

Heilbrun, Carolyn G. 1988. *Writing a Woman's Life*. New York: W. W. Norton.

Herndon, Marcia. 1974. "Analysis: The Herding of Sacred Cows?" *Ethnomusicology* 18(2):219–62.

———. 1993. "Insiders, Outsiders, Knowing our Limits, Limiting our Knowing (Emics and Etics in Ethnomusicology)." *World of Music* 35(1):63–80.

Herndon, Marcia, and Norma McLeod. 1983. *Field Manual for Ethnomusicology*. Norwood, PA: Norwood Editions.

Hewlett, Barry. 1991. *Intimate Fathers: The Nature and Context of Aka Pigmy Paternal Infant Care*. Ann Arbor: University of Michigan Press.

Hnatiuk, Volodymyr. 1896. "Lirnyky." *Etnografichnyi zbirnyk* 2:18–73.

Hobsbawm, Eric, and Terence Ranger, eds. 1983. *The Invention of Tradition*. Cambridge: Cambridge University Press.

Hofer, Tamas. 1968. "Comparative Notes on the Professional Personality of Two Disciplines." *Current Anthropology* 9(4):311–15.

———. 1969. "The Creation of Ethnic Symbols from the Elements of Peasant Culture." In *Nationalism in Eastern Europe*, edited by Peter Sugar and Ivo Lederer. Seattle: University of Washington Press.

Hoffman, Eva. 1993. *Exit into History: A Journey through the New Eastern Europe*. New York: Viking.

Hood, Mantle. 1960. "The Challenge of 'Bi-Musicality.'" *Ethnomusicology* 4(1):55–59.

———. 1982[1971]. *The Ethnomusicologist*. New Edition. Kent: Kent State University Press.

Hood, Mantle, Frank L. Harrison, and Claude V. Palisca. 1963. *Musicology*. Englewood Cliffs, NJ: Prentice-Hall.

Horlenko, V. P. 1884. "Kobzari i lirniki." *Kievskaia starina* 1:21–50 and 12:639–56.

Howes, David, ed. 1991. *The Varieties of Sensory Experience: A Sourcebook in the Anthropology of the Senses*. Toronto: University of Toronto Press.

Hrinchenko, M. O. 1939. "Muzyka ukraïns'kykh narodnykh pisen' pro Lenina i Stalina." *Narodna tvorchist'* 4:28–40.

Hrushevs'ka, Kateryna. 1927. *Ukraïns'ki narodni dumy*. Kyïv: Vydavnytstvo Akademii Nauk.

Hsia, R. Po-chia. 1988. *The Myth of Ritual Murder: Jews and Magic in Reformation Germany*. New Haven: Yale University Press.

Hutchinson, Patrick. 1994. "The Work and Words of Piping." In *Canadian Music: Issues of Hegemony and Identity*, edited by Beverly Diamond and Robert Witmer. Toronto: Canadian Scholars Press.

Iashchenko, Leopold. 1962. *Ukraïns'ke narodne bahatoholossia*. Kyïv: Vydavnytstvo Akademii Nauk.

———. 1970. *Derzhavna zasluzhena kapela bandurystiv Ukraïns'koï RSR*. Kyïv: Muzychna Ukraïna.

Idelsohn, A. Z. 1932. *Die traditionellen Gesänge der süddeutschen Juden*. Vol. 7: *Hebräisch-orientalischer Melodienschatz*. Leipzig: Friedrich Hofmeister.

Ignatieff, Michael. 1994. *Blood and Belonging: Journeys into the New Nationalism*. New York: Farrar, Straus, and Giroux.

Ihde, Don. 1986[1977]. *Experimental Phenomenology: An Introduction*. Albany, NY: State University of New York Press.

Ivanenko, Volodymyr. 1970. "Dovhe zhyttia v narodnii pisni—Klyment V. Kvitka." *Visti* 1(32):14–17.

Ives, Edward. 1980. *The Tape-Recorded Interview: A Manual for Field Workers in Folklore and Oral History*. Revised and enlarged. Knoxville: University of Tennessee Press. (First edition published in 1974 as *Manual for Fieldworders*. Orono, ME: Northeast Folklore Society.)

Jackson, Bruce. 1987. *Fieldwork*. Urbana: University of Illinois Press.

Jackson, Jean E. 1990. "'I Am a Fieldnote': Fieldnotes as a Symbol of Professional Identity." In *Fieldnotes: The Makings of Anthropology*, edited by Roger Sanjek. Ithaca: Cornell University Press.

Jackson, Michael. 1989. *Paths Toward a Clearing: Radical Empiricism and Ethnographic Enquiry*. Bloomington: Indiana University Press.

Jay, Robert. 1974[1969]. "Personal and Extrapersonal Vision in Anthropology." In *Reinventing Anthropology*, edited by Dell Hymes. New York: Vintage Books Edition, Random House.

Jones, William (Sir). 1792. "On the Musical Modes of the Hindus." *Asiatick Researches* 3:55–87. Reprinted in *Music of India*, by William Jones and N. Augustus Willard. 1962. Calcutta: Susil Gupta Private, Ltd.

Karpeles, Maud, ed. 1958. *The Collection of Folk Music and Other Ethnomusicological Material: A Manual for Field Workers*. London: The International Folk Music Council and the Royal Anthropological Institute of Great Britain and Ireland.

Kerman, Joseph. 1985. *Contemplating Music. Challenges to Musicology*. Cambridge, MA: Harvard University Press.

Khai, Mykhailo. 1989. "Au, autentyka! . . ." *Ukraïna* 45:17–18.

Kharkiv, Volodymyr. 1929. "Posterezhennia nad lirnykamy ta kobzariamy valkivs'koho raionu na zasidanni Etnohrafichnoï Komisiï VUAN." *IMFE* (Kyïv): f. 6–2, od. zb. 23(2).

———. 1930. "Dumy, psal'my (z melodiiamy)." *IMFE* (Kyïv): f. 6–4, od. zb. 194.

———. 1932. "Muzychnyi pobut robitnykiv Stalinshchyna." *IMFE* (Kyïv): f. 6–2, od. zb. 23(6).

———. 1937. "Fol'klorna ekspedytsiia upravlinnia v spravakh mystetstv pry RNK URSR 1936 roku." *Ukraïns'kyi Fol'klor* 1:129–30.

Khotkevych, Hnat. 1930a. *Muzychni instrumenty ukraïns'koho narodu*. Kharkiv: Derzhavne Vydavnytstvo Ukraïny.

———. 1930b. *Pidruchnyk hry na banduri*. Kharkiv: Derzhavne Vydavnytstvo Ukraïny.

Khvylia, Andryi. 1937. "Rozkvit ukraïns'koï narodnoï tvorchosti." *Ukraïns'kyi fol'klor* 1:29–30.

K-ii. 1928. "Orhanizatsiia muzroboty. Muzkor i ioho robota." *Muzka masam* 2:5.

Kingsbury, Henry. 1988. *Music, Talent, and Performance: A Conservatory Cultural System*. Philadelphia: Temple University Press.

Kircher, Athanasius. 1650. *Musurgia universalis, sive ars magna consoni et dissoni*. Rome: Francesco Corbelletti.

Kisliuk, Michelle. 1991. "Confronting the Quintessential: Singing, Dancing, and Everyday Life Among Biaka Pygmies (Central African Republic)." Ph.D. diss., New York University.

———. In preparation. *"Seize the Dance!" Performance and Modernity Among BaAka Pygmies*.

Klampfer, Josef. 1966. *Das Eisenstädter Ghetto*. Eisenstadt: Burgenländisches Landesarchiv. (*Burgenländische Forschungen* 51)

Kolberg, Oskar. 1961– . *Dzieła wszystkie*. Kraków: Polskie Wydawnictwo Muzyczne (ca. 68 volumes).

———. 1979[1867]. *Kujawy, część II. Dzieła wszystkie*, Vol. 4. Wroław: Polskie Towarzystwo Ludoznawcze.

Kolessa, Filaret. 1969[1910/1913]. *Melodiï ukraïns'kykh narodnykh dum*. Kyïv: Naukova Dumka [originally published in *Materialy do ukraïns'koï ethol'ogiï* 13 and 14, 1910 and 1913].

Kondufor, IU., ed. 1989. *Kul'turne budivnytstvo v ukraïns'kii RSR, 1941–1950*. Kyïv: Naukova Dumka.

———. 1992. *Represovane kraieznavstvo (20–30-i roky)*. Kyïv: Ridnyi Krai.

Koperzhyns'kyi, Kost'. 1929. "Kalendar narodnoï obriadovosty novorichnoho tsykly." *Pervisne hromadianstvo ta ioho perezhytky na Ukraïni* 3:14–98.

Koskoff, Ellen. 1993. "Miriam Sings Her Song: The Self and the Other in Anthropological Discourse." In *Musicology and Difference: Gender and Sexuality in Music Scholarship*, edited by Ruth A. Solie. Berkeley: University of California Press.

Koskoff, Ellen, ed. 1989. *Women and Music in Cross-Cultural Perspective*. Urbana: University of Illinois Press.

Krader, Barbara. 1980. "Ethnomusicology." In *The New Grove Dictionary of Music and Musicians*, edited by Stanley Sadie. London: Macmillan.

Krist, I. E. 1902. "Kobzari i lirniki kharkovskoi gubernii." *Sbornik kharkovskogo istoriko-filologicheskogo obshchestva* 15, ch. 2.

Kryms'kyi, Ah. 1928. *Zvynohorodshchyna z pohliadu etnohrafichnoho ta diialektolohichnoho*. Chastyna 1. Kyïv: Vseukraïns'ka Akadema Nauk.

Kuhn, Thomas S. 1962. *The Structure of Scientific Revolutions*. Chicago: University of Chicago Press.

Kunst, Jaap. 1959. *Ethnomusicology: A Study of Its Nature, Its Problems, Methods and Representative Personalities to Which Is Added a Bibliography*. 3rd ed. The Hague: Martinus Nijhoff. [First published as *Musicologica* in 1950 by the Royal Tropical Institute, Amsterdam.]

Kvitka, Klyment. 1928. "Do vyvchennia pobutu lirnykiv." *Pervisne hromadianstvo ta ioho perezhytky na Ukraïni* 2–3:115–29.

———. 1971/1973. *K. V. Kvitka. Izbrannye trudy v dvukh tomakh*. Volodymyr Hoshovs'kyi [Edited by Vladimir Goshovskii]. Moskva: Sovetskii Kompozitor.

———. 1985/1986. *Vybrani statti*, Vols. 1 and 2. Anatolyi Ivanyts'kyi, ed. Kyïv: Muzychna Ukraïna.

Lafitau, Joseph François. 1974–1977[1724]. *Customs of the American Indians Compared with the Customs of Primitive Times*, edited and translated by William N. Fenton and Elizabeth L. Moore. Toronto: The Champlain Society. Two volumes. [First published as *Moeurs des Sauvages Ameriquains, Comparées aux Moeurs des Premiers Temps*. Paris 1724.]

Landow, George. 1992. *Hypertext*. Baltimore: Johns Hopkins University Press.

Lapidus, Gail Warshofsky. 1978. "Educational Strategies and Cultural Revolution: The Politics of Soviet Development." In *Cultural Revolution in Russia, 1928–1931*, edited by Sheila Fitzpatrick. Bloomington: Indiana University Press.

Lawless, Robert. 1983. "On First Being an Anthropologist." In *Fieldwork. The Human Experi-*

ence, edited by Robert Lawless, Vinson H. Sutlive Jr., and Mario D. Zamora. New York: Gordon and Breach Science Publishers.

Lederman, Rena. 1990. "Pretexts for Ethnography: On Reading Fieldnotes." In *Fieldnotes: The Making of Anthropology*, edited by Roger Sanjek. Ithaca: Cornell University Press.

de Léry, Jean. 1578. *Histoire d'un voyage faict en la terre du Brésil*. La Rochelle: Antoine Chuppin.

Lévi-Strauss, Claude. 1969. *The Raw and the Cooked*. New York: Harper and Row.

Lieberman, Fredric. 1980. "Amiot, Jean Joseph Marie." In *The New Grove Dictionary of Music and Musicians*, edited by Stanley Sadie. London: Macmillan.

List, George. 1974. "The Reliability of Transcription." *Ethnomusicology* 18(3):353–77.

———. 1979. "Ethnomusicology: A Discipline Defined." *Ethnomusicology* 23(1):1–4.

Lomax, Alan. 1968. *Folk Song Style and Culture*. New Brunswick, NJ: Transaction Books.

———. 1976. *Cantometrics*. Berkeley: University of California Extension.

Lomax, John Avery, comp. 1910. *Cowboy Songs, and Other Frontier Ballads*. Introduction by Barrett Wendell. New York: Sturgis and Walton Company.

Lowenthal, David. 1985. *The Past is a Foreign Country*. Cambridge: Cambridge University Press.

Lucas, William. 1971. *Lazy Bill Lucas*. Wild 12MO1. 12 in. long play record, Buc, France.

———. 1972. *Lazy Bill and His Friends*. Lazy 12MO2. 12 in. long play record, Buc, France.

Luhovs'kyi, Borys. 1926. "Chernihivs'ki startsi." *Pervisne hromadianstvo to ioho perezhytky na Ukraïni* 3:131–177.

———. 1993. "Materialy do iarmarkovoho repertuaru ta pobutu startsivstva." *Rodovid* 6:87–120 [written in ca. 1926].

Lysenko, Mykola. 1978[1874]. "Kharkterystyka muzychnykh osoblyvostei ukraïns'kykh dum i pisen' u vykonanni kobzaria Veresaia." Kyïv: Muzychna Ukraïna [originally published in *Sbornik iugo-zapadnogo otdela russkogo geograficheskogo obshchestva* 1, 1874].

Lysty. 1926. "Lysty." *IMFE* (Kyïv): f. 8-kol. 3, od. zb. 2.

Malinowski, Bronislaw. 1962[1922]. *Argonauts of the Western Pacific: An Account of Native Enterprise and Adventure in the Archipelagoes of Melanesian New Guinea*. Reprint. New York: E. P. Dutton & Co., Inc.

———. 1989[1967]. *A Diary in the Strict Sense of the Term*. Preface by Valetta Malinowski, introduction by Raymond Firth, translated by Norbert Guterman, index of native terms by Mario Bick. Stanford: Stanford University Press.

Malynka, Oleksandyr. 1929 "Kobzari S. Vlasko ta D. Symonenko i lirnyk A. Ivanyts'kyi; ikhnii repertuar." *Pervisne hromadianstvo ta ioho perezhytky na Ukraïni* 1:105–28.

Manganaro, Marc, ed. 1990. *Modernist Anthropology: From Fieldwork to Text*. Princeton, NJ: Princeton University Press.

Marcus, George E. 1986. "Contemporary Problems of Ethnography in the Modern World System." In *Writing Culture: The Poetics and Politics of Ethnography*, edited by James Clifford and George E. Marcus. Berkeley: University of California Press.

Marcus, George E., ed. 1993. *Perilous States: Conversations on Culture, Politics, and Nation*. Chicago: University of Chicago Press. (*Late Editions* 1).

Marcus, George E., and Michael M. J. Fischer. 1986. *Anthropology as Cultural Critique: An Experimental Moment in the Human Sciences*. Chicago: University of Chicago Press.

Materialy z istorii. 1922. "Statuty Pershoï Kyïvs'koï Kapely bandurystiv." Materialy z istorii pershoï ukraïns'koï khudozhnoï kapely kobzariv, IMFE (Kyïv): f. 14-kol. 1, od. zb. 1.

————. 1934? "Repertuar ta marshruty Pershoï Kyïvs'koï Kapely bandurystiv 1921–1934." *Materialy z istoriï pershoï ukraïns'koï khudozhnoï kapely kobzariv*, IMFE (Kyïv): f. 14-kol. 1, od. zb. 6 [date is uncertain].

McAllester, David P. 1973[1954]. *Enemy Way Music: A Study of Social and Aesthetic Values as Seen in Navaho Music*. New York: Kraus Reprint Co.

————. 1989. Videotaped seminar, Brown University.

Merriam, Alan. 1960. "Ethnomusicology, Discussion and Definition of the Field." *Ethnomusicology* 4:107–14.

————. 1964. *The Anthropology of Music*. Evanston: Northwestern University Press.

————. 1967. "The Use of Music as a Technique of Reconstructing Culture History in Africa." In *Reconstructing African Culture History*, edited by Creighton Gabel and Norman R. Bennett. Boston: Basic Books.

————. 1977. "Definitions of 'Comparative Musicology' and 'Ethnomusicology': An Historical-Theoretical Perspective." *Ethnomusicology* 21(2):189–204.

Miller, Daniel. 1994. *Modernity—An Ethnographic Approach: Dualism and Mass Consumption in Trinidad*. Providence: Berg Publishers.

Minister, Kristina. 1991. "A Feminist Frame for the Oral History Interview." In *Women's Words: The Feminist Practice of Oral History*, edited by Sherna Berger Gluck and Daphne Patai. New York: Routledge.

Mitchell, Frank. 1978. *Navajo Blessingway Singer*. Edited by Charlotte Frisbie and David McAllester. Tucson: University of Arizona Press.

Montaigne, Michel Eyquem de. 1952[1580]. *Essais*. Paris: Editions Garnier Frères.

Musyku na front. 1931. *Muzyku na front sotsiialistychnoho budivnytstva (persha vseukraïns'ka muzychnaolimpiiada)*. Kyïv: Biuleten' ch. 1–3.

Myerhoff, Barbara, and Jay Ruby, eds. 1982. *A Crack in the Mirror: Reflexive Perspectives in Anthropology*. Philadelphia: University of Pennsylvania Press.

Myers, Helen. 1992. "Fieldwork" and "Field Technology." In *Ethnomusicology: An Introduction*, edited by Helen Myers. New York: W. W. Norton.

Myers, Helen, ed. 1993. *Ethnomusicology: Historical and Regional Studies*. New York: W. W. Norton.

Mykoliuk, A. 1929. "Do perevyboriv rad sel'budiv. Shcho povynni robyty muz. i khor. hurtku pidchas perevyboriv rad sel'budiv." *Muzyka masam* 3(4):18–19.

Nattiez, Jean-Jacques. 1990. *Music and Discourse: Toward a Semiology of Music*, translated by Carolyn Abbate. Princeton, NJ: Princeton University Press.

Nazina, I. D. 1989. *Belaruskaia narodnaia instrumental'naia muzyka*. Minsk: Navuka i Tekhnika.

Nettl, Bruno. 1964. *Theory and Method in Ethnomusicology*. New York: The Free Press of Glencoe.

————. 1983. *The Study of Ethnomusicology: Twenty-nine Issues and Concepts*. Urbana: University of Illinois Press.

————. 1984. "In Honor of Our Principal Teachers." *Ethnomusicology* 28(2):173–85.

————. 1985. *The Western Impact on World Music: Change, Adaptation, and Survival*. New York: Schirmer Books.

————. 1986. "Ethnomusicology." In *The New Harvard Dictionary of Music*, edited by Don Michael Randel. Cambridge, MA: The Belknap Press of Harvard University Press.

_____. 1989. *Blackfoot Musical Thought: Comparative Perspectives*. Kent, OH: Kent State University Press.

_____. 1991. "The Dual Nature of Ethnomusicology in North America: The Contributions of Charles Seeger and George Herzog." In *Comparative Musicology and Anthropology of Music: Essays on the History of Ethnomusicology*, edited by Bruno Nettl and Philip V. Bohlman. Chicago: University of Chicago Press.

_____. 1992. "Recent Directions in Ethnomusicology." In *Ethnomusicology. An Introduction*, edited by Helen Meyers. New York: W. W. Norton.

Neumann, Frederick. 1992. "Improper Appoggiaturas in the Neue Mozart Ausgabe." *Journal of Musicology* 10(4):505–21.

Noll, William. 1991a. "Economics of Music Patronage Among Polish and Ukrainian Peasants to 1939." *Ethnomusicology* 35(3):349–79.

_____. 1991b. "Porivnial'ne doslidzhennia mystetstva bardiv z perspektyvy etnomuzykolo-hii." *Rodovid* 2:37–40.

_____. 1993a. "Paralel'na kul'tura v period stalinizmu." *Rodovid* 5:37–41.

_____. 1993b. "The Social Role and Economic Status of Blind Peasant Minstrels in Ukraine." *Harvard Ukrainian Studies* 17(1/2):45–71. (A similar article in Ukrainian is in *Rodovid* 6:16–26, 1993.)

_____. 1994a. "Cultural Contact Through Music Institutions in Ukrainian Lands, 1920–1948." In *Musical Cultures in Contact: Convergences and Collisions*, edited by Margaret Kartomi and Stephen Blum. (*Australian Studies in the History, Philosophy and Social Studies of Music 2.*) Sydney: Currency Press.

_____. 1994b. "Rol' zhynok v muzychnomu zhyttii ukraïns'koho sela." *Rodovid* 9:36–43.

Nordstrom, Carolyn, and Antonius C. G. M. Robben, eds. 1995. *Fieldwork Under Fire: Contemporary Studies of Violence and Survival*. Berkeley, CA: University of California Press.

Oakeshott, Michael. 1991[1959]. "The Voice of Poetry in the Conversation of Mankind." In *Rationalism in Politics and Other Essays*, edited by Timothy Fuller. Indianapolis: Liberty Press.

Odarchenko, Petro. 1962–1963. "A Survey of Publications on Ukrainian Ethnography and Folklore in the Years 1957–1962." *The Annals of the Ukrainian Academy of Arts and Sciences in the United States* 10(1–2):92–110.

Ortner, Sherry B. 1973. "On Key Symbols." *American Anthropologist* 75:1338–46.

Ottenberg, Simon. 1990. "Thirty Years of Fieldnotes: Changing Relationships to the Text." In *Fieldnotes: The Making of Anthropology*, edited by Roger Sanjek. Ithaca: Cornell University Press.

Pike, Kenneth. 1954. *Language in Relation to a Unified Theory of Structure and Human Behavior*. Glendale, CA: Summer Institute of Linguistics.

Pillay, Jayendran. 1994. "Indian Music in the Indian School in South Africa: The Use of Cultural Forms as a Political Tool." *Ethnomusicology* 38(2):281–301.

Polotai, M. 1937. "Mystetstvo kobzariv Radians'koï Ukraïny." *Radians'ka Muzyka* 6:23–34.

Post, Jennifer C., Mary Russell Bucknum, and Laurel Sercombe. 1994. *A Manual for Documentation, Fieldwork, and Preservation*. Bloomington: The Society for Ethnomusicology.

Proiektyvnyi Plan. 1925. "Proiektyvnyi plan pratsi Pershoï Kyïvs'koï Kapely kobzariv na 1925 rik." *Tsentralnyi Derzhavnyi Arkhiv Zhovtnevoï Revolutsiï URSR* (Kyïv): f. 257, op. 1, sp. 189, ark. 306–7.

Qureshi, Regula Burckhardt. 1995. "Musical Anthropologies and Music Histories: A Preface and an Agenda." *Journal of the American Musicological Society* 48(3):331–42.

Rabinow, Paul. 1977. *Reflections of Fieldwork in Morocco*. Berkeley: University of California Press.

———. 1983. *Un ethnologue au Maroc, réflexions sur une enquête de terrain*, translated from English by Tina Jolas. Paris: Hachette.

Reck, David B., Mark Slobin, and Jeff Todd Titon. 1992. "Discovering and Documenting a World of Music." In *Worlds of Music*, general editor Jeff Todd Titon. New York: Schirmer Books.

Redfield, Robert, and Milton Singer. 1962. "The Cultural Role of Cities." In *Human Nature and the Study of Society: The Papers of Robert Redfield*, edited by Margaret Park Redfield, 1:326–50. Chicago: University of Chicago Press.

Reiss, Johannes. 1995. *Hier in der heiligen jüdischen Gemeinde Eisenstadt: Die Grabinschriften des jüngeren jüdischen Friedhofes in Eisenstadt*. Eisenstadt: Österreichisches Jüdisches Museum in Eisenstadt.

Reiterits, Anton. 1988. *Dörfl: Gebrauchsmusik in einem burgenländischen Ort*. Edited by Walter Deutsch and Helga Thiel. Eisenstadt: Burgenländisches Landesmuseum. (*Wissenschaftliche Arbeiten aus dem Burgenland* 80)

Repertuar. 1934. "Repertuar ta marshruty Pershoï Kyïvs'koï kapely bandurystiv 1921–1934." *Materiialy z istoriï pershoï ukraïns'koï khudozhnoï kapely kobzariv*, IMFE, f. 14-kol. 1, od zb. 6.

Rice, Timothy. 1977. "Polyphony in Bulgarian Folk Music." Ph.D. diss., University of Washington.

———. 1980. "Aspects of Bulgarian Musical Thought." *Yearbook of the International Folk Music Council* 12:43–67.

———. 1985. "Music Learned but Not Taught." In *Becoming Human Through Music*. Reston, VA: Music Educators National Conference.

———. 1988. "Understanding Three-Part Singing in Bulgaria: The Interplay of Concept and Experience." *Selected Reports in Ethnomusicology* 7:43–57.

———. 1994. *May It Fill Your Soul: Experiencing Bulgarian Folk Music*. Chicago: University of Chicago Press.

———. 1995. "Understanding and Producing the Variability of Oral Tradition: Learning from a Bulgarian Bagpiper." *Journal of American Folklore* 108(429):266–76.

Ricoeur, Paul. 1981a. "What Is a Text: Explanation and Understanding." In *Hermeneutics and the Human Sciences: Essays on Language, Action and Interpretation*, edited and translated by John B. Thompson. Cambridge, UK: Cambridge University Press.

———. 1981b. "The Model of the Text: Meaningful Action Considered as a Text." In *Hermeneutics and the Human Sciences: Essays on Language, Action and Interpretation*, edited and translated by John B. Thompson. Cambridge, UK: Cambridge University Press.

———. 1981c. *Hermeneutics and the Human Sciences: Essays on Language, Action and Interpretation*, edited and translated by John B. Thompson. Cambridge, UK: Cambridge University Press.

———. 1992. *Oneself as Another*, translated by Kathleen Blamey. Chicago: University of Chicago Press.

Rorty, Richard. 1979. *Philosophy and the Mirror of Nature*. Princeton, NJ: Princeton University Press.

Rosaldo, Renato. 1980. *Illongot Headhunting 1883–1974*. Stanford: Stanford University Press.

_____. 1993[1989]. *Culture and Truth: The Remaking of Social Analysis*. Boston: Beacon Press.

Roseberry, William. 1991a. "European History and the Construction of Anthropological Subjects." In *Anthropologies and Histories: Essays in Culture, History, and Political Economy*. New Brunswick, NJ: Rutgers University Press.

_____. 1991b. "Marxism and Culture." In *Anthropologies and Histories: Essays in Culture, History, and Political Economy*. New Brunswick, NJ: Rutgers University Press.

Rosendorfer, Herbert. 1983. *Briefe in die chinesische Vergangenheit*. Munich: Nymphenburger.

Roth, Gerhard. 1991. *Eine Reise in das Innere von Wien*. Frankfurt am Main: S. Fischer.

Roth, Joseph. 1978[1927]. *Die Flucht ohne Ende: Ein Bericht*. Munich: Deutscher Taschenbuch Verlag.

_____. 1977[1937]. *Das falsche Gewicht: Die Geschichte eines Eichmeisters*. Cologne: Kiepenheuer & Witsch.

Rousseau, Jean Jacques. 1768. *Dictionnaire de Musique*. Paris.

Sachs, Curt. 1962. *The Wellsprings of Music*. Edited by Jaap Kunst. The Hague: Martinus Nijhoff.

Sahlins, Marshall. 1985. *Islands of History*. Chicago: University of Chicago Press.

Said, Edward W. 1993. *Culture and Imperialism*. New York: Alfred A. Knopf.

Salazar, Claudia. 1991. "A Third World Woman's Text: Between the Politics of Criticism and Cultural Politics." In *Women's Words: The Feminist Practice of Oral History*, edited by Sherna Berger Gluck and Daphne Patai. New York: Routledge.

Sanjek, Roger. 1990. "The Secret Life of Fieldnotes." In *Fieldnotes: The Makings of Anthropology*, edited by Roger Sanjek. Ithaca: Cornell University Press.

Sanjek, Roger, ed. 1990. *Fieldnotes: The Makings of Anthropology*. Ithaca: Cornell University Press.

Schechner, Richard, and Willa Appel, eds. 1990. *By Means of Performance: Intercultural Studies of Theatre and Ritual*. Cambridge, UK: Cambridge University Press.

Schleiermacher, Friedrich. 1977. *Hermeneutics: The Handwritten Manuscripts*. Edited by Heinz Kimmerle, translated by James Duke and Jack Forstman. Missoula, MT: Scholars Press for Theory of Structure and Human Behavior.

Schneider, Albrecht. 1976. *Musikwissenschaft und Kulturkreislehre: Zur Methodik und Geschichte der Vergleichenden Musikwissenschaft*. Bonn-Bad Godesberg: Verlag für systematische Musikwissenschaft.

Schutz, Alfred. 1962. *Collected Papers*. The Hague: Martinus Nijhoff.

Schuursma, Ann Briegleb. 1992. *Ethnomusicology Research: A Select Annotated Bibliography*. New York: Garland.

Seeger, Anthony. 1987a. "Do We Need To Remodel Ethnomusicology?" *Ethnomusicology* 31(3):491–95.

_____. 1987b. *Why Suyá Sing: A Musical Anthropology of an Amazonian People*. Cambridge, UK: Cambridge University Press.

_____. 1992. "Ethnography of Music." In *Ethnomusicology: An Introduction*, edited by Helen Myers. New York: W. W. Norton.

Seeger, Anthony, and A Comunidade Suyá. 1982. *Música Indígena: A Arte Vocal dos Suyá*. 12 in. long play record and notes. São João del Rei: Tacape (007).

Seeger, Charles. 1965[1963]. "Preface to the Critique of Music." *Boletin interamericano de música* 49:2–24.

———. 1977. *Studies in Musicology: 1935–1975.* Berkeley: University of California Press.

Sharp, Cecil J. 1932. *English Folksong from the Southern Appalachians, collected by Cecil J. Sharp, Comprising two hundred and seventy-three Songs and Ballads with nine hundred and sixty-eight Tunes, Including thirty-nine Tunes contributed by Olive Dame Campbell.* Vol. 1. Edited by Maud Karpeles. London: Oxford University Press.

———. 1954. *English Folk Song: Some Conclusions.* 3rd. ed., revised by Maud Karpeles with an appreciation by Ralph Vaughan Williams. London: Methuen & Co.

Sheehy, Daniel. 1992. "A Few Notions about Philosophy and Strategy in Ethnomusicology." *Ethnomusicology* 36(3):323–36.

Shelemay, Kay Kaufman. 1988. "Together in the Field: Team Research Among Syrian Jews in Brooklyn, New York." *Ethnomusicology* 32(3):369–84.

———. 1989. *Music, Ritual, and Falasha History.* East Lansing: Michigan State University Press.

———. 1991. *A Song of Longing: An Ethiopian Journey.* Urbana: University of Illinois Press.

Shelemay, Kay Kaufman, and Peter Jeffery, eds. 1993. *Ethiopian Christian Liturgical Chant: An Anthology.* Volume 1: *General Introduction; Dictionaries of Notational Signs.* Recent Researches in the Oral Traditions of Music. Madison, WI: A-R Editions.

———. In press. *Ethiopian Christian Liturgical Chant: An Anthology.* Volume 3: *History of Ethiopian Chant.* Recent Researches in the Oral Traditions of Music. Madison, WI: A-R Editions.

Shelemay, Kay Kaufman, and Sarah Weiss, eds. 1985. "Pizmon: Syrian Religious and Social Song." Shanachie Records Corp., Meadowlark 105.

Shiloah, Amnon. 1995. *Music in the World of Islam: A Socio-Cultural Study.* Detroit: Wayne State University Press.

Shils, Edward. 1981. *Tradition.* Chicago: University of Chicago Press.

Slastion, Opanas. 1902. *Kobzar Mykhailo Kravchenko i iego dumy.* Kyïv: Ottisk iz zhurnala Kievskaia Starina, Mai.

Slobin, Mark. 1992a. "Ethical Issues." In *Ethnomusicology: An Introduction,* edited by Helen Myers. New York: W. W. Norton.

———. 1992b. "Micromusics of the West: A Comparative Approach." *Ethnomusicology* 36(1):1–88.

Slobin, Mark, and Jeff Todd Titon. 1992. "The Music-Culture as a World of Music." In *Worlds of Music: An Introduction to the Music of the World's Peoples.* 2nd ed., edited by Jeff Todd Titon. New York: Schirmer.

Smith, Barbara Barnard. 1987. "Variability, Change, and the Learning of Music." *Ethnomusicology* 31(2):201–20.

Smith, Carolyn D., and William Kornblum, eds. 1989. *In the Field: Readings on the Field Research Experience.* New York: Praeger.

Solomon, Susan Gross. 1978. "Rural Scholars and the Cultural Revolution." In *Cultural Revolution in Russia,* edited by Sheila Fitzpatrick, pp. 129–53. Bloomington: Indiana University Press.

Speranskii, Mykhailo. 1904. *Iuzhno-russkaia piesnia i sovremennyie ee Nosytieli.* Kyïv: ottisk iz zhurnala Sbornika istoriko-filologicheskago obshchestva v Nyzhiny, tom 5.

Spitzer, Shlomo. 1995. *Die jüdische Gemeinde von Deutschkreutz.* Vienna: Böhlau Verlag.

Stacey, Judith. 1991. "Can There Be a Feminist Ethnography?" In *Women's Words: The Feminist Practice of Oral History*, edited by Sherna Berger Gluck and Daphne Patai. New York: Routledge.

Stauben, Daniel. 1986[1860]. *Eine Reise zu den Juden auf dem Lande*. Augsburg: Ölbaum.

Stewart, David, and Algis Mickunas. 1990[1974]. *Exploring Phenomenology: A Guide to the Field and Its Literature*. 2nd ed. Athens: Ohio University Press.

Stocking, George W., Jr. 1974. "The Boas Plan for the Study of American Indian Languages." In *Studies in the History of Linguistics: Traditions and Paradigms*, edited by Dell Hymes. Bloomington: Indiana University Press.

Stocking, George W., Jr., ed. 1983. *Observers Observed. Essays on Ethnographic Fieldwork. History of Anthropology*. Vol. 1. Madison: University of Wisconsin Press.

Stoller, Paul. 1989. *The Taste of Ethnographic Things*. Philadelphia: University of Pennsylvania Press.

Stone, Ruth M. 1982. *Let the Inside Be Sweet: The Interpretation of Music Events among the Kpelle of Liberia*. Bloomington, IN: Indiana University Press.

Sugar, Peter. 1969. "External and Domestic Roots of Eastern European Nationalism." In *Nationalism in Eastern Europe*, edited by Peter Sugar and Ivo Lederer. Seattle: University of Washington Press.

Suppan, Wolfgang. 1976. "Research on Folk Music in Austria since 1800." *Yearbook of the International Folk Music Council* 8:117–29.

Tabachnyk, Dmytro, and Viktor Pohrebniak. 1989. "'Voroh narodu' i ioho kompaniia." *Sotsialistychna Kul'tura* 11:10–13.

Tarnas, Richard. 1991. *The Passion of the Western Mind: Understanding Ideas That Have Shaped Our World View*. New York: Ballantine Books.

Taruskin, Richard. 1982. "On Letting the Music Speak for Itself: Some Reflections on Musicology and Performance." *Journal of Musicology* 1(3):338–49.

Taussig, Michael. 1987. *Shamanism, Colonialism and the Wild Man: A Study in Terror and Healing*. Chicago: University of Chicago Press.

Theweleit, Klaus. 1988. *Buch der Könige*. Vol. 1: *Orpheus (und) Eurydike*. Basel/Frankfurt am Main: Stroemfeld/Roter Stern.

Tick, Judith, ed. 1993. *A Suite for Four Strings and Piano by Ruth Crawford*. Madison, WI: A-R Editions, Inc.

Titon, Jeff Todd. 1969. "Calling All Cows: Lazy Bill Lucas." *Blues Unlimited* 60:10–11 (March 1969), 61:9–10 (April 1969), 62:11–12 (May 1969), 63:9–10 (June 1969).

_____. 1976. "Son House: Two Narratives." *Alcheringa: Ethnopoetics* NS 2(1):2–9.

_____. 1980. "The Life Story." *Journal of American Folklore* 93:276–92.

_____. 1985. "Stance, Role, and Identity in Fieldwork among Folk Baptists and Pentecostals in the United States." *American Music* 3:16–24.

_____. 1988. *Powerhouse for God: Speech, Chant, and Song in an Appalachian Baptist Church*. Austin: University of Texas Press.

_____. 1989. "Ethnomusicology as the Study of People Making Music." Paper delivered at the annual conference of the Northeast Chapter of the Society for Ethnomusicology, Hartford, Connecticut, April 22, 1989.

_____. 1991. The Clyde Davenport HyperCard Stack. [Available via anonymous ftp on the

Internet from EthnoForum since 1992. For information on how to download it, send an electronic mail message to ETHMUS-L@UMDD.UMD.EDU.]

———. 1992. "Music, the Public Interest, and the Practice of Ethnomusicology." *Ethnomusicology* 36(3):315–22.

———. 1994. "Knowing People Making Music: Toward a New Epistemology for Ethnomusicology." *Etnomusikologian vuosikirja*, Vol. 6. Helsinki: Suomen Etnomusikologinen seura [Yearbook of the Finnish Society for Ethnomusicology].

———. 1995. "Meaningful Action Considered as Music." A reply to Roger Savage. Paper presented at the annual conference of the Society for Ethnomusicology, Los Angeles, CA, October 20–24.

Titon, Jeff Todd, gen. ed. 1992[1984]. *Worlds of Music*. 2nd ed. New York: Schirmer Books.

Titon, Jeff Todd, and Barry Dornfeld. 1992. "Representation and Authority in Ethnographic Film/Video: Production" and "Representation and Authority in Ethnographic Film/Video: Reception." *Ethnomusicology* 36(1):89–94, and 95–98.

Tomlinson, Gary. 1993. *Music in Renaissance Magic: Toward a Historiography of Others*. Chicago: University of Chicago Press.

Tsertelev, Kniaz. 1827. "O narodnykh stikhotvorieniiakh." *Vesnik evropi* 9:270–77.

Turnbull, Colin M. 1961. *The Forest People*. New York: Simon and Schuster.

Turner, Victor W. 1989[1969]. *The Ritual Process: Structure and Anti-Structure*. Ithaca: Cornell University Press.

Turner, Victor W., and Edward M. Bruner, eds. 1986. *The Anthropology of Experience*. Urbana: University of Illinois Press.

Tykhanov, P. 1899. "Chernigovskie startsy." *Trudy chernigovskoi gubernskoi arkhivnoi kommissii* 2:65–158.

Tyler, Stephen A. 1986. "Post-Modern Ethnography: From Document of the Occult to Occult Document." In *Writing Culture: The Poetics and Politics of Ethnography*, edited by James Clifford and George E. Marcus. Berkeley: University of California Press.

Vale, Sue Carole de. 1980. "Boas, Franz." In *The New Grove Dictionary of Music and Musicians*, edited by Stanley Sadie, 2:623–24. London: Macmillan.

Van Maanen, John. 1988. *Tales of the Field: On Writing Ethnography*. Chicago: University of Chicago Press.

Vlasiuk, Lesia, and Lidia Lykhach, eds. 1994. "Sofiia Tereshchenko. Dodatkovi pokazy do protokoliv slidstva." *Rodovid* 7:59–92.

von Rosen, Franziska. 1992. "Micmac Storyteller: River of Fire—The Co-Creation of an Ethnographic Video." *Canadian Folk Music Journal* 20:40–46.

von Rosen, Franziska, and Michael William Francis. 1992. *River of Fire*. VHS Videotape. Lanark, Ontario, Canada: Franziska von Rosen.

Wachstein, Bernhard, ed. 1926. *Urkunden und Akten zur Geschichte der Juden in Eisenstadt und den Siebengemeinden*. Vienna: Wilhelm Braumüller.

Wade, Bonnie C., and Ann M. Pescatello. 1977. "Music 'Patronage' in Indic Culture: The Jajmani Model." In *Essays for a Humanist: An Offering to Klaus Wachsmann*. New York: The Town House Press.

Warren, Carol A.B. 1988. *Gender Issues in Field Research*. Newbury Park, CA: Sage Publications.

Wax, Rosalie. 1971. *Doing Fieldwork: Warnings and Advice*. Chicago: University of Chicago Press.

Wengle, John L. 1988. *Ethnographers in the Field: The Psychology of Research*. Tuscaloosa: University of Alabama Press.

Werfel, Franz. 1944. *Between Heaven and Earth*, translated by Maxim Newmark. New York: Philosophical Library.

_____. 1982[1955]. *Cella oder die Überwinder: Vesuch eines Romans*. Frankfurt am Main: S. Fischer.

White, Anne. 1990. *De-Stalinization and the House of Culture*. London: Routledge.

Whitehead, Tony Larry, and Mary Ellen Conaway, eds. 1986. *Self, Sex, and Gender in Cross-Cultural Fieldwork*. Urbana: University of Illinois Press.

Widdess, Richard. 1992. "Historical Ethnomusicology." In *Ethnomusicology. An Introduction*, edited by Helen Meyers. New York: W. W. Norton.

Williams, Raymond. 1980. "Base and Superstructure in Marxist Cultural Theory." In *Problems in Materialism and Culture*. London: Verso Press.

Willis, William S., Jr. 1972. "Skeletons in the Anthropological Closet." In *Reinventing Anthropology*, edited by Dell Hymes. New York: Vintage.

Wischenbart, Rüdiger. 1992. *Karpaten: Die dunkle Seite Europas*. Vienna: Kremayr & Scheriau.

Witmer, Robert. 1991. "Stability in Blackfoot Songs, 1909–1968." In *Ethnomusicology and Modern Music History*, edited by Stephen Blum, Philip V. Bohlman, and Daniel M. Neuman. Urbana: University of Illinois Press.

Wolf, Eric. 1982. *Europe and the People Without History*. Berkeley: University of California Press.

Wolff, Larry. 1994. *Inventing Eastern Europe: The Map of Civilization on the Mind of the Enlightenment*. Stanford: Stanford University Press.

Wong, Isabel K.F. 1991. "Chinese Musicology in the Twentieth Century." In *Comparative Musicology and Anthropology of Music*, edited by Bruno Nettl and Philip V. Bohlman. Chicago: University of Chicago Press.

Zalta, B. 1991. Personal communication, March 16.

Zamora, Mario, and Bjorn B. Erring, eds. 1991. *Fieldwork in Cultural Anthropology*. New Delhi: Reliance Publishing House.

Index

Printed in the United States
17650LVS00004B/121